YOUR BOSS IS AN ALGO

What effect do robots, algorithms, and online platforms have on the world of work? Using case studies and examples from across the EU, the UK, and the US, this book provides a compass to navigate this technological transformation as well as the regulatory options available, and proposes a new map for the era of radical digital advancements.

From platform work to the gig-economy and the impact of artificial intelligence, algorithmic management, and digital surveillance on workplaces, technology has overwhelming consequences for everyone's lives, reshaping the labour market and straining social institutions. Contrary to preliminary analyses forecasting the threat of human work obsolescence, the book demonstrates that digital tools are more likely to replace managerial roles and intensify organisational processes in workplaces, rather than opening the way for mass job displacement.

Can flexibility and protection be reconciled so that legal frameworks uphold innovation? How can we address the pervasive power of AI-enabled monitoring? How likely is it that the gig-economy model will emerge as a new organisational paradigm across sectors? And what can social partners and political players do to adopt effective regulation?

Technology is never neutral. It can and must be governed, to ensure that progress favours the many. Digital transformation can be an essential ally, from the warehouse to the office, but it must be tested in terms of social and political sustainability, not only through the lenses of economic convenience. *Your Boss Is an Algorithm* offers a guide to explore these new scenarios, their promises, and perils.

Your Boss Is an Algorithm

*Artificial Intelligence, Platform
Work and Labour*

Antonio Aloisi
and
Valerio De Stefano

•HART•
OXFORD • LONDON • NEW YORK • NEW DELHI • SYDNEY

HART PUBLISHING

Bloomsbury Publishing Plc

Kemp House, Chawley Park, Cumnor Hill, Oxford, OX2 9PH, UK

1385 Broadway, New York, NY 10018, USA

29 Earlsfort Terrace, Dublin 2, Ireland

HART PUBLISHING, the Hart/Stag logo, BLOOMSBURY and the Diana logo are
trademarks of Bloomsbury Publishing Plc

A catalogue record for this book is available from the British Library.

A catalogue record for this book is available from the Library of Congress.

Library of Congress Control Number: 2022934284

ISBN: PB: 978-1-50995-318-9
        ePDF: 978-1-50995-320-2
        ePub: 978-1-50995-319-6

Typeset by Compuscript Ltd, Shannon
Printed and bound in Great Britain by CPI Group (UK) Ltd, Croydon CR0 4YY

MIX
Paper from
responsible sources
FSC® C013604

To find out more about our authors and books visit www.hartpublishing.co.uk.
Here you will find extracts, author information, details of forthcoming events
and the option to sign up for our newsletters.

ACKNOWLEDGEMENTS

Despite being a thrilling section, acknowledgements are always written at the end of an energy-draining experience. The risk is that – when creativity has been exhausted – only clichéd formulas come to the minds of the authors. While we cannot assure readers that we will be able to overcome this pitfall, we must confess that condensing our research, ideas and proposals in this book has been a privilege and a source of entertainment. Contrary to many academic tasks that may be very solitary, this journey has been a sociable one, and we are tremendously grateful for this.

This book was envisioned and written in Brussels, Madrid, Toronto, Geneva, Milan, Florence, Salento and Calabria. It owes much to the fresh air one can breathe in these places and, above all, to the friends, families and people that contribute to making them so welcoming. Without their support, we would have never had the strength and calm necessary to embark on such an adventure. Undoubtedly, this is no small thing: all this affection, perhaps even undeserved, is worth its weight in gold.

We must thank the institutions we belong(ed) to, respectively the IE Law School of IE University, Madrid, the Osgoode Hall Law School of York University, Toronto and (previously) the Catholic University of Leuven, in Belgium, for having generously stimulated and supported the research on the themes that are discussed in these pages. This book also benefited from insightful conversations with our talented colleagues, mentors, doctoral and university students and administrative staff whose contribution, sometimes not adequately recognised, has been decisive.

The research leading to this book project has received funding from the European Union's Horizon 2020 research and innovation programme under the Marie Skłodowska-Curie grant agreement No. 893888 'Boss Ex Machina. Mapping and understanding the technological transformation of managerial prerogatives in workplaces driven by machines, artificial intelligence and algorithms' as well as from the Odysseus grant 'Employment rights and labour protection in the on-demand economy' awarded by the FWO Research Foundation – Flanders.

We would like to thank Stefano Liebman, the teacher who ignited our passion for labour law and encouraged us (and continues to do so) in a thoughtful and unusual way, having adopted freedom as an anti-dogmatic teaching method. Our gratitude should be extended to Maurizio Del Conte, Elena Gramano and Giovanni Gaudio.

Many thanks to the terrific team at Hart Publishing and, in particular, to Roberta Bassi, Rosemarie Mearns and Linda Staniford who supported us through every stage of the writing process. The credit for this publication also goes to our Italian publisher, Giuseppe Laterza, who patiently granted autonomy and companionship. Thanks to Claire Banyard and Lia Di Trapani, the editors who generously cleaned up any unclear passages, helping us to make even the most complex content accessible to a broad audience. Many thanks also to the anonymous reviewers who promoted the publication of the manuscript.

The most relentless editor was Giuliana Morabito, to whom our most sincere thanks go. Many sections are now enjoyable only thanks to Antonella Zarra, who graciously tolerated the fanatical devotion to this project. Nastazja Potocka-Sionek, Andrea Garnero, Gianluca Greco, Lorenzo Micheli, Loredana Carta and Isabella Notarangelo were among the first to read the manuscript, and offered their comments with wisdom, openness and friendship. A big thank you also goes to Silvana Sciarra, 'tutelary deity' of all young(ish) Italian labour lawyers.

Our research and this book also hugely benefitted from the incessant exchanges and meetings we were privileged to have with friends and colleagues like Janine Berg, Jeremias Adams-Prassl, Miriam Cherry, Uma Rani, Nicola Countouris, Brishen Rogers, Claire Kilpatrick, Cindy Estlund, Martin Gruber-Risak, Six Silberman, Mark Graham, Luca Ratti, Frank Hendrickx, Silvia Rainone, Ilda Durri, Charalampos Stylogiannis, Mathias Wouters, Simon Taes, Piera Loi, Luisa Corazza, Matt Finkin, Vincenzo Pietrogiovanni, Ewan McGaughey, Alan Bogg, Tonia Novitz, Einat Albin, Veena Dubal, Ioannis Lianos, Adrián Todolí Signes, Phoebe Moore, Antonio Casilli and many others with whom we were lucky to discuss these topics – the full list would exceed any reasonable space constraints.

Thanks to the many family members (Anna Chiara and Lorenzo above all) and friends who had the opportunity to comment on earlier drafts of the book, suggesting changes and pointing out inaccuracies. Their generous encouragement improved our efforts. We are also deeply grateful to those who offered us the opportunity to present the core of the text at conferences, lectures and seminars, and to the journals, books, blogs and newspapers that hosted our contributions and interviews on these topics.

The text was finalised at the end of November 2021 and slightly updated in early February 2022. For this reason, it cannot take into account any subsequent developments, whether legislative or judicial. In any case, the sense of the reflections is independent of the contingent data and, hopefully, should withstand the impact of the news without too much disruption. Should that not be the case, feel free to reach out to us. Errors and inaccuracies are to be attributed exclusively to us (then again, to who else?).

Antonio Aloisi and Valerio De Stefano
Madrid and Toronto, February 2022.

TABLE OF CONTENTS

Introduction

In October 2015, after organising a conference session on platform work at the International Labour Office, we were invited to present our research to the European Parliament in Brussels. The Parliament's building is a maze and, as expected, we immediately lost our way among the corridors in search of the meeting room. We were rescued by an old classmate, who since our time together at university had become a parliamentary assistant. He met us by chance several floors away from the room where we were to speak and volunteered to accompany us. On the way there, he asked what had brought us to the EU Parliament. We replied that we had been summoned to talk about 'platform workers, like Uber drivers, you know'. He was flabbergasted: 'Isn't this a problem of antitrust and transport regulation? Why on earth', he questioned, 'are you labour lawyers interested in this?'. We replied that the most pressing issues we saw were the drivers' working conditions and their employment status. Being classified as self-employed workers, they could count on very little legal protection. It was also an entirely unbalanced relationship, due to the massive use of algorithms and other digital means of surveillance. We bet against him that soon this would be one of the most tantalising topics in the hectic debate on the future of work, and it would also help to shed light on other vital issues at the intersection between labour and emerging technologies, the use of artificial intelligence (AI) and extensive adoption of big data in workforce management.

It was an easy bet to win, let's be honest. From 2015 onwards, work for companies such as Deliveroo, Uber, Grubhub or online platforms such as Amazon Mechanical Turk, UpWork and Jovoto has made the front pages of newspapers around the world, thanks to multiple lawsuits that workers have filed virtually everywhere these businesses operate. Meanwhile, numerous other issues, much broader than the legal classification of workers, came to light. Platforms increasingly seemed a pilot test for nascent forms of algorithmic governance – the use of information technology to manage the labour force, from hiring to firing, involving constant performance appraisal powered by the large amount of information collected. These practices are now a common feature of our economies, affecting blue- and white-collar jobs well beyond the expanding boundaries of platform work. Many governments all over the world are pondering whether to step in to regulate in this field. Trade unions and labour rights advocates are demanding a more effective enforcement of existing legal frameworks. Meanwhile, research on this topic burgeoned: countless publications, conferences and seminars showcasing platform work in all its ramifications have been set up in the last few years.

Much ink has already been spilled. We have admittedly contributed our part to this deluge of research. We wrote many articles, essays and reports for international organisations. We were presenters in many academic, institutional and political initiatives, and we discussed these issues in our classes. We have learned a great deal from these experiences. We gained innumerable insights from audiences and fellow speakers who took part in these meetings. However, we must admit that, unsurprisingly, many of the questions we received during these discussions became recurrent.

Wouldn't it make sense – many people wonder – to turn a blind eye to the conditions of these precarious workers, given that they will soon be replaced by self-driving cars or remotely controlled drones? Shouldn't we be grateful for any form of algorithmic management replacing human arbitrariness with automated supervision, to finally get rid of human biases and market failures when hiring and managing workers? Shouldn't we instead concentrate all our intellectual resources on the professional skills that will be needed in a changing labour market? Wouldn't it be better to let wages and protections adjust, to avoid companies slamming even harder on the accelerator of full automation? Shouldn't we begrudgingly replace all these old-fashioned labour rights with modern, 'fluid' social security measures, including universal basic income? Don't we risk slowing down innovation and hindering technological development by granting twentieth century-style protections to the workers involved in the most innovative sectors of our otherwise crushed economies? Wouldn't it be easier to introduce lighter labour protection regimes to avoid the digital platforms running away from our countries in search of more welcoming shores?

No! Our sincere answer to all these questions is simple. And it is a firm response, honed during our years of research.

With this book we do not only aim to offer arguments in support of this blunt stance, but also to help redefine the issues on the table. We want to show how technology can be used to positively change our life and work, as long as we do not let the tech industry self-regulate by purporting to govern public decisions as the sole arbiter of our fate. We also want to discuss how new technologies will allow us to save time and energy by automating hazardous, menial, or repetitive jobs. At the same time, we warn that some connected tools risk subjecting everyone to invasive and relentless surveillance regimes, including at the workplace. The use of some of these devices, then, should be limited, if not banned altogether, to safeguard the fundamental values, rights and freedoms that govern our democratic societies.

If we were to listen to gurus of game-changing technologies, digital evangelists and their many cheerleaders stationed between public institutions and specialised magazines, we would end up being victims to a grave misunderstanding. Trying to govern innovation – they contend – would be pointless and harmful. Tech companies increasingly invoke government intervention in order to dictate rules on controversial issues such as misinformation and the fight against online hate, freedom of speech, or commercialisation of data rights, but no other legislative intervention ever seems to end well. Very few politicians attempt to discuss introducing rules to outlaw AI applications used to profile candidates when they apply for a job, to check their creditworthiness when people ask for a mortgage, or to assess personal risk factors when it comes to buying insurance. Regulating platform work, therefore, would be sheer madness. 'You don't want platforms to shut down, do you? We'd lose thousands of jobs! Not to mention the satellite activities supported by the apps. If there was no food-delivery, lockdowns and quarantines during the pandemic would have been hell for everyone'. It's as if the economies of some of the most industrialised countries in the world really could depend on the delivery of meals and parcels by bike to the point of accepting any condition imposed by these companies so they can do us the favour of staying solvent. Surely there should be a line.

In order to avoid these lapses of reason, we must first demystify a fallacy, namely the misconception that the state of progress is deterministically given ('things can only get better'). Too many observers and self-proclaimed disruptors lament the incapacity of current legislation to keep pace with the 'brave new world' by resorting to the argument of inevitability and irreversibility of innovation.[1] They often argue that we should tear the crusts off our old laws and rights, claiming that existing rules are irreversibly mouldy.

To dispel these die hard myths, suffice it to say that the impact of social changes is prominently determined by corporate decisions and, above all, by societal choices. Information and communication technology (ICT) only accelerates, validates and consolidates these changes. In short, it is certainly not the fault of digitalisation if work becomes precarious, nor can we impute exclusively to technology the ever-increasing disregard for the dignity of human work.[2] Although today the eponymous word 'Uber' is a global metaphor for all the phenomena of atomisation of work relations, as media keep quoting for example: 'Uber of dog-sitting', 'Uber of helicopters', 'Uber of laundry',[3] the modern trend of work commodification has certainly not been inaugurated by the California-based platform. Work arrangements that are parcelled out in countless discrete tasks (the single delivery of a pizza slice, the short online translation, the transcription of receipts, even the effort of tagging photos online to refine machine learning engines) and distributed in seamless micro exchanges that replace more stable and better regulated work relationships are simply the most well-known examples of a much wider tendency,[4] a phenomenon that ranges from casual work to subcontracting, from sham self-employment to franchising.

Discussing the impact of new technologies on freedom, democracy, justice and politics, Jamie Susskind wrote that many of the problems of our times have more to do with individual options and interests than with digitalisation itself.[5] Far from being set in stone, innovation takes the direction that we set, with our actions and aspirations, and moves at the speed that we impose on it. In short, all the great transformations are nothing more than a sum, sometimes virtuous, sometimes vicious, of countless personal and collective choices. There are no good and bad technologies per se, there are distorted or mindful uses of innovation. Thus, the quality of present and future work depends explicitly on how we conceive, negotiate and organise it. This will be one of our key messages throughout this book: the use of digital tools at work can and must be governed to ensure that technological progress favours the many and not the very few.

Of course, this is not about advocating less innovation, particularly where progress already lags behind. In too many areas, even in industrialised countries, fast internet connection is a mirage and other investments in new technologies fall short especially in terms of skills, high capacity networks and advanced solutions for businesses and public services, as revealed by the Digital Economy and Society Index (DESI).[6] The COVID-19 pandemic has made it clear, for example, how poor some digital infrastructures are, as well as how conservative corporate culture is when it comes to adopting new organisational patterns. Remote work has been vital during the emergency, to decongest commuting routes, mitigate the contagion risk, allow business continuity and keep people safe. But when fast internet is confined within the Zone 1 of big cities and firms impose micromanagement even on people working from home, growth is really kept at bay. Real innovation is scarce. Hence, we need more of it and for it to be better distributed and this is why we must all have a voice in managing its implications on people's lives and work.

At the same time, an overestimation of the wonders of new tech has monopolised the conventional debate on work. Yet, unlike in regard to medicine, electrification, biotechnology, infrastructure and air travel, the business applications of digital advancements seem to have very little ground-breaking effects in many areas. New technology today is often merely used to perform more effectively actions and functions that, in the past, involved using more energy (which is very welcome!) or that, in many cases, we were wary to implement due to values and principles, such as human dignity, which today may seem irrelevant. Think, for instance, of the collection and use of biometric data, intrusive facial recognition for authentication,[7] or private mass tracking to deal with health emergencies.

Often, a certain prevalent fatalism accompanies an attitude to downplay the scope of the ongoing shift. According to many observers, large segments of the workforce will still be engaged in traditional activities for a long time, sheltered from encroaching digitisation and the formidable competition of tech giants. We firmly disagree. Some sectors, in fact, may serve to test business models that, if successful, will be exported elsewhere. The contractual precariousness of these types of workers and the subjection to intrusive managerial practices in exchange for little job and income security are just some of the symptoms of the great transformation currently taking place.[8]

There are numerous studies which have described the advent of the newest technologies and mapped their corrosive effects on work.[9] They range from physical devices such as exoskeletons and 'wearable' electronic bracelets to immaterial tools such as algorithms and AI. On the brighter side, these technologies can process information in real time, preventing accidents caused by human errors and reducing the hazards and strain of certain routine and tedious tasks. At the same time, as we explain in the second chapter of this book, they enable so much meticulous and pervasive monitoring of workers that all too often leads to appalling abuses. We should not resign ourselves to the idea that to reap the benefits in terms of greater safety and relief of physical work fatigue we should accept surveillance habits unravelling at an increasing pace.

Some major technological breakthroughs also enable the allocation of many managerial functions to non-human agents ('management-by-algorithms'). Workers in manufacturing, logistics and office-based occupations can receive orders from an automated decision-making system, be continuously monitored by GPS trackers or digital log-stamps and fired for not achieving the goals set by computational tools measuring average community targets and the clients' level of satisfaction, with little (if any) possibility of redress. Many new technologies enable reconfiguring organisational procedures, workplace practices, talent acquisition, retention and enhancement. This results in a parallel erosion of job autonomy and skill depreciation: workers eventually experience loss of agency and a sense of alienation from their work, weakening abstract thinking while favouring persistent homogeneity.

Software are deployed to digitise scheduling, set promotion and compute remuneration – and this is where the platform businesses also come into play, as we discuss thoroughly in the third chapter. The division of labour carried out by some digital platforms conceals the activities of too many workers behind a curtain of invisibility, by disguising this work as automated. To put it bluntly: an army of ghost workers, as Mary Gray and Siddarth Suri describe them,[10] is obscured in the backroom of the wondrous digital economy, deputised as they are to trigger processes, to repair errors, to program code strings, or even to relocate bikes and scooters of shared-mobility businesses, or to cook a hamburger, store and deliver parcels. The dirty job of the new economy's second wave is not done by super intelligent machines, but by invisible, dispossessed machinists.

This is not an encouraging scenario. We end up being subject to innovation, rather than generating it. This is a betrayal of any 'emancipating' promise of digital technologies. They rose as a tool for libertarian 'rebels', they often turn into instruments of bureaucratic repression. They were supposed to simplify our lives, foster freedom and enable social connection, they instead have proved to be a trump card for surveillance, measurement, hegemonisation, blackmail, commodification, spamming, wiretapping, haranguing and punishment. They arrived as a space open to no holds barred competition, they have become a hunting ground for oligopolists perpetuating a tailspin of data extraction and digital enclosure in a world dominated by winner-take-all markets. They aimed to turn us into a new Prometheus, the titan who stole knowledge from the gods to offer it to men, instead they have handed us over to low value-added services that stoke frivolous desires and satisfy low-cost consumerism.[11] They were supposed to reduce inequalities, they ended up raising barriers, exaggerating imbalances and deepening social oppression.

The widespread reaction to all of this was sudden and thunderous. Socio-economic earthquakes often lead to political shockwaves.[12] Many of the electoral results of recent years, such as Trump's victory in 2016, the success of Brexiters in the UK and the bolstered electoral performance of extremist parties in many European countries, demonstrate a severe rejection of the inequalities that technological gaps have precipitated.

Law professors Alan Bogg and Mark Freedland have written that precarious work makes our democracies unstable, or at least less liberal.[13] It is difficult to disagree. To be sure, populist responses, as well as calming ones, only exacerbate the ailments that they are expected to cure. Even worse, they are often part of an agenda that has opposite hidden objectives. To give some examples: the people who voted to *Make America Great Again*, ensnared by the sirens of star-spangled protectionism, often found themselves paying the hefty bill for shameless anti-labour policies that harmed the middle class. Similarly, the UK's exit from the European Union and the desire to 'take back control' seriously threatens to weaken the many employment rights of British working people that EU membership helped to build.[14] Nevertheless, the deep roots of social vulnerabilities and resentment should not be overlooked or looked down upon. It is instead our duty to investigate the economic and social reasons of discontent, to mitigate their symptoms and correct their causes.[15]

To conclude, the point is not to indulge in a grotesque 'back to the good old times' attitude! Technology can be an indispensable ally, from the factory to the desk, from the warehouse to the office. It is critical, however, to constantly challenge it on the ground of social and political sustainability, not only through the lenses of economic convenience. For this reason, we direct our research toward fighting against a fanfare version of progress, which is nothing but a lot of talk and food delivery.

* * *

Our analysis springs from the premise that to shape the future it is necessary to take care of the present. One cannot speculate on the future of the work without investigating in depth today's unresolved issues and healing open wounds.

What happens to the jobs that will not be swept away by technology? Can flexibility and protection be reconciled to ensure that the existing regulatory frameworks uphold innovation? How can we negotiate the extent and intensity of increasingly insidious surveillance techniques? How should we regulate the processing of data collected in the workplace without abdicating fundamental values? How likely is it that the business model of gig-economy platforms spreads to other industries and emerges as a new productive paradigm? What investments and cuts are needed to sustain productivity? In what way is a fair distribution of the dividends of technological progress ensured? How should we adapt welfare systems to make sure non-standard workers are not left behind? Do we need a new social compact to reduce inequalities, contain resentment and expand opportunities? And what should go into it? What are the social partners and political players doing, and what can they do, to accompany the transition? Two even more fundamental questions must be answered: what are we willing to give up and what are we aiming for?

This book aims to address bewilderment, answer some doubts and offer realistic solutions. It deals with the three major vectors of change that are redesigning the modern world of work: automation, algorithms and platforms.[16] Together, these forces can bring us into a completely new work reality, for which we are not yet equipped. They are a moving target as they change rapidly and profoundly, along with the environments where they operate. These three transformative vectors affect the entire cycle of options available to entrepreneurs: potential dislocation of tasks and jobs, digitisation of decision-making processes, intensification of command-and-control roles, opportunities for outsourcing and effects on job quality and task discretion. We therefore need a compass to orient ourselves in this unchartered territory.

This book is based on the stubbornness of facts and is the result of several years of research across various methodological silos. Using case studies from across the EU, the UK and the US, it focuses on two classical dimensions of labour studies, the *individual* and the *collective* by marshalling both empirical and normative arguments. It starts from an assumption: rules do not necessarily halt economic activities. It is not true that our entire regulatory landscape is obsolete and to be thrown away. Nor is it true that we should make unchallenged room for new business models, by giving up attempts to govern work and technology. On the contrary, regulation is an ally of authentic innovation, since it allows a level playing field between competitors, prevents the abuse of dominant positions, enables the most daring experiments and protects their results. It also mediates between conflicting interests and lowers transaction costs, by ensuring determinacy and predictability in the application of the law, and rebalances disparities.

Your Boss Is an Algorithm moves on from legal problems to deal with the fundamental issues that affect the whole of society and concern those of us who want to shape an alternative path of the transformation of work. It is also a law book that adopts a socio-legal and comparative approach, while speaking everyone's language and drawing examples from everyday life. If we really needed to frame it in a literary genre, we would like to consider it as a dispatch from the work front. We hope that our readers will obtain enough insights to make up their mind independently. And we hope to make them aware of one important message: tech and its consequences are human phenomena, they depend strictly on the social and regulatory fabric on which they impact. They can, in short, be regulated and it is beneficial to do so quickly. Some tools are already there, some can be identified through collective discussion. The most crucial thing, however, is not to take mercurial innovation for granted nor to be afraid to manipulate it for the benefit of all. There is plenty of human leadership to exercise in writing the future history of innovation. Not only is this not impossible, it would not even be unprecedented. We hope to be convincing enough.

It's time to get started!

[1] K Roose, *Futureproof: 9 Rules for Humans in the Age of Automation* (London, Hachette UK, 2021).

[2] See generally VB Dubal, 'The Drive to Precarity: A Political History of Work, Regulation, & Labor Advocacy in San Francisco's Taxi & Uber Economies' (2017) 38(1) *Berkeley Journal of Employment and Labor Law* 73–136.

[3] Even the 'Uber of Washington', see E McGaughey, 'Uber, the Taylor review, mutuality and the duty not to misrepresent employment status' (2019) 48(2) *Industrial Law Journal* 180–98.

[4] L Hyman, *Temp. How American Work, American Business, and the American Dream Became Temporary* (New York, Viking Press, 2018).

[5] J Susskind, *Future Politics: Living Together in a World Transformed by Tech* (Oxford, Oxford University Press, 2018).

[6] The Digital Economy and Society Index (DESI) monitors Europe's overall digital performance and tracks the progress of EU countries in digital competitiveness. By providing data on the state of digitisation of each Member State, it helps them identify areas requiring priority investment and action. See https://digital-strategy.ec.europa.eu/en/policies/desi.

[7] C O'Murchu, 'Facial recognition cameras arrive in UK school canteens' *Financial Times* (17 October 2021) www.ft.com/content/af08fe55-39f3-4894-9b2f-4115732395b9.

[8] S Kessler, *Gigged: The Gig Economy, the End of the Job and the Future of Work* (New York, Random House, 2018). See also G Valenduc and P Vendramin, *Work in the digital economy: sorting the old from the new* (Brussels, European Trade Union Institute, 2016).

[9] PV Moore, M Upchurch and X Whittaker, *Humans and machines at work: Monitoring, surveillance and automation in contemporary capitalism* (Cham, Palgrave Macmillan, 2018).

[10] ML Gray and S Siddharth, *Ghost Work: How to Stop Silicon Valley from Building a New Global Underclass* (New York, Eamon Dolan/Houghton Mifflin Harcourt, 2019).

[11] We have been living 'Balenciaga lifestyles on Banana Republic budgets'. But the honeymoon seems to be over. See K Roose, 'Farewell, Millennial Lifestyle Subsidy' *The New York Times* (8 June 2021) www.nytimes.com/2021/06/08/technology/farewell-millennial-lifestyle-subsidy.html.

[12] CB Frey, *The Technology Trap. Capital, Labor, and Power in the Age of Automation* (Princeton, Princeton University Press, 2019).

[13] A Bogg and M Freedland, 'Labour Law in the age of populism: towards sustainable democratic engagement' in J López Labor (ed), *Collective Bargaining and Collective Action. Labour Agency and Governance in the 21st Century?* (London, Bloomsbury Publishing, 2019).

[14] T Novitz, 'Why Brexit will be bad for workers' (*Futures of Work*, 19 November 2018) https://futuresofwork.co.uk/2018/11/19/the-potential-impact-of-brexit-on-workers/.

[15] S Deakin, 'Luddism in the age of Uber' (*Social Europe*, 3 November 2015) https://socialeurope.eu/luddism-in-the-age-of-uber. See also D Susskind, *A World Without Work: Technology, Automation and How we Should Respond* (London, Penguin, 2020).

[16] In a sense, rewriting the trinomial described in A McAfee and E Brynjolfsson, *Machine, Platform, Crowd: Harnessing our Digital Future* (New York, WW Norton & Company, 2017).

1

Navigating Uncharted Waters

I. A Future Without Work? Raining on the 'Full Automation' Parade

Over the past few years, the 'future of work' has become a subject in itself, appearing in conferences and soon to occupy dedicated shelves in bookstores. There is no parliament, university, multinational, think-tank or trade union that has not yet launched a research group to deal with work and the Fourth industrial revolution.[1]

This should come as no surprise: work plays a fundamental role in daily life. As well as being a means of personal fulfilment, work enables interpersonal bonds and is a vehicle for social mobility: it contributes to defining a substantial piece of our identities.[2] In many legal systems, work – mainly of a subordinate, full-time and permanent nature, the so-called 'standard employment relationship'[3] – is a privileged, and sometimes irreplaceable, gateway to an integrated system of rights, obligations, protection and welfare. For many citizens, work takes up most of the day and is the main source of income.

A spectre, however, is haunting many analyses that revolve around the digital revolution: the imminent disappearance of (human) work. The mainstream debate is almost monopolised by a purely 'accounting' perspective on the number of jobs that will be lost due to automation and what to do about it.[4] We thus end up relying solely on statistics, rejoicing or despairing depending on whether a positive or negative balance can be highlighted on the quarterly spreadsheets. 'Automation anxiety' seeks solace in the charts.[5] This unsettling interpretation of the changes underway has replaced in-depth analyses – most of the common assumptions about the technological transformation of work have a hyperbolic nature. Genuine investigations about both the concrete uses of technologies and the ways to augment human capabilities without replacing them are almost completely neglected. Any reflection on how to redesign workspaces, rethink the content and shape of jobs, adjust contractual arrangements and reinvent collective action strategies fares even worse.

In this context, even the most insignificant story in the news becomes an incontrovertible sign of some unparalleled and unstoppable trend. Human microchip implants to monitor workers, the many professions replaced by computers, big data sacking slackers, the AI that will unleash bloody world conflicts, the 'social credit' card to compile the ranking of the most reliable humans, 3D shopping and design in the Metaverse thanks to the wondrous means of virtual reality ... these are just some of the stories that are circulating, inspiring public and private conversations on the subject.

Nevertheless, such preoccupations are not new. The same anxieties recurrently reappear on the stage of economic history, demanding attention. It may be useful to look to the past to see the future. In this regard, there is a pertinent meme showing three different covers of *Der Spiegel*, the popular German weekly magazine, side by side. It features the first pages of the March 1964, April 1978 and September 2016 issues respectively. The headlines ranged from an alarming 'Automation in Germany, the arrival of robots', to a worried 'The computer revolution: how progress causes unemployment', to a disastrous 'You're fired! How computers and robots steal our jobs – and which jobs will be safe'. In all three cases, an anthropomorphised robot is represented in the act of getting rid of a worker. The only substantial difference between the 1978 cover and the 2016 cover is regarding the worker: in the former it is a blue-collar worker, in the latter a clerk.

In truth, no profession is intrinsically immune to the digital revolution and, on the contrary, the classic polarising vision (manual work on one side, cognitive work on the other) is unable to capture the complexity of the present situation. A lawyer, a doctor, a consultant and a manager run similar or even worse substitution risks than a nurse, a postman, a cook or a driver. While danger zones are expanding, 'safe' areas are most likely located at the intersection of existing industries and job positions. In fact, hybrid professions are being created such as big data architects, algorithm analysts, computer scientists specialised in legal knowledge, computational linguists and robotic-prosthetic trainers.[6] Alongside these, many more traditional jobs will resist technological modernisation: health and home care assistants, marketing professionals, educators, security personnel, comedians, domestic workers and caretakers.[7]

In many areas, humans will still retain an unassailable competitive advantage over machines, and they will benefit from unprecedented alliances with smart robots and AI.[8] However, how can we be sure not to sacrifice these opportunities on the altar of technocratic *laissez faire*? A not-so-silent world race between rival powers to secure a leading position in technological fields is taking place, and Europe is lagging behind. To counter this trend, we need to heavily invest in those intangible infrastructures with a secure and extensive return over time: education and training. The problem, however, is that it seems to be more obvious to perpetuate wealth through financial gains and not, instead, by investing in the talent of people who work, further tilting the playing field toward capital over labour.

Efforts to guess the exact nature of the next technological advance are doomed to fail.[9] At the same time, it is almost impossible to predict what skills will be in demand in the years to come, given how little we know about what advanced labour markets are going to look like. We know what activities might disappear, but we have no idea what might arise. We do know, however, that too many people lack the basic digital skills that will be crucial in the future. Thus, massive investments in vocational training and the development of quality apprenticeship and well-paid traineeship schemes should be part of the answer. A big issue, in the years to come, will be that the most vulnerable and precarious workers are the same people who will have the least access to training and learning programmes. This has been the case for decades, unfortunately. In addition, many of the organisational models that are mistaken for innovative tend to generate unstable and poor-quality jobs.

The main threat to labour is the slow and persistent downward pressure on the value and availability of work exerted by general purpose technologies.[10] Even worse, those who lose their jobs have very little chance of finding any decent jobs in a different sector. Regulators and analysts should be more aware of this vicious circle in which we risk getting stuck.

In the meantime, there is much uncertainty about how to frame the issue from a legal perspective. Although this raging dispute is not likely to be resolved within academic circles, it may severely affect policy responses and the way in which regulators design accompanying measures. Therefore, as suggested by NYU professor Cynthia Estlund,[11] employment law scholars cannot afford to ignore this discussion among economists and business leaders.

Today, workers face a routine-biased transformation, eliminating the more repetitive midlevel tasks in clerical occupations and on factory floors. At the same time, labour markets are experiencing a simultaneous growth in the bottom and top of the skill distribution accompanied by a substantial contraction of middle-skill jobs, resulting in a growing polarisation 'between satisfying and rewarding work for some, and a growing cadre of workers who experience a tyranny of technology over their work tasks, routines and remuneration.'[12] Game-changing technologies 'hollow out' the distribution of jobs into either high-paying skilled positions or low-paying routine ones through the destruction of mid-range jobs. According to the data,[13] the substitution effect seems to have much more chance of working in the mid-range, while looking at the areas below and above in the work and skills map it is easier to come across the complementarity effect. The scenario is not very reassuring. Only highly skilled workers see their productivity increase because of technology and benefit directly from it. For everyone else, the news is much more worrying.[14]

All these concerns are more than justified. But when governments intervene on the issues raised in these debates, the responses are all too often erratic, brief and inadequate. To get out of this dead end, courage and investment are needed. It is not enough, however, to offload this responsibility to political authorities; businesses should also take on the task of constantly upskilling their workforce and providing people with appropriate training.[15] Among other things, their ability to succeed in markets that are ever competitive and hungry for innovation depends on it.

A. The 'Robocalypse' is Postponed to a Later Date

Are we headed towards the end of work as we know it? The apocalypse, or rather the 'robocalypse', could be approaching, and real workers are in danger of coming off rather badly.[16] Many commentators are ominously repeating that job-killing innovation is heading at full speed towards the replacement of human labour.

This cataclysmic narrative – albeit in good faith – has served as a rhetorical weapon to justify deregulation of the labour market and the resulting erosion of protection and immiseration of working conditions. It has also helped to spread the commonplace notion that social institutions are 'rigid' and 'antiquated' while labour protection would strangle innovation in the cradle. Even worse, mainstream discourses have associated this scenario with a more or less explicit threat – if automation promises to make human work redundant, the only strategy to make workers competitive would be to remove constraints and protection – offloading risks from businesses onto workers and welfare systems. In short, the idea that machines, if not smarter, will at least be cheaper than workers, is claimed by any entrepreneur that wants to compete unfairly.

The COVID-19 pandemic caused experts to forecast an upsurge in automation and an accompanying reduction in manpower intensity for many reasons. First, technology substituting for human labour is not affected by illness ('robots never call in sick' was the catchy headline; 'nor do they complain or unionise', the likely afterthought). Secondly, machines offer cost-saving prospects for firms. It is no mere accident that the same storyline has gained traction during previous recessions.[17] Thanks to exogenous shocks, automation happened in bursts, especially for those roles considered too expensive in automatable occupations.[18] However, recent data shows that the current narrative is wrong.[19] There is little evidence of growing interest in automation, and even the pandemic, with its rules on distancing, has only had a modest impact. It has not increased the adoption of robots, although aggregate unemployment has risen, and the feasibility of 'in-presence' labour has been severely compromised.[20] While positively shifting public attitudes toward the uptake of new technology, mainly in customer mindsets, the pandemic has also brought to our attention the usually hidden human network that is the backbone of the smooth operation of our digital world.[21]

It is undeniable, though, that companies leverage temporary economic depressions to 'permanently restructure in ways that informalize work',[22] in such a way as to make worker self-organisation more difficult and encourage regulatory arbitrage. In turn, a general 'take-it-or-leave-it' attitude may play a role in curbing contestation and collective claims. Certain cutting-edge business strategies are thus anything but revolutionary.[23] Very often, they end up freezing productivity and encouraging inefficiencies. Moreover, gutting labour regulation has not proved to achieve great results so far. By contrast, in the absence of solid work arrangements and stable relationships, the interests of the firms and those of the workers are misaligned and tend to drift apart, especially when it comes to developing new skills and internal innovation. Competitiveness, therefore, ends up being hampered.[24]

Granted, the current developments are unpredictable and the relationship between innovation and employment remains unclear. In the face of doom-filled forecasts, optimists are too quick to recall, almost in mocking tones, a long series of predictions about the reduction of working hours, which turned out to be exaggerated. In the midst of the Great Depression, in *Economic Possibilities for our Grandchildren*, John Maynard Keynes described a plausible dawn of 2030 when a US citizen would wake up with very little work to do, thanks to public investment in innovation and technological progress.[25] This prediction, unfortunately, is late in coming true – as you may have noticed after having set your alarm for tomorrow morning to avoid being late for work.

The reopening of the debate has been freshly stimulated by the publication of the much cited and highly contested working paper quantifying prospective human redundancy due to susceptibility to computerisation, *The Future of Employment: How Susceptible are Jobs to Computerisation?*. In this paper, Oxford researchers Carl Benedikt Frey and Michael Osborne argued that 47 per cent of total US employment is vulnerable to automation 'relatively soon, perhaps over the next decade or two'.[26] The two authors – relying on the contribution of AI experts – assessed the probability that a given occupation, in a sample of more than 700 professions, would be affected and eventually replaced by advanced machinery such as AI-driven applications, with jobs in logistics, production and administrative support particularly vulnerable. The occupations were then designated as 'high, medium and low risk', depending on 'their probability of computerization'.

The exercise has been repeated with many adjustments and country or sector-specific adaptations. A flurry of authors has shared similarly sinister messages. By adopting the Frey and Osborne model, other academics estimated figures would rise to 54 per cent, if the model is applied to European countries, or even 57 per cent, when the same method was used to assess the risk of automation in OECD countries.[27] Past research shows that the boldest predictions only provide unsatisfactory answers. The problem with many studies, on taking a closer look, was in considering the occupations and not the tasks. Within the same job, only some specific tasks can be automated. What will happen in the future?

After considering the variety of workers' tasks within even the same occupation, instead of the average task content of all jobs in each occupation, several authors have re-evaluated the estimate claiming that, on average across the 21 OECD countries, only about 9 per cent of jobs risk being entirely automated, while almost half of workers will experience a radical change in their tasks. The Organisation for Economic Co-operation and Development (OECD) has long tried to explain how technology transforms the structure and content of work relations, rather than directly affecting the total job count. This is because job destruction in certain sectors is offset in other fields. These processes, however, are often accompanied by geographical and economic imbalances, not only between states but also between different areas of the same country, with the 'richer' areas even more affected by divergences and inequalities.[28]

Over the years, the methodology used by Frey and Osborne has been strongly criticised: occupations considered as high-risk often still contain a substantial share of tasks that will be almost impossible (or too costly and difficult) to automate in the future. What is more, the likelihood of substitution does not always result in actual replacement. Many authors have therefore overestimated the speed and intensity of the process by which machines will take over from human beings. This linear extrapolation, which extends trends for a certain group to totally different groups, seems to overlook the principle of comparative advantage and the social organisation of the production process. Being merely concerned with the pace at which tech performance improves, a purely numerical approach says very little or nothing about the qualitative aspects of the change, that are extremely difficult to forecast.

From the vantage point of the present, pessimistic predictions have not corresponded to actual developments. However, there appears to be a large-scale revival of such flawed arguments. Therefore, it is still interesting to examine in more detail why the gloomiest projections have not materialised so far. On the one hand, it is important to discuss the 'lump of labour' fallacy (the misconception that there is a fixed amount of work available). It is wrong to assume a stable stock of jobs, as the amount of work available can theoretically increase with no real limit. Besides, job losses can be absorbed by other sectors and workers can specialise in new and complementary tasks, thus shifting the composition of work.[29] On the other hand, it must also be considered that the transformation of the world of work is not only tech-determined: demographic and societal phenomena, globalisation, migration, climate and health emergencies, but also changes in lifestyles contribute significantly to reshaping labour markets. This view has gained acceptance in mainstream economics, but it is taking a long time to establish itself as a significant fact among policymakers.

If the direct impact of innovations aimed at increasing productivity leads to the destruction of jobs when production and prices remain constant in the short term, the introduction of certain machines – in particular those leading to the partial automation of a given job or the reduction of prices and the launch of new products – has beneficial 'spill-over' effects on employment.[30] In practice, more efficient production pushes prices down, increases purchasing power and generates greater demand for goods. The result should then be the creation of more jobs than those lost, or even new economic activities, better paid, in different and more productive sectors (with a consequent net positive outcome at aggregate level).[31]

In the US, it was feared that the introduction of automatic teller machines (ATMs) 50 years ago would make banking occupations redundant. Instead, the lower costs of branches prompted banks to open new offices, even in remote locations, which in turn attracted a growing number of customers. At the same time, thanks to the complementary effect, bank tellers could focus on providing financial guidance, instead of having to merely hand out cash. The result was a material growth of jobs in the sector, in spite of the initial predictions, and a gradual change in the tasks of workers: going from simple tellers to financial advisers. The real trouble is that this trend did not lead to a parallel increase in wages.[32] Undoubtedly, in order to generate positive effects, it is necessary that companies do not opt – or are not allowed – to entirely freeze or leave the wealth of productivity increases captured by capital rather than by labour.

The race to estimate the likelihood of computerisation, without considering the heterogeneity of functions and tasks 'wrapped' in the same job, left much to be desired. More recently, research has focused on the single task rather than the entire job, when assessing the risk of automation. These studies are based on the method adopted by David Autor of Boston's MIT and his co-authors, who have shown that occupations are much more multi-faceted than people believe.[33] As is clear to all, jobs consist of performing a bundle of different tasks, not all of which are at risk of robotic replacement. A large slice of activity is still difficult to automate, as these are actions that require a mix of human-exclusive skills, including abstraction, improvisation, critical thinking, analytical judgement, relational or social intelligence, not to mention perceptive and manipulative skills as well as physical dexterity. Nor should geographical difference be overlooked: a job with a high risk of automation in a certain area of the world could be safe from automation in a different area. And vice versa.[34]

As we go on to argue below, there are several limits to automation. The first is connected to the difficulty of unpacking and programming activity that may seem trivial yet involve a considerable deal of expertise. There is 'tacit' knowledge, either personal or procedural, developed with practice and buried in our subconscious. And it is extremely difficult to articulate these human capabilities in standard protocols: it is the human limit to automation. Let us console ourselves that so many intellectual and manual activities, from the most mundane to the sublime, cannot be computerised because we would not be able to fully decode their components and transfer them to an intelligent machine.[35] As the philosopher Karl Polanyi tried to say, we are able to do more than we can explain.[36]

Secondly, robots are far from becoming mainstream in many jobs where human labour is still preferred, mainly due to its comparatively low cost and the still significant practical challenges involved in their automation. This limit is particularly worrying, as it depends on the large availability of poorly paid jobs. A gradual yet seemingly inexorable process making workers expendable or interchangeable constitutes a valid alternative to full automation.[37] As a consequence, in the era of disruptive technologies, we are witnessing a proliferation of bad jobs instead of having them automated away.[38]

II. The Digital is Political. Adopting a 'Human in Command' Approach

Many professions have disappeared. To name but a few: lamplighters, lift operators, switchboard workers, travel agents, military sentries. In other sectors, the number of employees has dropped dramatically, such as within agriculture. However, work still exists. The long list of wrong assumptions and the studies deflating the most dramatic estimates of computerisation should alleviate some anxiety.

Nonetheless, it is not enough to read into the most reassuring analyses of labour economists to dismiss the questions posed by the digital transition of work and breathe a sigh of relief. The news that the end of the world of work is not nigh challenges us even more to broaden our views. Before delving into the legal analysis of the digital transformation, it is useful to ask ourselves what the room for intervention in such a rapidly changing context is.

We must thus remember that while in the last century the process of industrial-isation was followed, in many countries, by a trend towards more stable and secure work relationships, the current transition has so far generated a countermovement to this. The signature contractual schemes of the platform economy take the form of under-regulated relations between a client and a 'disposable' contractor – to put it simply. And yet, in a contradictory way, while legislative action is being taken to reduce the alleged rigidity of standard employment, many observers still call out the inability of traditional labour regulation to adapt to new business models. One of two things is true, however: either the flexibility-enhancing reforms have led to nothing concrete, or they were invoked with the sole purpose of getting rid of some responsibility.

While we are unsure of the effects of certain practices (outsourcing, fissurisation, casualisation) on competitiveness and efficiency,[39] the suspicion is that many tech giants, as well as many self-proclaimed innovative companies, have feet of clay. Their current modus operandi, which is certainly effective when it comes to 'moving fast and breaking things', is bound to crumble in the long run, both finan-cially and operationally. Many IPOs (the process by which a private company sells shares of stock to the public) have failed despite promising the world and investors have been forced to foot the bill to avoid collapse.[40] Conversely, various apps that adopt a classic business model, with standard employees, still thrive on the market. When it comes to achieving results in the long term, a simple rule applies: solid is better than liquid, or at least this is what several business cases seem to teach us.[41]

All of this means that the rise of digital technologies can and must be governed. Innovation does not take place in an institutional, political, socio-economic and cultural vacuum. It occurs in ingrained value sets and webs of norms. Nevertheless, the dominant opinion on technology advances the entirely erroneous and disin-genuous idea that rules on the introduction of new technologies at the workplace cannot be put in place, or – even worse – that it is not appropriate to govern their consequences on jobs. Any attempt to manage the effects of digital innovation would strangle the spirit of innovation and lead to severe economic losses. Plus, standards introduced in the last century cannot possibly keep up with the ground-breaking models launched in recent years.

These conjectures, once again, must be rejected. Regulations aim to alleviate the potentially harmful effects of the use of technological devices on the quality and quantity of the work. Rules to mitigate the most invasive and harmful effects of the use of technological devices on the health and safety, privacy and the human dignity of workers already exist in a number of industrialised, emerging or devel-oping countries.[42] Think of the prohibition on using a polygraph on job applicants or employees, the protection of personal data or the recent right to disconnect. Many legal systems have long adopted rules to address the social impact of mass redundancies and job losses, including those linked to automation and technological conversion. Many international and European legal standards mandate for these rules and require business to adequately inform and consult trade unions and workers' representatives and to involve public bodies before proceeding with mass layoffs.

Other examples are clear to everyone. During the pandemic, massive furlough and short-time work schemes have been implemented, with simplified rules, in order to grant relief to businesses short of liquidity and at the same time support workers' income. Even countries where this would have been unimaginable, such as the UK or the US, introduced these programmes. EU institutions have promptly invested 100 billion euros to assist sectors in difficulty (750 billion euros were later endowed through the 'NextGenerationEU' plan).[43] Many 'small-government' pundits as well as countless anti-EU militants were forced to beat a hasty retreat under the circumstances.

A negative economic impact of this type of regulation has never been proven. On the contrary, a strong involvement of public institutions and social partners in the management of potential mass redundancies is associated with high levels of productivity and competitiveness.[44] Data from the Cambridge Centre for Business Research shows that an adequate body of labour law rules has a positive effect on employment rates, reduces unemployment and stimulates innovation.[45]

It is time, then, to disprove the rambling proclamations of those who insist on painting labour law as red tape for businesses. As the OECD has made clear,[46] collective bargaining – to be discussed in the final section of this book – helps to reduce inequalities. It can foster the dissemination of best practices in the fields of personnel management, training programmes, occupational health and safety, the introduction of new technologies, early retirement packages and incentive schemes – all of which can be useful tools for small and medium enterprises to face the challenges of the current transition. Collectively negotiated solutions enable businesses to respond to demographic and digital change by adapting their work organisations to new market needs in a more flexible and pragmatic way than any possible legal reform.

However, we should not delude ourselves by thinking that a package of rules, enlightened as they may be, is enough to dismiss the challenges arising from automation and the digital revolution. Current regulation, for example, can tone down the most dramatic consequences of redundancies, but cannot prevent them, especially when new machinery and organisational processes can allow for substituting a huge number of jobs in a short time span.

History does not necessarily repeat itself. It is said that the main difference between the first industrial era and the current one rests on the fact that while rudimentary technologies were predominantly labour-enabling, today's innovation is eminently labour-replacing. Certain characteristics of the Fourth industrial revolution, combined with the persistent global crisis and exacerbated by the shock caused by the pandemic, could generate consequences that are extremely complicated to govern and that can strain existing regulatory frameworks and industrial relations models.[47] Moreover, the almost monopolistic nature of many technologies will not help. It is almost certain that the rules on collective redundancies alone will not be sufficient to dissolve the imbalances exacerbated by the digital transition, but to proclaim their irrelevance or the outright helplessness of public decision-makers is preposterous.

Debunking many myths about the end of work, therefore, cannot lead to cheap triumphalism. We cannot rule out that jobs in the future will be inferior, in number and quality, to the work of today.[48] In any case, there is an urgent need to refocus the crux of the discussion, trying to decode the consequences of automation, digitisation and 'gigification' from a qualitative point of view. Deeper changes, as explained by Eurofound – the EU agency promoting the improvement of living and working conditions – often require an adaptation of organisational practices, social institutions and even governance frameworks. To do this, an effort of analysis is needed to assess elements of continuity and discontinuity, avoiding being blinded by what is most familiar to us, before experimenting with new interventions.

Although automation and digitalisation have been under close observation by jurists since the advent of the microprocessor, the meteoric rise of new platform enterprises – hybrid organisational modules and ultra-atypical contract formats, straddling self-employment and subordinate work – seems to have taken experts and commentators by surprise, who have perhaps turned too hastily to classical resources, in search of interpretative tools to be used in this new phase. In order to avoid Pavlovian conditionings, a pragmatic attitude is needed, aiming at a more effective and flexible application of the existing rules, as well as a reclamation of ambiguous rules and uncertainty, moving beyond technical fixes. To those who admonish that 'reins and restraints' risk condemning countries that are in themselves scarcely innovative and prone to perennial backwardness, it is also necessary to answer that this is not the time to give up intransigence. As we shall see, the European institutions have also launched the battle for a sustainable digital future, leading the way for a global tech governance movement. It is crucial to dovetail new models with existing regulation and fine-tune legislation to accommodate new initiatives. But for this to happen, attention and strategic planning are urgently needed.

Progress, both technological and social, needs to be steered and the direction is defined by its desired objectives. The work of the future is in desperate need of political and social institutions that build up consensus around visions that are not taken for granted. Instead of a self-driving future, it is important to strive to design and implement a model that sees the human being at the helm, with human decision-makers 'at the wheel' of technical and social change, as called for by the European Economic and Social Committee (EESC), an authoritative consulting body of the European Union.[49] Reflecting on AI and new automated decision-making systems, the Committee has defined an approach that, by promoting a strong sense of agency, places the human being – citizens and workers – at the centre of choices as a precondition for sustainable, accessible, safe and beneficial digital transformation. Technology is fine, but it is human beings who guide its adoption and regulation. Machines remain machines and people retain control over them, reads an EESC opinion calling for broad involvement in the development of advanced systems, 'to ensure the worker still has sufficient autonomy and control (human-in-command), fulfilment and job satisfaction'.[50]

In order to achieve this goal, governments, researchers and experts cannot assume that a regulatory framework to mitigate the damaging effects of labour market shocks does not exist or is impossible to apply. The regulation of collective redundancies resulting from company reorganisations, data protection rules and the criteria for access to social protection are a given throughout the European Union.[51] The standards of the International Labour Organisation also offer guidance on these issues. As rightly pointed out by legal academic Joshua Fairfield, 'law plays a critical role in anticipating and guiding, in naming and shaping, technological change'.[52] On this basis, there is an urgent need to define legislative measures that strengthen fundamental rights, establish minimum standards and impose due-process safeguards. It is essential to balance complex and opposing interests. Negotiating the transition and governing change are the only recipes that can ensure a future that lives up to the most ambitious expectations.

We can let our fears define us. Or we can make our aspirations prevail. Whatever face change has, it cannot happen accidentally: it is important that it is the result of conscious choices that answer a simple question: not *how much*, but *what* work we want.

---

[1] For a definition, see K Schwab, 'The Fourth Industrial Revolution. What It Means and How to Respond' (*Foreign Affairs*, 12 December 2015) www.foreignaffairs.com/articles/2015-12-12/fourth-industrial-revolution.

[2] J Suzman, *Work. A History of How We Spend Our Time* (London, Bloomsbury, 2020).

[3] The 'employment relationship' is an umbrella definition, of which the 'standard employment relationship' is only one modality. The former 'expands the coverage of EU labour regulation from a narrower scope limited to a "contract of employment", based on the criterion of subordination of the employee to the employer'. See Eurofound, *Employment relationship* (2011). The 'standard employment relationship' is 'understood as work that is full time, indefinite, as well as part of a subordinate and bilateral employment relationship'. See ILO, *Non-standard employment around the world: Understanding challenges, shaping prospects* (Geneva, International Labour Office, 2016) 7.

[4] For a critical point of view on this ideological dispute, M Vivarelli, *Innovation and employment: A survey*, IZA Discussion papers, No. 2621, 2007.

[5] C Estlund, *Automation Anxiety. Why and How to Save Work* (Oxford, Oxford University Press, 2021).

[6] RE Susskind and D Susskind, *The Future of the Professions: How Technology will Transform the Work of Human Experts* (Oxford, Oxford University Press, 2015).

[7] S Kolhatkar, 'Welcoming Our New Robot Overlords' *The New Yorker* (23 October 2017) www.newyorker.com/magazine/2017/10/23/welcoming-our-new-robot-overlords.

[8] DH Autor, 'Why are there still so many jobs? The history and future of workplace automation' (2015) 29(3) *The Journal of Economic Perspectives* 3–30.

[9] C Mims, 'New Research Busts Popular Myths About Innovation' *The Wall Street Journal* (18 September 2021) www.wsj.com/articles/new-research-busts-popular-myths-about-innovation-11631937693.

[10] The term 'general purpose technology' describes modern, versatile multifunctional methods of producing that are impactful enough to have a protracted aggregate impact. TF Bresnahan and M Trajtenberg, 'General Purpose Technologies "Engines of Growth?"' (1995) 65(1) *Journal of Econometrics* 83–108. See also M Ford, *Rule of the Robots: How Artificial Intelligence Will Transform Everything* (New York, Basic Books, 2021).

[11] C Estlund, 'What Should We Do after Work: Automation and Employment' (2018) 128(2) *Yale Law Journal* 257–326. For instance, skill obsolescence and enhanced mechanisation could prompt large restructuring operations, whose social implications should be mitigated. Anticipating the advent of new demands could inform reskilling processes. Alternatively, fewer jobs may usher in downward competition on wages and other conditions for the jobs that survive the turbulence.

[12] G Mundlak and J Fudge, 'The Future of Work and The Covid-19 Crisis' (*Futures of Work*, 5 June 2020) https://futuresofwork.co.uk/2020/06/05/the-future-of-work-and-the-covid-19-crisis/.

[13] D Acemoglu and P Restrepo, 'Automation and new tasks: How technology displaces and reinstates labor' (2019) 33(2) *Journal of Economic Perspectives* 3–30.

[14] A specific division of labour has been and is the condition of the possibility of digital automation. Eurofound, *Automation, Digitisation and Platforms: Implications for Work and Employment* (Luxembourg, Publications Office of the European Union, 2018).

[15] I Ferreras, *Firms as Political Entities: Saving Democracy Through Economic Bicameralism* (Cambridge, Cambridge University Press, 2017). But see A Lowrey, 'Low-Skill Workers Aren't a Problem to Be Fixed' (*The Atlantic*, 23 April 2021) www.theatlantic.com/ideas/archive/2021/04/theres-no-such-thing-as-a-low-skill-worker/618674/.

[16] Although there is a lack of strong scientific evidence, the narrative of the imminent end of work has been stubbornly diffused, fuelled by dozens of texts that have long remained at the top of the charts all over the world. See, among others, E Brynjolfsson and A McAfee, *The Second Machine Age: Work, Progress, and Prosperity in a Time of Brilliant Technologies* (New York, WW Norton & Company, 2014); M Ford, *The Rise of the Robots: Technology and the Threat of a Jobless Future* (New York, Basic Books, 2015); J Manyika, 'Technology, jobs, and the future of work' (McKinsey Global Institute, Executive Briefing, 2017), available at www.mckinsey.com/featured-insights/employment-and-growth/technology-jobs-and-the-future-of-work, J Manyika et al, 'Disruptive technologies: Advances that will transform life, business, and the global economy' (McKinsey Global Institute, Report, 2013). See also RJ Gordon, *The Rise and Fall of American Growth: the U.S. Standard of Living since the Civil War* (Princeton, Princeton University Press, 2016) arguing that technological progress is less disruptive than it appears, and that workers will face a modest risk of replacement.

[17] *The Economist*, 'Robots Threaten Jobs Less Than Fearmongers Claim' (*The Economist*, 10 April 2021) www.economist.com/special-report/2021/04/08/robots-threaten-jobs-less-than-fearmongers-claim. JE Smith, *Smart Machines and Service Work: Automation in an Age of Stagnation* (London, Reaktion Books, 2020) 76.

[18] W Knight, 'Now You Can Rent a Robot Worker – for Less Than Paying a Human' (*Wired*, 18 January 2022) www.wired.com/story/rent-robot-worker-less-paying-human/.

[19] A Georgieff and A Milanez, 'What Happened to Jobs at High Risk of Automation?' (*OECD*, 25 January 2021).

[20] Future of Work Commission, 'The Impact of Automation on Labour Markets: Interactions with Covid-19' (*IFOW*, 2021).

[21] S Amrute, 'Automation Won't Keep Front-Line Workers Safe' (*Slate*, 9 April 2020) https://slate.com/technology/2020/04/automation-coronavirus-frontline-workers-protection.html.

[22] S Amrute, A Rosenblat and B Callaci, 'Why Are Good Jobs Disappearing if Robots Aren't Taking Them?' (*Points Data&Society*, 16 June 2020) https://points.datasociety.net/why-are-good-jobs-disappearing-if-robots-arent-taking-them-9f8d4845302a?gi=1d7e4897b64b.

[23] K Crawford, *The Atlas of AI* (New Haven, CT, Yale University Press, 2021).

[24] A Lindbeck and DJ Snower, *The Insider-Outsider Theory of Employment and Unemployment* (Cambridge, MA, The MIT Press, 1988); T Boeri and P Garibaldi, 'Two tier reforms of employment protection: A honeymoon effect?' (2007) 117(521) *The Economic Journal* 357–85. See also J Eeckhout, *The Profit Paradox: How Thriving Firms Threaten the Future of Work* (Princeton, Princeton University Press, 2021).

[25] JM Keynes, *Economic Possibilities for our Grandchildren, Essays in Persuasion* (New York, Harcourt Brace, 1930) 358–73. See also A Toffler, *Future Shock* (New York, Random House, 1970); D Ricardo, *Principles of political economy and taxation* (London, G Bell & Sons, 1891); D Bell, 'The Coming of

the Post-Industrial Society' (1976) 40(4) *The Educational Forum* 574–79; J Rifkin, *The End of Work: The Decline of the Global Labor Force and the Dawn of the Post-Market Era* (New York, GP Putnam's Sons, 1995).

[26] Despite having more than 9,500 citations on Google Scholar in January 2022, the study was presented in 2013 and more recently accepted in a peer reviewed journal. The delay shows that the scientific review process was troubled. CB Frey and MA Osborne, 'The future of employment: How susceptible are jobs to computerisation?' (2017) 114 *Technological Forecasting and Social Change* 254–80. The authors also seem to have tuned down their message ('Our estimates have often been taken to imply an employment apocalypse. Yet that is not what we intended or suggested'). C Benedikt Frey and MA Osborne, 'Automation and the future of work – understanding the numbers' (*The Oxford Martin Blog*, 13 April 2018) www.oxfordmartin.ox.ac.uk/blog/automation-and-the-future-of-work-understanding-the-numbers/.

[27] M Arntz, T Gregory and U Zierahn, *The risk of automation for jobs in OECD countries: A comparative analysis* (OECD Social, Employment and Migration Working Paper, No. 189, 2016).

[28] OECD, *OECD Employment Outlook 2019: the future of work* (Paris, OECD Publishing, 2019).

[29] DH Autor, 'Why Are There Still So Many Jobs? The History and Future of Workplace Automation' (2015) 29(3) *The Journal of Economic Perspectives* 3–30.

[30] E Morath, 'Automation isn't killing jobs, study says, but may be keeping income in check' (*The Wall Street Journal*, 8 March 2018) www.wsj.com/articles/automation-isnt-killing-jobs-study-says-but-may-be-keeping-income-in-check-1520505311?tesla=y.

[31] J Mokyr, C Vickers and NL Ziebarth, 'The History of Technological Anxiety and the Future of Economic Growth: Is This Time Different?' (2015) 29(3) *The Journal of Economic Perspectives* 31–50; D Acemoglu and P Restrepo, *Robots and Jobs: Evidence from US Labor Market* (NBER Working Paper, No. 23285, 2017). Indeed, the effect of the widespread recourse to digital tech 'will be felt more in the content of work, rather than in its volume'. D Spencer, M Cole, S Joyce, X Whittaker and M Stuart, *Digital Automation and the Future of Work* (Luxembourg, European Union, 2021).

[32] According to the authors, the economists Acemoglu and Restrepo, large and robust negative effects of robots are estimated on employment and wages across commuting zones. See D Acemoglu and P Restrepo, *Robots and Jobs: Evidence from US labor markets* (NBER Working Paper, No. 23285, 2017).

[33] DH Autor, *The 'task approach' to labor markets: an overview* (NBER Working Paper, No. 18711, 2013). See also DH Autor and D Dorn, 'The growth of low-skill service jobs and the polarization of the US labour market' (2013) 103(5) *American Economic Review* 1553–97.

[34] E Anthes, 'The shape of work to come: Three ways that the digital revolution is reshaping workforces around the world' (2017) 550 *Nature* 316–19.

[35] DH Autor, *Polanyi's Paradox and the Shape of Employment Growth* (NBER Working Paper, No. 20485, 2014).

[36] M Polanyi, *The Tacit Dimension* (London, Routledge & Kegan Paul, 1967). See also G Colvin, *Humans Are Underrated: What High Achievers Know That Brilliant Machines Never Will* (London, Penguin, 2016).

[37] Indeed, the question is not simply 'whether a job can be mechanised but if it is economically worthwhile given the cheap labour available', which reduces the incentive for companies to innovate. P Flemin, 'Robots and Organization Studies: Why Robots Might Not Want to Steal Your Job' (2019) 40(1) *Organization Studies* 23–38.

[38] S Raisch and S Krakowski, 'Artificial Intelligence and Management: The Automation–Augmentation Paradox' (2021) 46(1) *Academy of Management Review* 192–210; E Stewart, 'Robots were supposed to take our jobs. Instead, they're making them worse' (*Vox*, 2 July 2021) www.vox.com/the-goods/22557895/automation-robots-work-amazon-uber-lyft.

[39] A Lo Faro, 'Core and contingent work: a theoretical framework' in E Ales, O Deinert and J Kenner (eds), *Core and Contingent Work in the European Union: A Comparative Analysis* (Oxford, Hart Publishing, 2017) 7–23.

[40] T Bradshaw and A Mooney, 'Disaster strikes as Deliveroo becomes "worst IPO in London's history"' *Financial Times* (31 March 2021) www.ft.com/content/bdf6ac6b-46b5-4f7a-90db-291d7fd2898d.

[41] G Barber, 'This Company Hires Gig Workers – as Employees' (*Wired*, 13 January 2021) www.wired.com/story/company-hires-gig-workers-employees/.

[42] JE Cohen, 'What Privacy is For' (2013) 126 *Harvard Law Review* 1904–33.

[43] S Giubboni, '«In a spirit of solidarity between Member States». Noterella a prima lettura sulla proposta della Commissione di una «cassa integrazione europea»' (*Eticaeconomia menabò*, 6 April 2020) www.eticaeconomia.it/in-a-spirit-of-solidarity-between-member-states-noterella-a-prima-lettura-sulla-proposta-della-commissione-di-una-cassa-integrazione-europea/. See also M Ferrera, J Miró and

S Ronchi, 'Walking the road together? EU polity maintenance during the COVID-19 crisis' (2021) 55(5–6) *West European Politics* 1329–52.

[44] R Solow, 'We'd Better Watch Out' (*New York Times Book Review*, 12 July 1987) ('We see the computer age everywhere, except in the productivity statistics'). See J Triplett, 'The Solow Productivity Paradox: What Do Computers Do to Productivity?' (1999) 32(2) *The Canadian Journal of Economics* 309–34.

[45] See also M Sandbu, 'Europe's social model is a source of productivity' *Financial Times* (4 May 2021) www.ft.com/content/31b43bee-82cf-4fe9-9b3d-6cc2a630f3fa.

[46] OECD, *Negotiating Our Way Up: Collective Bargaining in a Changing World of Work* (Paris, OECD Publishing, 2019).

[47] A Toeffler, *The Third Wave: The Classic Study of Tomorrow* (Bantam, New York, 1980).

[48] DA Spencer, 'Fear and hope in an age of mass automation: debating the future of work' (2018) 33(1) *New Technology, Work and Employment* 1–12.

[49] Opinion of the European Economic and Social Committee on 'Artificial intelligence – The consequences of artificial intelligence on the (digital) single market, production, consumption, employment and society' (own-initiative opinion) (2017/C 288/01).

[50] ibid. See also I Bartoletti, *An Artificial Revolution: On Power, Politics and AI* (London, Indigo Press, 2020).

[51] The regulatory framework for collective redundancies and the classical mechanics of trade union law, for example, ensure that the industrial relations system functions properly and that cooperation between the parties involved promotes sustainable economic solutions. In addition, robust labour law institutions are associated with the good performance of the German labour market, which has maintained stable employment levels even during the economic crisis, as argued by O Bohachova, B Boockmann and CM Buch, *Labor Demand During the Crisis: What Happened in Germany?* (IZA Discussion Paper, No. 6074, 2011). Other studies find a positive relationship between strong collective institutions and productivity: S Deakin, C Fenwick and P Sarkar, 'Labour law and inclusive development: the economic effects of industrial relations laws in middle income countries' in M Schmiegelow and H Schmiegelow (eds), *Institutional Competition between Common Law and Civil Law: Theory and Policy* (Heidelberg, Springer, 2014) 185–209.

[52] JAT Fairfield, *Runaway Technology: Can Law Keep Up?* (Cambridge, Cambridge University Press, 2021) 5. See also S Deakin and C Markou, 'The Law-Technology Cycle and the Future of Work' (2018) 158(2) *Giornale di diritto del lavoro e di relazioni industriali* 445–62. But see GE Marchant et al (eds), *The Growing Gap Between Emerging Technologies and Legal-Ethical Oversight: The Pacing Problem* (New York, Springer, 2011).

2

A Changing Labour Market

I. The Consequences for the 'Jobs that Remain'

The anxiety of a future-without-jobs can be easily justified. It is of little use, though, unless we investigate the effects brought about by automation and digitisation on 'jobs that remain'. These are occupations that are not replaced by game-changing technologies, but which – in various forms – are displaced by digital transformation. In practice, these include almost every job in existence today.

Those who have been working for more than 30 years have experienced first-hand the power of the internet and digital tools in the workplace. The newcomers have certainly metabolised the technological grafting more quickly, often by contributing directly to the adoption of new IT-driven models. They are also already prepared for (or resigned to) dynamic careers. The human and professional histories of both the digital 'migrants' and the 'natives' dovetail together every day at the workplace. The progressive lengthening of working life results in several generations, from newbies to prospective retirees, based in the same office or factory. Despite their diverse attitudes towards hierarchies, information sharing and the use of tech tools, everyone is expected to deal directly with innovation and different ways of working.[1] The pandemic, by forcing businesses to adopt 'distanced' and remote solutions to adapt to physical lockdowns, also encouraged greater digitalisation in the workplace.

As mentioned, only certain tasks, the most monotonous, repetitive and predictable ones, can be completely automated. This calculation factors in at least three main elements. Are alternative options technically feasible? Are they affordable? And are they otherwise convenient? Much has been written about this imperfect, path-dependent equation. It is worth reiterating that any forecast about the automation of a job must deal with certain considerations that are often overlooked by analysts and policymakers.

First, we consider the content of the job, a combination of quality, professionalism, and complexity.[2] In this assessment, the factual, regulatory and contractual conditions that define the job itself also come into play and help to determine its value. What does this mean? Before replacing a worker with a (more or less) intelligent machine, or before reorganising a process using a mechanical or digital tool, a firm will assess the state of play of the technology and, therefore, the actual abilities of the prospective robot candidate, and then consider the cost and return of such an investment. All alternative options will be explored if the change is particularly costly. Therefore, to analyse the peculiar organisational processes of the 'Second Machine Age',[3] it is necessary to concentrate on the interaction between atoms and bits, on the one hand, and the terms and conditions of employment, on the other. This leads to cases where automation is not economically viable or technically possible.[4]

Years ago, the *New York Times* hosted a series of works of fiction labelled 'op-eds from the future', to be read as if written 10, 50 or even 200 years from now. In one of these, Brian Merchant tried to describe a 'fully automated' and 'human-free' Amazon fulfilment centre.[5] The year is 2034, and the report makes it clear from the outset that the plant just inaugurated by Bezos is anything but automated, despite the abundance of mechanical arms in charge of packing and self-driving mobile pallets responsible for storing items. At the time of the launch, after the toast, a janitor working for a subcontracting company had to clean up the mess after the party and remove the shards of a shattered bottle of champagne from the oversized autonomous vacuum cleaner. The narrator's voice is that of one of the maintenance managers, hired on a rigorously self-employed basis by a third-party contracting company, together with a troupe of engineers in charge of software control and glitches-fixing, cleaners and other contingent workers called to intervene every time a robot breaks down. Instructions and rebukes travel by cable and the premises are constantly remotely monitored. The machine-first environment, devised with the hope of avoiding a human workforce, is rather clunky, inhospitable and insecure: there is no ventilation system, little light and too many dangerous interchanges. Collisions and injuries are frequent. It is almost impossible in theory for these invisible workers to form a union and fight unsafe conditions, being all engaged by different entities. It is also difficult in practice, given the lack of interaction, the high turnover of employees and the absence of any class consciousness. At the end of the day, the most bewildering element of the op-ed is its adherence to the present, and the author himself has used this plot device to illustrate more freely a condition that already unites many of the American giant's warehouses and stores.

You no longer need to use your imagination. In January 2018, Amazon Go opened in Seattle. This is the first 'just-walk-out shopping' supermarket without cashiers where it is possible to shop 'contactless' in the name of speed and efficiency, thanks to an immersive system of sensors, computer vision and barcode readers throughout the store, and leave without going through tills, not even automatic ones, before receiving a simple notification of your receipt for your purchases. Obviously, in spite of the announcements made about the 'fully automated shop', the shelves are regularly stocked by real workers, who also oversee the preparation of fresh or baked goods. Something similar has happened in the company's warehouses. Thanks to inventions developed by Kiva, a robotics firm later purchased by Amazon, the assembly line has been flipped, and robots carrying shelves approach workers ('stowers' and 'pickers'), who occupy a separate space, instead of the other way around.[6] If anything, these experimental projects are indicative of how many companies are testing new organisational practices in a piecemeal, comical and chaotic way,[7] 'relying on humans to smooth out the rough edges' of dysfunctional innovations – as anthropologists Alexandra Mateescu and Madeleine Clare Elish wrote in a Data & Society report.[8]

Merchant's examples illustrate how the chimera of full automation feeds on a gradual devaluation of work. It is important to consider the factors that contribute to defining the nature of a given job, focusing on how and to what extent the digital components are able to emphasise or diminish the individual's contribution. Again, technology plays a far from neutral role as it can lead to a slow and deep erosion of wages.[9] By increasing the invasive potential of surveillance systems, parcelling out tasks to ease their outsourcing and adopting automated decision-making processes, tech innovations end up accelerating the process of robotisation and, in the long run, may bring about the end of good jobs for humans. Unfortunately, this gradual transformation seems to have paralysing effects on the responses of governments and social partners to vulnerable workers. Precarisation, low wages and automation thus risk becoming enforced stages of a steady journey towards the end of decent work. Simultaneously, contractual degradation, deregulatory chaos and feeble enforcement are also paving the way towards replacing well paid work with low-cost options.

Between learned stereotypes and the ingrained biases of programmers infiltrating software, members of disadvantaged groups end up permanently excluded from the roles in which they have traditionally been under-represented, in an endless tailspin of segregation by means of statistics. Algorithms are engaged in computing the law and 'automating society'[10] in regard to the most sensible tasks in some particularly important areas such as health care, insurance, education,[11] customs and immigration, crime prediction and even the administration of justice.[12] By crunching the datasets that record previous decisions and patterns of groups who share similar skills or backgrounds, these systems learn from the past and encourage unfair choices, or define new levels of injustice. Failures that have not been remedied serve as the basis for future wrongdoing.

When, instead, humans and machines work together, the result can be an insurance against obsolescence: this is how real added value is generated.[13] However, these kinds of readymade assessments are rarely carried out rationally, for very different but equally dangerous reasons. Often the need to achieve short-term results (in terms of volume, sales and profits) entails erratic and counterproductive decisions. In other cases, the managerial – but also the political and trade union – culture is not accurate enough in making forward-looking calculations. Moreover, the progressive compression of collective bargaining power, which is the result of a series of trends that will be analysed in the final chapter, dampens the possibility of jointly co-determining the organisational reconfiguring of the firm, which has always been a core element of negotiation and improvement. In short, to distribute risks and privileges not only efficiently, but also sustainably, it takes a good dose of courage, altruism and foresight – all qualities that are increasingly rare.

Any thorough investigation into the future of work must focus on the complementary relationship between workers and cutting-edge tools as, after all, the adoption of technology is primarily perceived as an organisational choice. To begin with, we ought to acknowledge a reality: machines and algorithms do not necessarily steal jobs, but they certainly transform them, not necessarily for the better. For the 'workers who remain', game-changing technology can be a hostile antagonist, but also a valuable ally. From the agricultural, manufacturing and mining sectors, to the service industry, and passing through sectors with great potential such as crafts, tourism and the cultural and media industries, digital innovation has already reaped the benefits (the disadvantages will be discussed later in this book). It has helped to streamline operational flows and production cycles, to reboot the business organisation of many companies, and to strengthen the abstract component of tasks. The introduction of computerised tools has also facilitated the development of new skills and the advent of new professions.

In many cases, both tangible and intangible infrastructures have accelerated timescales, reduced costs, expanded client portfolios, optimised resources and increased profitability. This is why we speak of 'valuable allies'. Think of the equipment that protects the health and safety of workers, the devices that replace human beings in heavy or risky operations, the intelligent chips that prevent accidents or flag malfunctions, the tools that have robotised menial activities. Consider also the convenience of affordable technology. Or the precision that can be achieved in revision and control processes, the possibility of serialising off-the-shelf production, the ability to engage potential buyers or investors on the other side of the globe and to test creative ideas with 'demo' prototypes before launching new entrepreneurial initiatives, benefiting from management support services and cheap data collection and storage. Technology is not an enemy in itself, it is the constrictive and restraining uses of it that represent a looming threat.

It is not surprising, therefore, that labour law and all other social sciences are in such turmoil these days. It is a sign of the 'flesh and blood' character of these sciences, of their intimate, conflictual and inherent link with the economic context and its main actors. Labour law is not alone, anyway, many other legal disciplines today face a renewed relationship between humans and machines, and need to understand how to handle the delicate legacy of over 100 years of liability principles, health and safety doctrines and criminal responsibilities. When it comes to labour, the relationship between blue-collar workers and machines has shaped the prevailing notion of the people to whom labour law protection is addressed. Whole segments of labour regulation have been conceived to regulate and improve working conditions in the industrial context: from working time regulations to rules protecting women and minors, from compulsory insurance in case of accidents to vicarious liability, from rules on rest periods to the procedure-based law of mass redundancies. The supposed purely industrial relevance of labour and employment law is misleading. Nonetheless, this view has some undeniable roots in reality and still shapes the generalised idea of who the main beneficiaries of labour protection are.

If we take a look at movies, the prevalence of the industrial environment is striking;[14] from the British *Full Monty*, which hit the box office and tells the story of six unemployed steel industry workers in Sheffield, to the Spanish *Los lunes al sol* ('*Mondays in the Sun*'), inspired by the process of restructuring of the shipyards in Gijón, Galicia, to the Italian *Il posto dell'anima* ('*The Soul's Place*'), portraying a dispute involving one of the many small tyre factories in the industrial suburbs, and the acclaimed *Made in Dagenham*, dramatising the 1968 Ford sewing machinists strike where female workers walked out demanding equal pay, resulting in landmark regulatory achievements. Although there is no lack of 'atypical' stories of call centres, knowledge workers, outsourced cleaning services, domestic workers, unpaid internships, unemployment benefits and active labour market policies, even movies have accustomed us to a scenography made up of factory gates, assembly lines, welding departments, crowded canteens, unionists in distress, loft offices and dim locker rooms.

It is also because of this scenario that those who deal with labour regulation are faced with an immeasurable paradigm shift. Suddenly, the scenes transform, the protagonists change and we must decide what to keep of the original screenplay. Just to give a few examples, while the workplace is becoming porous and ubiquitous, with the advent of homeworking partially marking the end of 'the office' as we know it, and the Metaverse potentially allowing an unprecedented combination of digital and physical 'workplace experiences',[15] the prerogatives conventionally belonging to management are intensified and replaced, not necessarily with a human face. Working time opens up immeasurably, to stick to the 'always connected' imperative, but remuneration packages do not always take into account periods of stand-by or on-call, let alone commuting time to reach the workplace. They encourage unbridled competition (just think of piece rates and performance-based pay) rather than it being based on projects, objectives and results.

In an ambitious attempt to put things into perspective, this Chapter maps the most illustrative examples of automation and digitalisation practices in factories and, more generally, in the 'everywhere' workplace. The aim of the following pages is to discuss the changes that are affecting a new, uneven, dispersed workforce that is already confronted with the arguably new rules of the Fourth industrial revolution.[16] First, solutions will first be considered, discussing specific cases of better security, flexibility and competitiveness guaranteed by technologies. Secondly, company practices that make human work standardised, invisible and powerless will be reviewed, ranging from algorithmic management to pervasive surveillance, and considering the digital piecework of 'digital janitors'. The aim is to broaden the view, including *people* who are involved in the on-the-ground process of digital acceleration, and look beyond the technologies.

Although the cases examined here refer to rapidly growing sectors, which are probably overhyped in the eyes of scholars and public opinion, the underlying trends potentially involve almost all types of businesses, regardless of their size and location.

II. Technology at Work

Let us perform a small non-scientific experiment: how many centimetres away from you is your smartphone while you are scrolling through these pages? Where is it, if you are not using it to read this book? And when was the last time, after a flash notification on the screen, you unlocked and voraciously consulted it?

Here is the paradox. Just as in a didactic little story described by David Foster Wallace, we are so immersed in the digital soup that we can no longer distinguish its ingredients, nor are we able to imagine an existence outside this 'natural element'. Like young fish incapable of responding to an older fish swimming the other way and asking them: 'Morning, boys. How's the water?', we might answer: 'What the hell is technology?' to the question 'What is technology like today?'.

This is a difficult question, which we struggle to answer. To our rescue comes Gerd Leonhard, in identifying three essential features of the recent digital transition. It is *exponential*, because it evolves at a rapid rate, *re-combinatory*, because its breakthroughs can complement themselves, and *interdependent*, because many innovations have a discernible ability to self-refine.[17]

Technological devices allow us to collect and manipulate reality data, and almost represent a cell membrane between ourselves and the outside world. Does it still make sense to distinguish between these two spheres? There is a dimension of our multiple lives where the online and offline coexist (philosopher Luciano Floridi calls it 'onlife', or 'phigital' – should you prefer a newly coined expression). This is not necessarily a bad thing, if you think of the endless opportunities of liberation from work and related inefficiencies and waste, or even autonomy at work, that these devices can offer. On closer inspection, even fire, the wheel or stone tools are nothing other than elementary innovations, discovered or forged with a common goal: to make life easier, to bring comfort to the daily toil, or to free up time. A large percentage of the digital tools that surround us in social, professional and private contexts do the same thing. Seen in this perspective, the digital transformation could be nothing more than the continuation of Prometheus' ambition by other means,[18] in a multi-millenary quest going from flint to silicon.

Both in the most acute phases of national lockdowns and after restrictions were relaxed, the use of digital instruments reached astonishing heights, confirming their role as 'privatised utilities' for workers, employers and public institutions.[19] Nevertheless, the relevance of digital automation was important well before the pandemic hit. As a result, this exogenous incident could serve as a litmus test to corroborate the accuracy of pre-existing theories on expanded managerial powers, skill displacement and efficiency enhancement.

Are we on the brink of some watershed moments? Or is it true that, in nature, things change gradually? A lingering question worth asking is what machines, algorithms and platforms have in common with the previous forces redesigning human history, such as steam, electricity and microprocessors, which have been used to categorise previous industrial shifts.[20] The fundamental underlying asset central to these new technologies is data, particularly personal ones,[21] without which new technologies could not operate in such efficient and effective ways. 'Big' or 'smart' data capture and processing now constitute the essential backbone of digital operators' strategies, ensuring sustained advancements in reprogramming business models and redeploying complex activities thanks to the large availability of devices and enhanced computational power.[22]

In recent decades, as in a *The Jetsons* episode filled with excessive ambient computing, homes, factories, offices and laboratories have been packed with screens, LEDs, speakers, voice assistants, smart thermostat and buttons. There is no doubt that new risks have emerged giving rise to new and worrying questions. We will also explore 'datafication' (or 'informatisation', to borrow from Shoshana Zuboff's work[23]) – the practice by which every movement, either offline or online, is traced, revised and stored as necessary, for statistical, financial, commercial and electoral purposes.[24]

IT tools are also becoming the medium on which almost all jobs are based. From the biologist in the laboratory to the plumber, from the mechatronic engineer to the court clerk employee, from the sommelier to the barista: every job has a growing reliance on digital operations. In many industries, technology is highly beneficial. It is undoubtedly thanks to technology that we are able to produce more clean energy at lower costs. The automation of stables has transformed the lives of farmers, as they can make use of sensors and cameras, ensuring animals can be fed on time and minimising waste. The same is true with GPS devices used to monitor cattle on the farm, a recent example of agricultural technology ('agtech'), a sector now also introducing tools that analyse distinct portions of the soil to calculate the precise proportions of water and nourishments needed to fertilise them. Another example is medical equipment that mitigates the risks associated with many common diseases: minimal, wearable equipment that constantly tracks insulin levels or measures blood pressure, promptly sending alerts regarding anomalies, thus averting disaster. Or even miniaturised surgical devices to be swallowed or injected to reduce invasiveness as well as lessen errors during operations where superhuman precision is required.

This amazing turnaround demands that we look at things differently. The following three sections give an account of the advantages produced by innovation, particularly in the manufacturing and service sectors. The challenge is to make the most of the trends, including the technological ones, that are reshaping the world of work and ensure this does not come at the expense of fundamental values and principles. It is an urgent matter as in this day and age humans and robots often collaborate, living under the same roof and sharing work environments. Starting from three observation points ('robofacturing', remote work and labour intermediation) we report on their positive impacts. In doing so, however, we will also highlight the related risks, which may be intrinsic but much more frequently are the result of deliberate abuses of technologies. Appreciating their benefits can and should be done, but without pretending that they are always free of side-effects.

A. Smart Robots, IoT and Manufacturing: Mind the Machines with Minds

Despite the changes to the manufacturing sector over the past 30 years, factories are the quintessential workplace in the collective imagination. This affinity with assembly lines was down to the design of urban areas, which host varying sizes of industrial parks, now occupied by the shells of abandoned factories. The last century has left us with a heritage of entire towns shaped by their relationships with factories and workshops – mill towns built to house workers, town-planning schemes altered to offer services in previously run down areas, roads widened to allow for heavy vehicles, and expanded ports to allow for the ease of transporting goods. Of course, in the last few years the cases of far too many barred gates, weed-infested steel and automaking mills have filled the headlines.[25] These buildings which, sometimes abruptly, had adapted to accommodate all sorts of production, are now being abandoned. This process affects the economic, social and also mental well-being of entire regions and generational groups.[26] Offshoring, bankruptcies, crises, 'dinosaur' industries as well as buy-outs, even self-financed by workers, are recurrent expressions when it comes to news reporting on the manufacturing ecosystem. This is why the world of factories cannot be indifferent to us: because of the magnitude of the earthquake swarm that crosses it and for the scale of the consequences that each shift causes.

Data show that workers in the manufacturing sector account for only 7.9 per cent of total employment in the US currently, as opposed to 22 per cent in 1970. Aaron Benanav explains that 'over the same period, manufacturing employment shares fell from 23 percent to 9 percent in France, and from 30 percent to 8 percent in the UK. Japan, Germany, and Italy experienced smaller but still-substantial declines'.[27] On the other hand, the share of workers employed in the services sector has skyrocketed, reaching 80 per cent in the US and 70 per cent in EU countries.[28] This trend is not confined to industrialised countries alone – as one might mistakenly believe. Even in developing countries, particularly in sub-Saharan Africa, there is a transition of workers from the agricultural to the service sector, which already accounts for 58 per cent of added value.[29] In any case, although the manufacturing sector has been giving way to an ever more aggressive tertiary sector (which is sometimes daringly termed 'quaternary'), it is still crucial in modern economies. In spite of the steep decline, many of the challenges for the future of work, from the green transition to workforce and managerial upskilling, are based in this sector.[30]

Increasingly, the rise of high-precision robotics has rekindled the hopes of this sector, inspiring hopes of a phoenix-like rebirth from its ashes. Unexpectedly, the number of jobs in the automotive sector in Germany has been growing as the number of machines increases, in a context in which the unemployment rate is also falling. In short, machines have never gone away and it is understandable that today they are living a new life – they have also progressively entered not only industrial environments, but also domestic ones as they assist people in various activities, often taking the place of domestic and care workers (a promisingly lucrative area, given the ageing population trend).

In recent legislatures, in the wake of a policy strategy first conceived in Germany, policymakers and social partners of various countries were forced to deal with a new chapter in the endless collection of public plans to support the digital conversion. In Italy, for instance, the 'Industry 4.0' strategy, later renamed as a more inclusive 'Firm 4.0', started a programme of economic subsidies, mostly in the form of tax credits to support research and development (R&D) investments in technology together with incentives on investments in start-ups and innovative small businesses and education funds for all levels (and PhD scholarships). This programme was expected to unleash so-called additive manufacturing, including the Industrial Internet of Things (IIoT), big data analytics, augmented reality, 3D printing and advanced industrial robotics.[31] It envisaged the creation of cyber-environments, with minimal human contribution. The synergies among machines span the streamlining of cycles and the creation of new processes or products. This kind of domestic strategy aims at encouraging factors such as innovative machineries and personnel training, with a view to promoting reshoring processes, in other words the return home of manufacturing from abroad.[32]

In sectors such as mechatronics or automotive, and also in the chemical, logistics and shipbuilding industries, automated processes are already extensively used. Smart, connected machines are expected to become more prevalent, thanks to large investments that could reduce the price of available products and increase their commercial use.[33] Past growth in sales confirms the forecast, with 30 per cent more sales between 2016 and 2018. Industry 4.0 strategies promote plans for the general reconfiguring of industrial production by integrating standard practices with state-of the-art technologies.[34] The model promises to send the old assembly line into retirement, by replacing it with less top-down processes and more interdependent systems. With a proper 5G connection, the new equipment can interact autonomously both with supplier companies, entrusted with maintenance and updates, and with the sales network and consumers, allowing for the adaptation of production and the tracking of orders. In short, all this should shift manufacturing towards the tertiary sector, confirming the importance of the role of data in the management of resources and equipment.

Wearable and handheld technologies are also on the rise. It has been estimated that the global wearable technology market would be worth $81.5 billion in 2021, an 18.1 per cent increase from $69 billion in 2020.[35] From warehouses to factories, bracelets and smart clothing have replaced more traditional tracking and reporting tools. At the same time, exoskeletons – basically artificial muscles that can be worn by humans – are helpful in operations where physical strength is required. Alongside these devices, goggles that simulate virtual reality environments and software that assess the key parameters of assembly lines are also increasingly common. Technology is a major asset, freeing workers from hard, fatiguing, risky or unpleasant tasks, for instance through visual or voice assistance systems.

Automated equipment has made many activities less burdensome and, in many cases, has encouraged progress in new areas.

In both high-precision and less sophisticated sectors, tools incorporating chips, AI components and other digital widgets have been used for some time. There is no doubt that, when it comes to checking for precautionary purposes or to detect errors or anomalies, machines can be more accurate than the human senses: first and foremost sight, touch and hearing. Here too, the most sensational stories are about a process of genuine 'augmentation' of human capabilities by means of technology: precision glasses, protective gloves, mechanical arms, interconnected helmets, badges checking on vitals, as well as the possibility of supporting people with chronic diseases through constant monitoring.

This is a whole new work environment where feelings of autonomy can thrive, thanks to the possibility of experimenting with new methods, but also where being subject to the strict hegemonic role of managers can become a stark reality. New health and safety risks can emerge, also in terms of stress, which in turn lead to forced turnover burnouts, as specified in a recent report by the UC Berkeley Labor Center, which investigated developments in the logistics industry because of the adoption of new technological devices and new logistic arrangements in warehouses.[36] The research shows how the changing expectations of consumers in terms of variety of supply and speed of delivery, coupled with the pressure wielded by giants such as Amazon, have pushed medium and small businesses to unprecedented experimentations that are now becoming the norm.[37]

Machines end up causing new problems, linked to accidents, psycho-physical stress, musculoskeletal disorders, and, more generally, they contribute to developing a work culture where greater stress leads to exhaustion to the detriment of 'associates' ('workers' in the company jargon).[38] Credit goes to the 'proprietary productivity metric' known as Associate Development and Performance Tracker ('ADAPT'), a technological system employed to assess worker performance and to warn and coach those who fall behind.[39] By using 'privileged and confidential' data, less than one year after the publication of Merchant's letter from the distant future, investigative reports have revealed that the deliberate attempt to privilege experimentations over health and safety (for humans) constituted Amazon's model. The Center for Investigative Reporting found that, from 2016 to 2019, injury rates have been more than 50 per cent higher at Amazon's robotic fulfilment centres than its traditional ones, with dangerous records hit during Prime Day 2019 (a revenue-boosting sales period together with Black Friday, Cyber Monday and many other seasonal shopping events), with nearly 400 serious injuries recorded across the USA.[40] The new normal, therefore, could be warehouse jobs that are 'part-human, part-robot',[41] where production quotas are ratcheted up 'to the point that humans can't keep up without hurting themselves'.[42] The hidden cost of the 'Buy Now' button is a brutal management strategy that deliberately normalises burnout.[43]

It is now time to investigate what a smart machine is. To give an accurate description of it, we refer to the definition given by Maria Chiara Carrozza, a professor of bioengineering at the Sant'Anna School of Advanced Studies, and to the very first documents developed by EU institutions on the subject.[44] According to Carrozza, a robot is a smart physical system, equipped with sensors and actuators. It incorporates AI components, connected to software and systems capable of learning, to which the activity of processing information and developing advanced forms of 'decision-making' can be assigned. More than anything else, a robot is extremely adaptable and capable of making autonomous employment-related decisions without human intervention. It uses online storage systems, located in remote servers, which elaborate data collected by the sensors. This allows it to be perceptive and able to move in unstructured and unfamiliar spaces.

Following a useful taxonomy prepared by labour law professor Valerio Maio, the machines 'at the service of work' can be put into three categories.[45] The first one is the 'herculean' industrial robot, designed to operate inside the company in a space distinct from other workers – basically a caged machine – accessible only in exceptional cases for updating or maintenance interventions. Secondly are the 'cobots', namely 'collaborative robots', constructed to operate in an open context, they can fit on a desktop and work in close contact with personnel, properly trained and equipped with adequate safety devices. The third type is the most sensible one, the multifunctional robot assigned to the worker as company equipment and, therefore, having constant interaction with the worker outside the company, thanks to natural language recognition capabilities.

What does a robot look like? It is curious to note how literature and the arts have predated technology to give us a familiar and perhaps too anthropomorphic representation of the machines we work with.[46] The European Parliament also could not resist this, passing a resolution whose opening reads: 'From Mary Shelley's Frankenstein's Monster to the classical myth of Pygmalion, through the story of Prague's Golem to the robot of Karel Čapek, who coined the word, people have fantasised about the possibility of building intelligent machines, more often than not androids with human features'.[47] *Vaste programme!*

In recent years, short videos produced by companies such as Boston Dynamics have gone viral, capturing the somersaults and leaps of some humanoids working in intricate places such as warehouses and forests, with dancing demonstrations and parkour exercises. The jewel of the crown, Atlas, is even able to gracefully train in the gym and to be kicked and pushed by his obnoxious human instructors. Those who watch are almost led to hope that the robot will give them two well-deserved slaps. More recently, an ironclad and fairly terrifying looking dog joined the club. It doesn't take much to be fooled, 'adorable clips are more than just a way to combine fun with mobility-competency testing and more than a marketing gimmick'.[48] Videos are meant to accustom the public to the robots, distracting us from the dangerous (for humans) context in which they could be used, perhaps sooner than we expect.

In 2016, the Hong Kong-based firm Hanson Robotics launched Sophia, one of the first humanoids with a feminine lifelike appearance to be taught (or programmed with, to be precise) more than 60 facial expressions and demeanours that mimic humans.[49] It has sensors and cameras that make it able to identify the objects around it and support eye contact. Since its launch, Sophia has been giving interviews and inaugurating conventions of investors interested in progress in this field.[50] In 2017, the United Nations Development Programme in Asia and the Pacific chose it as the first 'Innovation Champion'.[51] It is the first non-human to be appointed to this institutional role; not that the position of digital champion has ever been prestigious, to be honest maybe it was time to outsource it to robots. But the list of praises and prizes is rather long. Shortly beforehand, Saudi Arabia had granted Sophia an honorary citizenship, triggering a lengthy controversy over the peculiar choice of treating an object as a citizen. Many questioned the assignment of rights and duties to a social robot, and whether AI is comparable to human consciousness. According to its critics, Sophia takes advantage of its potential users. The real master stroke was to create a product that would satisfy the expectations of its interlocutors both verbally and in physiognomics, in a matchless mix of engineering, gender stereotypes and in the self-complacency of its users.[52]

Even if it is just an astute PR stunt, the Saudi Arabian initiative is not an entirely isolated one. In 2017, the European Parliament prepared a study and passed a resolution calling on the EU Commission to explore and assess the implications of different legal solutions when establishing a 'Civil Law of Robotics'.[53] Among these, the Parliament mentioned: establishing an obligatory insurance scheme for specific categories of robots, similar to the one valid today for motor vehicles; and the creation of a compensation fund, allowing the manufacturer, the programmer, the owner or the user to benefit from limited liability as long as they contribute to the fund. More interestingly, the Parliament suggested 'creating a specific legal status for robots in the long run, so that at least the most sophisticated autonomous robots could be established as having the status of electronic persons responsible for making good any damage they may cause, and possibly applying electronic personality to cases where robots make autonomous decisions or otherwise interact with third parties independently'.[54]

When defining the requirements a smart robot should meet, the Parliament proposed to look for at least four features: the acquisition of autonomy through sensors and/or by exchanging data with its environment ('inter-connectivity') and the trading and analysing of those data (with as an optional criterion, self-learning from experience and by interaction); having at least a minor physical support; the adaptation of its behaviour and actions to the environment ('perceptivity'); and absence of life in the biological sense ('abiologicity'). The resolution, therefore, suggested a chain of autonomous behaviour, aimed at the subsequent validation of automated decision-making processes with the view of making all potential responsibilities clear, if needed. The text does not go so far as to equate robots with human beings in terms of rights and duties. It is interesting to note, however, that in an exchange with *The Verge* magazine, the rapporteur of the initiative, former Luxembourg socialist MEP Mady Delvaux, drew a parallel between 'electronic personality' and 'legal personality', which has long been granted to corporations.

When Sophia was granted Saudi citizenship, Joanna Bryson, a professor of computer science and a researcher in human-robot interaction, firmly cautioned against granting rights to robots, saying it is like 'having a supposed equal you can turn on and off'. Having a 'citizen that you can buy' at a trade fair entering workplaces is anything but a smooth process.[55] Before the situation gets out of hand, it is therefore necessary to consider all the implications of this possible socio-legal revolution.

Beyond questions on the capacities of robots, there are intricate issues still relevant today whose roots go back centuries. Legal personality has proved crucial for economic development since it allowed the separation of personal assets of investors from those of corporations. This asset partitioning enabled the development of innovative, and therefore risky, entrepreneurial initiatives that would not have been conceivable if investors had responded with all their personal resources had things gone wrong. It allowed for trade and development. But it also contributed to paving the way for large scale exploitation and Western colonialism. More directly, legal personality and the corporate form have also been abused in order to dodge responsibility in many fields, including the environmental field. When it comes to labour issues, these misapplications can be detrimental for workers' rights in many areas, for instance by fragmenting bargaining units, thus creating obstacles for workers' freedom of association and the possibility of meaningfully engaging in collective bargaining as well as diluting occupational health and safety responsibilities.

Recognising legal rights and obligations to non-human beings, therefore, is far from being a neutral process. It can prove beneficial, but it can also lead to unforeseeable harms that put other parties in jeopardy. Introducing electronic personality for robots could allow their owners to shed responsibility and leave anyone interacting with these robots, including commercial partners, creditors, customers and workers, with no meaningful redress in case of damage. Nor can it be ruled out that by assigning them rights and duties robots could be progressively equated with human beings in the future, particularly if AI is designed to develop features that increasingly simulate human consciousness.[56]

There is also a crucial point that intersects law and ethics. Granting legal personality to corporations is an evident legal fiction. Companies do not exist in the real world. Even if they own tangible assets such as industrial machines and digital servers, one cannot bump into them on the street. On the contrary, robots have a specific physical dimension and often share a space with human workers. Therefore, granting electronic personality to intelligent machines and allocating rights and duties to them has nothing to do with the ploy of treating companies as legal entities. Giving electronic personality to a physical object like Sophia risks conflating human beings and humanoid machines. This has unpredictable consequences in terms of respect for the human dignity of people who have to work, alongside machines with rights, in a context of subordination, where they are subject to the authority of managers, whether direct or indirect. The result could be a state of perennial alienation and isolation, potentially leading humans to feel like mere 'speaking tools' (this is how slaves were defined in Ancient Rome to distinguish them from utensils and 'half-speaking' livestock). The resulting risk of dehumanisation cannot be overestimated.[57]

B. Remote Work, Out of Sight and Out of Place?
Beyond the Pandemic Panopticon

Freedom is within reach of a good Wi-Fi connection. As long as it works. The digital acceleration has dismantled the traditional unity of working time, space and action, contributing to deconstructing the classic firm's coordinates.[58] Increasingly, in all sectors where there is no need for non-substitutable manual activities to be carried out, a reassembly of the physical elements of work relationships is occurring. On the one hand, working hours and shifts are becoming longer due to the need to combine work duties with family or business needs, linked to dealing with multi-location virtual teams or clients located in far-flung areas. On the other hand, well before the pandemic hit, the 'ubiquitous work environment' has been expanding. Various cognitive tasks, even complex ones, can be comfortably carried out almost anywhere – in the dining room, on the train, in a waiting room, while travelling or in a café, albeit at the mercy of the availability of chargers and electrical sockets.

The lockdowns spurred 'the most extensive mass teleworking experiment in history' for both middle class occupations and 'knowledge workers': offices were left unoccupied all at once, almost overnight.[59] Forty per cent of employees in the EU started working remotely full-time; for almost one in four workers, it was the first time of adopting this mode.[60] This revolution, however, started long ago. As early as the 1980s people started talking about telework and,[61] at the same time, questioning the sustainability of a '9-to-5' model.[62]

In the recent past, the prototype of the new, agile worker corresponded to the digital nomads or freelancers organising their schedule at their own pace and renting a desk in one or more co-working spaces in urban areas or exotic destinations.[63] These environments are equipped to host knowledge workers, born out of the need to share expenses and develop a professional network. Today, remote work is an option that many employees can enjoy, following collective agreements and new company policies that thoroughly regulate the way it is to be implemented. It is an opportunity for all parties involved – a chance to increase productivity and competitiveness, promote a better work-life balance and, just as importantly, benefit from a form of company welfare, while saving on company costs for office spaces and unnecessary travel. Appreciation for this model is now widespread, to the point that many experts hastened to proclaim the death of the office as we know it.

These flexible templates also respond to the assumption that new forms of work shun former rigid and siloed schemes, avoid fixed hierarchical structures and pursue the thrill of organisational self-determination, using technology in an empowering way.[64] The crumbling of the walls of offices and cubicles, as well as the blurring of the firm's boundaries, bear witness to the overcoming of the rigidity of roles, hierarchies and duties, as well as the gradual disappearance of a model whereby commitment was exclusively measured by face-time.

Before praising the supposed modernity of remote work, it is necessary to disprove a misunderstanding. When it comes to remote and dematerialised environments, people assume that the new generation of jobs and professions are completely free from space-time parameters. In reality, all too often their distinguishing feature is an expansion of time and space, potentially caught between comfort and inconvenience.

Remote work, flexible working time and co-working spaces also show the overlap between employment and self-employment; it is thus essential to notice the universal scope of transformations and the movement from the model of subordination to that of autonomy, and vice versa. This change is realised 'anytime' and 'anywhere',[65] with a risk of flexible work schedules becoming potentially dangerous habits of overworking. The need for escape, therefore, is still here: in the case of remote work, employees skip crowded offices, annoying interruptions and traffic jams, in the case of co-working workers avoid the loneliness of their living room.

In some ways, working from home has undoubtedly been a relief for those who were used to spending long days in front of a screen or those who suffered exhausting commutes in densely populated metropolises or from poorly connected hinterlands. Remote work can meet workers' demands for flexibility and it has significant advantages for societies at large. It is also contributing to reversing the brain drain towards countries where well educated young people choose to migrate to find fulfilling professional advancement.[66] It can reduce city congestion and pollution and it lowers energy consumption at corporate headquarters. It can generate new professional opportunities for people with reduced mobility, attracting workers with specific needs and reconciling the work-life balance. There are downsides too. The need to interact with remote managers, colleagues and clients leads to an intensification of schedules and a perennial, suffocating state of alert, all at the expense of down time or private life. In the last two years, according to surveys,[67] predominantly women also had to carry out additional and unpaid education and caring duties (think of when home-schooling was the norm) or face challenging or abusive household conditions. The sudden shift has disproportionately impacted new hires, who have had less proper training, or have been penalised due to the difficulty of collaborating with senior colleagues.

As previously mentioned, modern labour regulation has taken on precise connotations at the same time factories, workshops and offices have come into existence. Both its individual and collective dimensions were defined in this context. Regarding the collective side of labour regulation, the colocation of workers in the same place acted as a trigger for trade union activity. Understandably, the fragmentation of the model impairs classical worker voice resources. Workplaces have always had a legal duty to allocate powers and responsibilities. Managers can easily organise and monitor work performance, but they are also required to put in place health and safety measures and to comply with working time regulations. This becomes a lot more complex when there are a variety of work environments.

The topographical alteration of working environments and the fluidity of working hours caused by the always-on-call mode leads to a state of constant connection that is difficult to restrain. Workers are under pressure to over-perform and multi-task, always ready to 'go beyond the call of duty'. Recent studies provide an incongruous picture of the situation. There is no longer the need to be physically at the workplace, yet the time spent in the office is lengthened, a circumstance which is sugar coated by the introduction of social activities and made easier with the provision of services to cope with the absence of any free time (some businesses take care of laundry, run errands, etc). Simultaneously, there is an increase in the use of marginal or involuntary part-time work for large, and often over-qualified, segments of the workforce, with disproportionate implications for women and young people. This division between those who spend too much time at work and those who would like to work more but cannot, is a striking testimony to the societal inability to rethink work by making adequate use of the potential of digital innovation.

Disregarding the subtleties of the numerous popular definitions, it must be noted that, as far back as 2002, the European Framework Agreement on Teleworking was signed to regulate the terms and conditions of people working remotely by establishing a general principle of non-discrimination between tele-workers and comparable workers at the employer's premises in terms of workload and performance standards.[68] The EU framework instigated multiple domestic initiatives. In 2017, the French labour code was reformed to relax the legal framework in order to encourage telework, including on an occasional basis. The French law included the possibility of extending the option of '*télétravail*' (remote working) also 'in the event of exceptional circumstances, in particular of threat of epidemic, […] to allow the continuity of the business activity and to protect employees'. Similarly, in 2017 Italian lawmakers intervened to regulate remote working – locally dubbed 'agile working'. The law aimed at encouraging hybrid voluntary formulas – those who work a few days remotely connected from outside the office have the right to equal treatment in relation to office-based workers. Agile workers have the right to breaks and insurance protection against occupational accidents and diseases. The Spanish Labour Code lays down provisions for '*trabajo a distancia*' (remote working). In 2021, additional provisions were introduced to avoid any direct or indirect discrimination for workers providing their services remotely, including gender-based discrimination and discrimination by reason of age, length of service, professional category or disability.

At the beginning of the pandemic, people turned to technology in search of a remedy. Sadly, it quickly became clear that there are no digital solutions to organisational or cultural age-old problems. In many countries, emergency measures removed some formal requirements to the adoption of work-from-home arrangements. This spurred a transition to rigid homeworking dictated by precautionary purposes. Businesses have been able to activate remote working in a simplified way. This radical working pattern was mainly used as a measure to flatten the infection curve while rescuing a significant number of jobs rather than as a radical yet voluntary (and so far, niche) organisational policy. An unorthodox pattern envisioned to enhance elasticity and agency was rebooted to allow business continuity, resulting in an unexpected increase in workload. Remote workers found them-selves working longer hours in the absence of a dedicated office or desk space.[69] For white-collar jobs, paid working time encroached on the time once spent on leisure or with family, with little capacity to switch off given the expectation of permanent devotion to the 'home office'.

There is no lack of positive practices, typically the result of far-sighted collec-tive agreements and specific company protocols.[70] These agreements cover conditions allowing the switch to remote work, information about the monitor-ing devices and policies, and good practices for collaboration with colleagues. On closer inspection, this benefited those organisations that had previously planned for this and, for example, equipped their workers with the relevant secure software. Conversely, those companies that suddenly had to coordinate teams of dispersed workers without prior planning suffered from their lack of preparation.

Far from being a benchmark, this crisis-driven arrangement, however, has little to do with the authentic model of remote working, which should be based on a twofold fundamental premise: workers' free choice and alternation between in-house and remote periods. Hopefully, however, the difficulties encountered during the pandemic will not become excuses – neither to let those who have not arranged work flows compatible with remote work in due time off the hook, nor to dismiss a work model with huge potential benefits as a passing fad.

Regrettably, remote work is an opportunity that not all managers were willing (or culturally equipped) to offer, even when public authorities strongly recommended it or made it compulsory.[71] Small and medium enterprises hesitantly implemented remote working and then swiftly discouraged it at the earliest opportunity. Many local politicians, for instance, encouraged people to go 'back to work' – by which they mean 'back to the office', as if remote work was the same as a holiday – to help economic activities in urban areas.[72] This reveals a widespread reluctance to extend unsupervised autonomy, let alone the inability to overcome an often toxic work environment. This is overly paradoxical, as the evidence suggests that commit-ment increased in a situation when managerial control was inevitably limited. Corporate conventional wisdom was proved wrong, the pandemic did not create a 'hellscape for productivity'.[73] However, too many managers and policymakers do not seem to understand that hierarchies can be flattened and companies can still continue to be successful.

The short-sightedness of personnel organisation policies was overwhelmingly evident during the months of stay-at-home policies. The first data shows that not much progress was made to foster reciprocal trust and result-based schemes.[74] Less reassuringly, in the face of a mass exodus from corporate spaces, many managers and executives reacted with alarm, with more controlling measures.[75] Many firms and institutions, unable to draw up work plans based on objectives, verifiable deliverables and multilateral accountability, increased the number of online meetings and hastened to implement panopticon-like software (to meas-ure for example the time spent online, the number of keystrokes or the list of websites visited).[76]

Those who worked from home had to deal with apprehensive line managers obsessively looking over their shoulders to reduce cyberslacking under the mistaken assumption that employees work absent-mindedly or do not stay motivated without being monitored. Surveillance applications used to retain control have boomed at an unparalleled rate. Preliminary data shows that in April 2020, demand for tracking tools surged by 54 per cent and was on average 58 per cent higher in 2021 than it was before the pandemic.[77]

The crisis has been a marketing chance as well as the opportunity to finetune existing applications. *Activtrack* inspects the programs used and tells bosses if an employee is unfocussed, spending time on social media. *OccupEye* records when and for how long someone is away from their workstation.[78] *TimeDoctor* and *Teramind* keep track of every task conducted online. Similarly, *Interguard* compiles a minute-by-minute timeline that monitors all data such as web history and bandwidth utilisation and sends a notification to the managers if workers pick up anything suspicious. *HubStaff* and *Sneek* routinely take snapshots of employees through their webcams every five minutes or so to generate a timecard and circulate them to boost morale. *Pragli* synchronises professional calendars and music playlists to create a sense of community; it also features a facial recognition that could display a worker's real-world emotion on their virtual avatar's face. Anecdotes are sinister, for example in the case of a customer service agent for an American financial tech company, whose boss without any prior notification started instructing him through his headset.[79] More prosaic applications are used to replicate online the experience of 'corporate camaraderie' with gossip rooms, watercoolers or 'not-so optional happy hours [to] create a sense of togetherness'.[80]

While there is an abundance of reports about 'fringe software vendors', it is commonly overlooked that all applications, including the seemingly innocuous ones such as Microsoft and Google tools to automatically gauge workers' productivity,[81] aggregate all sorts of data into simple charts or graphs that give managers a high-level view of what employees are doing.[82] The same goes for free collaborative ecosystems, cloud spaces and shared repositories, which are now more indispensable than ever before for remote teams but are too expensive to be developed internally or through proprietary technologies.

Overreliance on metrics risks narrowing an organisation's focus on simple activity rather than on decision making, performance and accomplishments.[83] Accordingly, workers are encouraged to control their own tasks thanks to an array of self-tracking dashboards.[84] Yet, data may be misleading. Transparency regarding productivity scores and the extent of monitoring is far from established. Moreover, there is no evidence that productivity metrics are closely correlated with the outcome. As a result, they raise concerns about their accuracy and interpretation, particularly in inexperienced hands and without going through workforce consultation. This lack of trust can impact negatively on workforce morale.

The advent of 'portable offices' and remote working also brings with it the need for new protection, such as the right to disconnect, namely that is, the right not to be reached by work-related communications outside working hours.

Several countries introduced this kind of protection to avoid overworking.[85] The result, however, is paradoxical: a right to disconnection is recognised mainly to the benefit of those workers who should already have that right. This shows how, regrettably, remote workers' time is too often still tied to office hours. Disconnection often remains a luxury for the few who can afford it.

The French Supreme Court paved the way to this right with some judgments in the early 2000s. In 2016, the French lawmakers followed suit by amending the *Code du Travail* with measures evocatively titled 'Adapting the Labour Law to the Digital Age'. The last country on the bandwagon is Portugal, which is also a hot destination for radical remote workers. A new law has been passed which bans managers from contacting workers outside of office hours and monitoring them at home; it also forces employers to pick up the tab for expenses incurred by employees.[86] To deal with the right to disconnect, some multinationals have opted for outright server shutdown after certain hours, others have negotiated flexible limits with the unions. More generally, however, a quantum leap is yet to be made to promote the sustainability of workloads.

On the other hand, endless discussions have been taking place about taking commuting time into account when counting working hours. Right at the beginning of 2020, the Swiss government set an example, allowing the home-office journey to be considered working time for some civil servants. In the past, the Court of Justice of the European Union has also ruled in this regard.[87] Working on these routes is promoted, encouraging the residents of overcrowded city centres to look for accommodation in suburbs or in the dormitory districts.

Alongside remote work, the format of co-working has for some time seemed revolutionary, so much so that even the most avant-garde companies have begun to pull down walls and partitions to make way for shared workspaces and rest areas. Today, this trend reveals all its flaws. Hubs of shared spaces have mushroomed everywhere, the result of a modular conversion to hospitality – with abandoned offices being refurbished or new spaces built expressly to accommodate freelancers or brand new small businesses. There are now dozens of these spaces in large cities. In the meantime, from spaces born for mutual support, co-working has inspired many, contributing to the definition of new, completely out of control, business epics. Many reports document the pitfalls faced by the creative classes.[88]

The loneliness of the digital nomad is only partly mitigated by the sharing of co-working or co-living spaces, where costs are often anything but cheap. Take, for instance, the case of WeWork calling off its stock exchange listing – the company formerly being the poster child of businesses offering shared rental workspaces by presenting them as an immaterial infrastructure at the service of a sect of innovators. The goal was to 'to elevate the world's consciousness' thanks to a near-celestial workplace aesthetic and shared-living spaces supporting 'a community of creators [who] leverage technology to connect people'. The founder resorted to an unfortunate parallel: 'So we're definitely not a real-estate company. Just like Uber is the sharing economy for cars, and Citibike for bicycles, we're the sharing economy for space'.[89] The operation, supported by SoftBank, an investment fund with a passion for revolutionary yet cash-burning businesses, soon turned out to be disastrous. Today, WeWork has had to get rid of its founder (by paying him a billion and a half euros), rapidly closed some projects and dismissed thousands of guiltless employees. As many observers wrote, this flop is an example of a situation where there is a huge mismatch between public resonance and business solidity.

It is too early to say whether, after a frantic expansion, the honeymoon with communal workplaces has come to an end. In successful cases, mere real estate operations are complemented by extensive training and learning programs for community members. This is how workers can connect to the future – Wi-Fi, an open space and a shared kettle are no longer enough. Similarly, to be effective and authentic, remote work requires a qualitative managerial leap, shifting the evaluation of work performance to outcomes rather than mere physical attendance or micromanagement. We need to set aside prejudices and must bet on organisations based on trust and responsibility.[90] This challenge is a systemic one,[91] not a sectoral one, involving the rethinking of management theories and models.

C. Selective Affinities: Matchmaking is the New Recruiting

Whether regarding a mortgage, a romantic date or a targeted advert banner, increasingly algorithms make decisions for and about us. As modern 'gatekeepers to our life experience',[92] they basically work to match us: to a bank, a potential partner, an offer. The same happens at work. On the basis of aggregated information and data, a number of software programs aimed at efficiently filling vacancies determine whether a candidate is sufficiently qualified for a given job, well before scheduling a live interview for a job opening. This is where a new function of technology, which until recently had remained under human control, operates – often coming to ambiguous conclusions[93] without revealing what led to such a response.

An algorithm can be described as a hierarchy of abstract, formal and adaptable instructions for a software to complete an activity pursuing a desired outcome, as defined by human agents, thanks to probabilistic evaluations of datasets.[94] Unlike humans, with different ideas of what that outcome should be, 'algocratic' systems are not hampered by bias.[95] They are not moody, nor can they be deceived or bribed. According to mainstream opinion, algorithms are true champions of objectivity, technical quality or science,[96] programmed to treat all candidates in the same way and avoid any partiality. For tech-optimists, relying on such a system for the profiling of prospective recruits has an unquestionable merit: it allows choices to be made without the most fallible component of human nature, by eliminating unconscious bias. This applies to the entire 'funnel' of recruitment, from targeting the best candidates to sourcing CVs and managing the application, running background screening and remote interviews.[97] This is too good to be true, given the immense complexity of handling a large pool of aspiring candidates making it difficult to narrow down workers deserving consideration. And in reality, it isn't true at all. Various scholars, data in hand, highlight the dark side of automated recruiting and workplace decision-making processes. Algorithms, wrote the programmer Cathy O'Neil, are nothing more than 'opinions embedded in mathematics'.[98] Additionally, if machine learning accompanies these systems, the result is an avalanche of uncontrollable effect, on a mass scale.

Discrimination thus becomes an underlying feature, as explained by law professor Ifeoma Ajunwa in highly documented studies.[99] Blocking years of birth in a dropdown menu of a website is enough to exclude entire cohorts, or using Facebook filters to direct a certain job advertisement to an audience that fits with the rest of the company. It is even possible to compile questions about university study or career progression in a way that indirectly penalises women irrespective of their other qualifications, as they are more likely to have gaps in their CVs due to family responsibilities. For example, Amazon had to scrap a tool aimed at uncovering passive candidates as it showed bias against female candidates, because their applications lacked 'masculine' wording, reflecting male dominance across the tech industry. Amazon's AI system had 'taught itself that male candidates were preferable'.[100] The same applies to those who may have gaps in full-time employment, having experienced difficulties in finding a job during a recession. If there is one thing where algorithms are unbeatable, it is the ability to introduce or develop prejudices related to gender, race and social origin by using proxies for sensitive data. If the data from the past reflect discriminatory practices, the results will also be discriminatory ('garbage in, garbage out', as computer scientists say). We thus end up enforcing predictions and decisions guided by past actions and the set of values that informed the programming of the system.[101] Importantly, in the context of the EU, legal redress remedies are only partially equipped to challenge new forms of multidimensional discrimination, which is the result of the dynamic and composite nature of algorithms used to make correlations.[102]

There are unconscious, and even less controllable processes linked to the incorrect interpretations of certain data. If, for example, the statistics on the frequency of car accidents were to indicate the city centre as a being risky area because of high levels of traffic, the mere fact of living downtown would lead to higher insurance pricing for the residents. This does occur in many big cities, especially outside Europe, where the centre is often populated by minorities who cannot afford to live in expensive suburbs. The algorithms of insurance companies may have not been intentionally programmed to discriminate against members of minority communities, however the apparently neutral correlation of the data produces a discriminatory result.[103] (It is interesting that crucial information about driving behaviour, which would back up such decisions, is totally ignored.) Accordingly, in search of tenure maximisation, an employer observed that commuting time was the single prominent variable that determined the reduction of turnover – the untold truth, however, was that such a factor strongly correlates with housing affordability and race.[104]

As should already be clear, the absorption of incomplete or distorted social patterns leads to further disadvantages and historical disparities for excluded and vulnerable communities, thus reinforcing legacies of misogyny, racism and authoritarianism.[105] It encourages a form of tax on poverty, especially when these systems are adopted by governments or public administrations entrusted with managing unemployment benefits, dependent allowances, housing subsidies or even predictive policing.[106] Political scientist Virginia Eubanks detailed that the lack of flexibility and the inability to obtain explanations whenever one feels unduly penalised by an automated process are frequent decisive shortcomings of automated decision-making systems.[107] The extent of this imbalance is likely to be endemic, with outcomes falling somewhere between Kafkaesque and Dickensian. Challenging errors is an uphill battle.[108]

Profiling in the pre-hiring stages is an increasingly widespread model of recruitment, and today it also deploys AI-based facial and speech analysis to track emotions, personality traits and behaviour. Many businesses, especially large ones, are using these systems, convinced that technology is much more reliable and affordable than a flesh and blood head-hunter in the quest for 'talent' in high-volume, entry-level job openings. 98 per cent of Fortune 500 companies use algorithmic or data-driven systems during the hiring phase.[109] A large multinational company that owns several brands of food and hygiene products, reportedly asks its potential salespeople to answer a number of questions on their mobile phones. The results are sorted by AI systems that have been programmed with all the interviews that led to a successful past hire. The evaluation is based on gesturing (smiles, glances, shudders), but also on the use of verbs in the passive form, the prevalence of the pronoun 'I' over 'we', the choice of words and their complexity, and the length of sentences. This would eliminate those who do not embody the required model.[110] The mechanism is also used in respect of freelancers, who are now selected after AI systems have reviewed a catalogue of contractors online, using information, reviews and details operated by platforms like *Smarterer*, among others.

The filtering is entrusted to 'black boxes' that collect information, process statistics and deliver judgements based on keywords found in the CVs uploaded online. Data can be collected from various sources, inside and outside the workplace, such as the number and length of phone calls, the list of websites browsed during working hours, the tone and content of conversations between colleagues, but also the list of places visited, tracked through geolocation and tags on personal social media. If we add the potential of 'natural language processing', namely the computerised analysis of textual documents, one can obtain a hyper-detailed picture, comprising some personal traits probably unknown to the workers themselves.

An online service symbolically called *Predictim* guarantees the possibility of carrying out profiling activities thanks to systems scanning every sentence written on social media to infer an applicant's personality. HireVue, a Utah-based leading company in the sector, claims it can measure people's 'employability' by using cameras and algorithms to determine who has what it takes to be hired against its database of more than 25,000 samples of facial and linguistic information (from brow raising to smiling, from chin raising to lip tightening). Using half a dozen questions selected by the prospective employer, HireVue computes up to 500,000 data points and facial features. These are the 'ingredients' of the score assigned to each person examined. The success index is constructed on the basis of these metrics, including skills, grit, learning attitude, conscientiousness and responsibility, family history, propensity to consume and personal stability. Inferring 'happiness from a smile, anger from a scowl, or sadness from a frown' is, at best, absurd.[111] Even worse, this method underestimates cultural differences, and draws from a universal sample in an oversimplistic way. Researchers contend that the system is a 'blend of superficial measurements and arbitrary number-crunching that is not rooted in scientific fact'.[112] And indeed, in January 2021, HireVue announced it would no longer use facial analysis for job assessment purposes, after concluding that 'for the significant majority of jobs and industries, visual analysis has far less correlation to job performance than other elements of our algorithmic assessment'.[113] However, language and verbal data still represent a key element in the appraisal of applicants' employability to deduce personality qualities such as openness to experience, conscientiousness, extraversion, agreeableness and emotional stability.[114] Apparently, to make their graduates competitive, some US universities plan to introduce courses in which the fundamentals of this pseudo-science are taught. Gaming the system with strategic keywords and smiles may therefore be about to make its way into academic curricula. The more effective any of these systems are, the greater the risk of creating a corporate monolithic culture where each new worker follows the profile of the previous one: an irreversible process of homogenisation.

The logic behind automated hiring is to allow HR managers to dig deep, by identifying skills, potential, aptitudes and inclinations that are well matched to the advertised position, also taking into account previous experiences and ongoing projects. It has the added merit of widening the boundaries of the local labour market and the pool of candidates. The fact that there is an excess of 'suppliers', as opposed to a small number of 'buyers', puts the latter in an advantageous situation. Uncertainty marks every step of the recruitment process, it is almost impossible to assess qualities such as dedication, good attitude and reliability, both on the side of the prospective employer and of the jobseeker. This chronic uncertainty causes a misalignment between profiles and offers and, in theory, risks paralysing companies. On the other hand, meticulous selection of prospective employees, albeit time consuming and costly, tends to reap rewards in terms of stable relationships and low turnover, paving the way for long-lasting and fruitful partnerships, which lead to increased productivity and success.[115]

Current regulations may offer inadequate protection against these kinds of inaccurate assumptions. Before the EU General Data Protection Regulation (GDPR) came into force in 2018, confirming the longstanding position of the EU as an international leader in the field of data protection, the European Data Protection Board had stated that the collection of data from applicants' personal profiles must be limited to what is necessary and relevant for recruitment to a given position, provided that they are duly informed and the data is destroyed after the procedure is completed, whatever the outcome.[116] This enforcement agency, whose mission is to issue general guidelines to promote a common interpretation of EU data protection rules, has specified that practices such as tracking mouse and keyboard movements or on-screen activities are forbidden in the EU as they amount to disproportionate surveillance methods that are at odds with the domestic legal tradition of privacy and personal dignity.[117]

The GDPR protects people against 'automated individual decision-making' and 'profiling', by creating barriers to AI-enabled practices of worker recruitment and management.[118] Article 22, in particular, bans the implementation of decisions 'based solely on automated processing, including profiling, which produces legal effects' or which 'similarly significantly affects' any data subject unless strong safeguards are provided.[119] Commenting on Article 22, Recital 71 mentions expressly 'e-recruiting practices without any human intervention'. Pseudonymised data which can still easily identify data subjects also fall within the scope of the Article. Courts and other interpreters will determine whether, albeit only referring to solely automated models, the GDPR can also rule out that minor, nominal human interventions that are entirely subservient to automatic decisions exempt such systems from the scope of Article 22.[120] It must be assumed that actions limited to rubber-stamping inexplicable choices taken elsewhere do not disempower the application of the general prohibition laid down in Article 22, which instead is meant to trigger the adoption of a 'human in command' approach in data processing.[121]

On closer inspection, the ban of automated decision-making processes features a significant list of exceptions. Profiling or algorithmic management is still allowed if it: '(a) is necessary for entering into, or performance of, a contract between the data subject and a data controller', (b) is authorised by Union or Member State law, which also specifies appropriate measures to protect the rights, freedoms and legitimate interests of the data subject, and '(c) is based on the data subject's explicit consent'.[122] The ban on automated individual decision-making processes does not apply straightforwardly in the employment context. Decisions in the HR department, such as e-screening of a large number of applications, could fall into the scope of exceptions allowed by Article 22(2), being 'necessary for entering into, or performance of, a contract'. However, appropriate measures must be adopted by the employer 'to safeguard the [worker]'s rights and freedoms and legitimate interests, at least the right to obtain human intervention on the part of the controller, to express his or her point of view and to contest the decision' and even 'to obtain an explanation of the decision reached', according to Recital 71.[123] There is the possibility to derogate from the general prohibition only in the presence of express consent. However, since workers are rarely 'in a position to freely give, refuse, or revoke consent', according to the European Data Protection Board (EDPB), 'lawful basis [for data processing at work] cannot and should not be consent',[124] due to the disparity in bargaining power.

The GDPR has also set a non-negotiable limit, algorithmic decisions cannot be based on sensitive data such as health conditions, sexual orientation, political, ideological and trade union opinions or ethnic origins, unless the person concerned consents, or the processing is necessary for reasons of public interest. In order to avoid the ambitious purpose of Article 22 remaining only on paper,[125] at the local level, legislation and collective negotiation are the most convincing response to automated decision-making, ensuring that it complies with transparent criteria and that human agents retain final control and accountability for any decision affecting workers, establishing a model of collective oversight.[126] This solution is backed up by the GDPR, stating that Member States may introduce, by law or by collective agreements, 'specific rules to ensure the protection of the rights and freedoms in respect of the processing of employees' personal data in the employment context, in particular for the purposes of the recruitment, the performance of the contract of employment, [...] management, planning and organisation of work, equality and diversity in the workplace, health and safety at work, [...] and for the purpose of the termination of the employment relationship'. Such rules shall 'include suitable and specific measures to safeguard the data subject's human dignity, legitimate interests and fundamental rights' (Article 88 GDPR).[127]

The overarching framework of the GDPR does not operate without outside influence; rather, it is a cornerstone element of a very complex, perhaps intricate, multi-source regulatory architecture. Member States can introduce specific internal measures with regards to employee monitoring and data processing at work. Moreover, data protection authorities' role is also crucial to ensure that the privacy of workers is not invaded when it comes to monitoring their activities. Individual consent is not enough, and these rights are not waivable. According to a solid legal tradition, in many EU jurisdictions a prior consultation phase with workers' representatives or their authorisation are inescapable preconditions for the introduction of surveillance equipment, including those used in the hiring process. This procedural rule constitutes a lawful basis for personal data collecting and processing, that must be supported by proof of a legitimate company interest behind such activity. Domestic legislation and case law ensure that workers' representatives are involved through information, discussion and codetermination. Failure to comply with these requirements may result in the impossibility of using data and information unlawfully captured and could also lead to sanctions.

Too often, however, observers underestimate the full extent of certain technologies. Despite its undoubtedly protective value, the EU GDPR risks becoming rapidly outdated and unable to effectively face all the new challenges raised by AI and machine learning technologies in regard to personal data. Sandra Wachter, a lawyer at the Oxford Internet Institute, has criticised this EU Regulation because it only focuses on data collection and neglects the processing of data. Once these are legitimately obtained, in her opinion, no limits exist on inferential analysis, namely the process through which algorithms extract recurring patterns from large amounts of data and advance real-time predictions. All this would remain a no-man's-land.[128] There are, however, good arguments to the contrary. It would be unreasonable to limit the collection of data which is based on concrete facts (eg, that someone buys a lot of junk food) and not to limit the inferences that the algorithms draw from this data (eg, predicting a certain state of health of that same individual). The European Data Protection Board claims that inferences are covered by the GDPR. However, the need to even discuss this aspect raises more than one question over the EU lawmakers' awareness of the risks.

From a theoretical point of view, there are other fundamental dilemmas. Algorithms are not programmed to be 'wise'. On the contrary, when they receive a task, they carry it out in the most effective way possible, to the detriment of the critical flexibility typical of human beings. The point, then, is how to interact with a system that does not recognise values and principles? We should avoid getting trapped in generic disquisitions on the ethics of AI and digital technologies, and rely instead on human rights protection instruments. A landmark reference in Europe is Article 8 of the European Convention on Human Rights (ECHR), protecting the right to private and family life, home and correspondence.

The Court of Human Rights in Strasbourg has interpreted this provision as a ban on excessive and disproportionate remote monitoring of workers. In 2018, the Council of Europe also adopted a Protocol to modernise the 1981 'Convention for the Protection of Individuals with regard to Automatic Processing of Personal Data'. The updated Convention sets out the right of every individual 'not to be subject to a decision significantly affecting him or her based solely on an automated processing of data without having his or her views taken into consideration' (Article 9). This protection does not dramatically differ from that established by the GDPR, whose effectiveness, however, is not comparable, also in the light of its market-oriented objectives. In line with the case law of the European Court of Human Rights, businesses can be expected to prove that any algorithmic hiring and profiling systems they put in place are not discriminatory and comply with other European norms and principles.

Triggering a reversal of the burden of proof must arguably be made easier. This expectation serves to counter the refusal of many 'algorithm barons' to make processes explainable and accountable, by invoking trade secrecy and intellectual property as shields, as if they were the secret ingredient of Nutella, with the huge difference that chocolate spread does not make decisions about our life (at most, about our waistline). Any attempt not to disclose the functioning of statistical decision-making systems should be dismissed.[129] Among other things, these refusals are deeply contradictory – confidentiality is demanded for oneself to the detriment of everyone else's privacy. The potential damages of unjust and unaccountable technologies must be contained by enforcing all the available legal tools. The importance of being able to explain the operational logic allowing data subjects to understand the consequences of certain conducts cannot be overstated, especially in light of Articles 13–15 GDPR on information and access rights.[130] This set of information can be key to bringing a prima facie discrimination case, thus deterring the employing entity from relying on software provided by third parties without ensuring the technical understanding of its implications. Being able to verify the logic used in automated decision-making processes, and to assess their criteria and consequences is vital, especially for the application of anti-discrimination rules. For example, EU case law recognises that employers may be held responsible for the biased conduct of a client towards their workers,[131] as well as for proxy discrimination.[132] This is why it is important to trace the chain of automatic decisions back to the source.

III. Work at the Service of Technology

Flesh and bone workers often maintain data-driven tools that are expected to complete apparently novel, and yet 'human-powered', functions. This is how workers end up stuck in a collection of algorithms that cynically manage them and give them the sack without a second thought. This is also how work disappears before our eyes while it is taken over by emerging technologies that, to date, have a hard time distinguishing a chihuahua's snout from a blueberry muffin,[133] and thus need constant oversight and support. The common denominator boils down to a process of 'total wiring' of work, to produce, collect and process as much data as possible.[134] Watchwords include: extract, profile, supervise, target, squeeze out, sell off.

It would be too easy to label this trend as an advanced form of the Taylorist model, that is, the set of management strategies based on both separating conception from execution and minimising discretion to obtain increasingly uniform and measurable outputs thanks to segmentation. Although the cultural background is precisely the one encapsulated in 'scientific management' strategies, proposed by Frederick Taylor at the beginning of the twentieth century, the most recent practices are writing a whole new chapter in the history of work being stripped of its significance. It seems as if modern production models are based on an exaggerated idea of Taylorism, something that its fiercest proponents could not have imagined.

To begin with: automation is by no means synonymous with greater autonomy for humans. Consequently, an examination of digital artefacts must include a deep dive into the alteration of the (already unbalanced) power relationship between management and workers.[135]

Even outside of the world of work, the frivolous nature of technology is making way for a trend that started decades ago in retail.[136] In many sectors, customers are increasingly recruited to carry out tasks that were once fulfilled by regular employees. They have to book their own appointment via apps or complete a check-in procedure before arriving at the airport (but not too early!). Bring your own device to work in peace, scan the barcode yourself (whether in museums, cinemas, railway stations or university libraries), or even compose the ingredients of the salad on screen, using the 'automated' till before queuing up to pay. It is the 'DIY' model, recently revitalised by the need to limit interactions due to risk of infection during the pandemic. Similarly, workers are encouraged to indicate their availability, track themselves, rate colleagues and have flexible hours in a fishbowl-like environment.[137] They personally participate in generating insights into workplace dynamics, from booking spaces in 'hot desk' models to identifying less productive moments of the day.

Without indulging in nostalgia for the good old days, we must note that the underlying assumption of the current model is a peculiar concept of autonomy, one that sees us transformed into personal assistants or replacing other occupations, feeling overwhelmed and trapped in a maze of unpredictable misunderstandings.[138] We should not be indifferent to these incessant efforts to outsource activities that represent the core of some business models and transfer them to third parties (sometimes to the users of the service themselves). *Tout se tient.* All the more so since, as discussed, it is the way the work is 'valued' that determines its fate. How much is an activity worth that, at some point, we are encouraged to do on our own? How meaningful in the eyes of a company is a series of tasks that can be easily performed by clients? Undoubtedly, we are faced with a self-fulfilling prophecy along a chain of professional devaluation, leading to understaffed teams, fungibility of tasks, partial automation but above all wage erosion, intensified competition and shrinking levels of protection.

In short, faith in progress to improve our lives is decidedly misplaced if it disregards these fallouts. It can turn into complete mistrust if we consider some worrying examples of the thin line that divides our private and professional identities. Every time we handle a tech device, inevitably connected to its 'cloud', we should be considering how much it actually belongs to us. Months ago, the case of an IT manager from the media company *Quartz* made the news. The poor bloke was given a counterfeited iTunes gift card. Despite a 15-year history as an impeccable customer of Apple's services and frequent purchaser of its products, he was cut off from his account because of a fraud he was a victim of, with devastating consequences. Not only did he lose all digital files bought or stored over the years (e-books, audio tracks, films, photos, to the tune of a good 15,000 dollars), he was also cut off from using his devices for work, as they need constant updates to run at maximum efficiency. This was a disaster on all fronts, made even worse by the impossibility of challenging the sanction which, as the customer service department did nothing more than reiterate, was 'in compliance with the terms and conditions' he had blindly accepted, after agreeing (like we all do) to 'have read, understood and agree'.

The case was finally resolved, not least thanks to the professional connections of the client who, after regaining possession of his account, simply denounced the incident, in the hope of preventing similar mishaps from happening again. But obviously the same reasoning applies to all Apple's contenders, Tesla or Google or Microsoft or Nintendo or Epic Games or Samsung or Sony, for two reasons. First, digital tools are never entirely ours. Most of their performance is almost exclusively dependent on the parent company, be it for remote assistance, access to virtual accounts, storage programs, cloud services or even underhand obsolescence tactics. Also, switching to competitors is expensive and complicated, because of a lock-in effect that makes any migration very impractical or expensive – forcing us to give up some of the digital materials due to incompatibility. The long-promised interoperability between different proprietary systems was never really delivered.[139] This is something employers, but also labour scholars and policymakers, tend to ignore when analysing the pros and cons of algorithmic management and people analytics.

How many times do you end up seduced and abandoned by apparently must-have promotions that turn out to be just another gateway to paid services or, in the worst-case scenario, to mere tests to be withdrawn in case of failure? And what about our treasured digital possessions? Isn't there a risk for all of us to be stuck with a bundle of services or goods, over which neither we nor our employers have any meaningful control? Doesn't it make sense to rethink how the adoption of AI-enabled management tools entrusts subjects who only respond to commercial logics with a substantial portion of our personal and professional lives? It is about time we raise much more strongly the question of how to regain independence and to ensure that we can seamlessly migrate from one provider to another.

If data is the lifeblood flowing through the veins of any work model at the service of technology, surveillance applications benefit from users and workers who are ready to share data in return for insignificant rewards.[140] The tech companies' storytelling, in turn, encourages constant measurement, in the name of wellness programmes or with the help of internal gamification systems, namely the adoption of entertaining practices in professional contexts. The perils of the deal with the devil, that consumers too often sign in exchange for unlimited, personalised and convenient access to seemingly free services, have been widely studied and tackled by regulatory actions.[141] On the contrary, the consequences of a too generous approach to personal data sharing at work have so far been widely neglected.[142]

All this adds up to a widespread trend, oscillating between authoritarian and hypochondriac approaches, which lead 'data subjects' to disseminate a disproportionate number of digital 'fingerprints' and 'breadcrumbs'. The market for sports or personal tracking applications is skyrocketing: daily step counts, gait, heart rate, menstrual cycles, sleep analysis.[143] Not to mention the many pictures shared online, from which it is almost too easy to infer not only relationships and location, but also economic conditions, political affiliations, professional predispositions and possible illnesses. It is delusional to pretend that a smartphone that can tell us if we snore at night is unable to record all kinds of conversations during the day, extracting and clustering information for resale to the highest bidder, be it a bank, a company or law enforcement.[144] Sleeping peacefully has never been so overrated, one might say.[145]

What has this to do with work? Everything. By September 2020, in Europe over 40 per cent of firms had adopted at least one algorithm-powered technology, while a further 18 per cent was considering implementing one in 2021.[146] We are at an inflection point. The ground under our feet is fragile and the risk of an avalanche is severe. For this reason, it is up to all of us to demand much more when it comes to regaining control over critical information infrastructure, from tech companies and, above all, from regulators. We must fight against the notion that 'if you are not paying for the product, you are the product'. This does not have to be the case. Demanding more power for ourselves, more confidentiality and less hidden data collection, is far from too much to ask. The goal is to prevent a climate of widespread anxiety where suspicion is normalised and the 'sanctity of information integrity' violated.[147] But it will not happen if we surrender to fate or believe the fallacy that imposing strict rules and severe sanctions is always an obstacle to progress. As long as the lobbyists in Silicon Valley say this, it is perfectly predictable, but it is not an acceptable response from regulators.

By providing a more cautionary tale of the rapidly changing digital transformation of work, we now discuss the 'genetic variation' that is unfolding in terms of breadth and instantaneity of information captured, accumulated and evaluated.[148] This shift also affects the very essence of managerial power, which now exceeds the capacity of any human gaze or bureaucratic management. Workers in many industries, both ordinary and tech-intensive, are witnessing a move from direct observation to technocratic control and are experiencing augmentation of bosses' prerogatives due to widespread, deceptive and rigid forms of power.[149] All workers are exposed to all-pervading, real-time and relentless domination that is not confined to the workplace and to working time. Unfortunately, this increase is not adequately limited by the protection defined by legislation or collectively negotiated by social partners. While a more effective enforcement of existing rules would in theory offer meaningful counterweights, wide-ranging transformations make gaps in protection systems and loopholes in regulation even more conspicuous.

A. 'People are Numbers': Count or be Counted

In HR and management circles, there is a great anticipation of the possible uses of the increasingly popular 'workforce analytics' techniques. This is the effective use of large troves of data and metrics about staff to control, measure and dissect performance, plan rewards and incentives, devise mechanisms for promotion and investment in skills and provide instantaneous feedback. Literature shows that control is magnified, up to a state of near-constant and intimate evaluation by supervisors, colleagues or even simple consumers, at the cost of workers' autonomy, not to mention the risk of algorithms spiralling out of control and making errors with no possibility of control, redress or correction.

The devices from which information can be extracted are countless. They range from tablets to badges, from email inboxes to storage clouds, from infrared and barcode scanners to keyboards and touchpads.[150] A cool backpack with radio frequency identification devices (RFID, the same as those found on credit cards) was a recently sought after corporate gift. The whereabouts of the bag can be tracked at all times. This probably means that workers' locations are also regularly tracked. Incidentally, some companies are experimenting with 'smart' office chair cushions and subcutaneous bionic chips.[151] A small incision and workers no longer need to worry about carrying keys and badges – all important passwords travel with them.

Labour regulation in many countries allows managers to use tools that enable the monitoring of workers' behaviours when there are reasonable grounds to do so, for instance, to track productivity, protect a company's assets (including intellectual property), ensure compliance with occupational health and safety, manage risks, mitigate responsibilities and prevent detrimental activities, hazards and frauds. A certain degree of control is embedded in the employment relationship. Sometimes, the law requires that workers' representatives or public authorities are consulted or approve the introduction of these tools.[152] The problem is that it is not so easy to distinguish between surveillance tools and any other equipment that is critical to a worker's performance and thus does not require any collective or public authorisation. CCTV cameras are definitely surveillance tools, but what about an ordinary laptop? Does it not allow as extensive monitoring as a camera, in principle? Or rather, if personal traits with no connection to protected characteristics are algorithmically identified and lay the ground for unfair treatment (such as an outdated browser from which a software infers that the candidate is connected to a public library in a specific neighbourhood, and associates her with a certain racial background),[153] how can non-discrimination law be effectively mobilised in court?

The multifunctional nature of the tech devices allows implementing management practices that take advantage of a wealth of information obtained either on purpose or accidentally. They are introduced to remedy internal flaws, fine-tuning expensive processes as well as improving efficiency and competitiveness. This happens in real time, with razor-sharp precision. Sensors and chips are not yet so precise, but they are becoming more refined through the analysis of proxies that, by approximation, provide extensive but not always accurate pictures, even about a worker's mental status. We are, sometimes, very close to 'neuro-surveillance' practices, the modern version of the faulty lie-detector,[154] through the analysis of biometric data such as heartbeat, tone of voice, facial expressions and, in even more extreme cases, brain waves.[155] It is the final realisation of one of the most deep-seated human dreams – reading other people's minds to adjust one's conduct, anticipating behaviours, perceiving reactions and preventing any objections.

It is no coincidence that many of these applications have been previously tested in the military to provide real-time mapping of fatigue, anxiety or irritation. They can also be deployed in much more everyday contexts, though. For instance, they can be used to infer the probability that a team member is about to resign and change company. Thus, managers that aspire to retain the best workers can design personalised bonus plans, which exclude those who would have stayed on staff anyway, as McKinsey and Company wrote in a report.[156] These practices replicate a marketing logic and apply 'price discrimination' techniques that charge different prices for the same service depending on the client's propensity to spend – something currently being examined by several antitrust authorities.[157] In short, we must be careful to ensure that the dream of mind reading does not turn into a dystopian nightmare.

New systems are programmed to 'identify statistical correlations from a range of data points which no human mind has consciously identified as "relevant", continually absorbing new information and seeking new correlations as they learn'.[158] The cost-effective combination of digitalisation, comprehensive information and pervasive monitoring contributes to further unbalance the information and power asymmetries between the parties of a work arrangement. This renders the workforce even more 'naked' in the eyes of managers.[159]

Workers are often required to fill in self-assessment and data collection forms, inexpensively contributing to corporate strategies aimed at downsizing personnel costs. This also nourishes internal rankings of humans, who have no idea they are under observation. Ratings are all the more questionable the more 'improbable' the parameters chosen to measure productivity are. Just think of the algorithms that compute how many emails sent by each of us get forwarded to other recipients within a team. According to their developers, the more your emails are forwarded the more you are a company 'influencer' or a 'change-maker'. And it doesn't matter if these ideas are patently idiotic and only forwarded for a good laugh, or if excellent ideas are proposed in in-person meetings or over coffee. If you think that nobody would come up with such an absurd system, think again. Introduced in the strongly regulated banking sector to discover potential insider dealing or illegal operations, this is now a very popular metric in major law firms and consultancy companies.[160]

Forms of wide-ranging algorithms were used to cluster items and obtain a sense of workflow bottlenecks or deviant conducts in the recent past.[161] Essentially, the use of data was *observational* or *descriptive*, nothing more than a sometimes tumultuous, concise and imprecise digital attempt to eerily portray reality through numbers and statistics. Nowadays, a greater dependence on inferential analytics, favoured by machine learning, helps managers to disentangle patterns and generate predictions regarding team dynamics, future behaviours and career prospects thanks to probabilistic evaluations of datasets.[162] *Predictive* analyses are conducted in accordance with a set of programmed objectives, 'relying on sophisticated statistical modelling to spot patterns or correlations in the data'[163] and to make informed HR decisions on everyday issues.[164] Initially adopted in anti-terrorism and police programmes, these practices enable managers to predict internal threats and flag suspicious behaviours. Whenever a system signals abnormal activities, such as excessive downloads, emails to dubious recipients or access from unusual locations, reports are made to managers who are responsible for dealing with these doubts and acting accordingly. At the same time, the overwhelming system of tacit punishments and rewards is also used to prompt compliance, thus further redesigning power dynamics with near-perfect information. Powerful data-driven company policies are aimed at subtly manipulating human conducts or, at least, opportunities.[165] Workers' choice is brutally constrained by *prescriptive* or *preemptive* algorithmic tools, which coercively 'shap[e] an environment in which there are no alternatives to performing the work as prescribed'.[166] Tech can subtly change the workers' reasonings, as discussed in the next paragraph. Paradoxically, in some cases, this model leaves workers with the sense of being the owners of their actions.[167]

Despite repeated attempts to crack the internal logic of these so-called 'black boxes', their ultimate components are so complex and intricate that they keep workers, and often also managers, in the dark about policies that, although partially automated, respond to specific organisational needs and reflect organisational choices.[168] This approach also biases the appraisal against new tasks or spontaneous or collaborative activities, as they are hardly prone to measurement. While making instructions more cogent, the constant threat of disciplinary action discourages out-of-the-box initiatives and unplanned endeavours, thus impairing creativity and promoting subservient behaviours in monolithic workplaces. Preparatory activities, auxiliary actions, safety double-checks and reports are essential to the overall performance – at the same time, they can be excluded from direct evaluation, and often from remuneration too. Moreover, in a work context, any reasonably complex project is interdependent with other colleagues' jobs and 'therefore individual performance is hard to disentangle from group performance'.[169] Rather than being reduced, surveillance-related stress increases problems with the result that collective welfare and profitability both get squeezed by high turnover rates (which in turn disperse the knowledge accrued over time), occupational diseases and – not so ironically – reduced productivity.

One of the leading companies in this industry, the Boston-based Humanyze, was founded by Ben Waber together with some of his MIT colleagues. Their key product is a 'sociometric' badge, wearable during working hours and fitted with a microphone, location sensor and accelerometer. It is a badge similar to the one everyone uses to open turnstiles, log their presence or even just access the network printer. On closer examination, however, their primary function is collecting information, using sensors to measure whether or not the 'participant' [aka the worker] is in motion, their proximity to other badged users, whether they are talking or not, and the frequency and duration of in-person interactions.[170] The data collected is then analysed to retrace personal networks within a workplace and to determine how employee interactions affect performance. With a disarming and almost suspicious spontaneity, the company ensures that the badge does not record or measure the content of conversations, web activity, or personal activities outside the office.[171] However, it is not clear how the tool is programmed to exclude certain details.

More precisely, the aim is to examine collaboration flows at work, understand how teams interact in the offices and identify the critical factors for success. This electronic timecard ends up in a logbook that keeps track of performance. No more surveys, observations or focus groups, the people at Humanyze promise.[172] Unsurprisingly, they are not the only ones. There is *Cogito*, which is widely used in call centres and promises to make workers more efficient thanks to instant feedback,[173] IBM's *Watson* to predict employee performance and the likelihood that they will resign and *Percolata* which uses sensors to assign a 'true productivity' score for each worker and draw up an internal ranking. The COVID-19 pandemic and the forced recourse to remote working have caused a surge in demand for this type of allegedly miraculous software.[174] In the USA, the number of large employers using tools to spy on workers has doubled since the onset of the pandemic to 60 per cent, according to Gartner.

Manual labour, of course, is not spared. When workers in one of Amazon's warehouses scattered around the US filed a complaint before the National Labour Relations Board claiming that they had been fired for engaging in legally protected activity, Amazon answered that people were fired because an internal algorithmic system had identified them as 'poor performers' – local management had no say in the decision, as they could not govern or even understand the algorithms.[175] As always, the step from a supporting to a controlling tool is a short one, and this has caused some alarm. Think of the possibility for using these tracking devices to detect any hint of workers' organisation, flagged, for instance, by the gathering of several bracelet signals in one place, which could lead to participants immediately being summoned before supervisors to contain any possible agitation. Very recently, software creating heat maps in order to track (and avert) collective organisation risk has sparked intense outrage.[176] In the meantime, Amazon has patented a new type of tracking wristband that vibrates to help warehouse workers locate items more quickly, and Walmart is testing harnesses that surveil the motions of staffers.[177]

One of the latest arrivals in the business of surveillance is Domino's Pizza which, in Australia and New Zealand, has launched a new tool, enabling customers to verify if they have received the correct pizza. Alongside this customer care function, the 'DOM Pizza Checker' – based on machine learning, AI and sensors – purportedly aims at standardising the service quality. It ensures that the result does not fall below average, by scanning freshly baked pizzas, checking their shape, seasoning and cheese, and comparing them with the 'standard pizza' saved in memory. Cooked and traced with love. Meanwhile, clients receive photo updates of the perfect pizza on the way – perfect for Domino's, of course. At the end of the day, the company claims, it is a training programme, not a Big Brother of the Pepperoni. Now, as two Italians who have lived abroad for a long time, you can rest assured we take pizza VERY seriously. Even we have to admit, however, that this is overkill. Irony aside, the instrument is linked to a reward system and a warning channel – so it undoubtedly presents disciplinary features, beyond its training purpose. Another example is McDonald's spending lavishly to purchase a start-up specialising in voice recognition systems for orders.

Some time ago, the digital publication *Buzzfeed* published a detailed story about *Ziosk*, a system to collect customer reviews which is very popular among US restaurant chains and independent restaurants. As reporter Caroline O'Donovan noted, tools like *Ziosk* 'allow customers to channel frustrations that would otherwise end up on public platforms like Yelp (or TripAdvisor) – which can make or break a restaurant – into a closed system that the restaurant controls. This protects the business and gives them access to valuable data, but it also effectively puts the customer in the position of evaluating and effectively managing their servers'.[178]

Therefore, businesses remain sheltered from the tantrums of unhappy customers, but still collect data and reviews in their internal databases, which are not subject to any form of collective oversight. All in all, it becomes yet another device for governing the workforce, which, with no screening to weed out discrimination, also risks storing biased opinions and taking them at face value.

In general, according to case law, the expectation of privacy on the part of employees in American workplaces can be 'reasonably' limited as they are using equipment owned by the employers and fulfilling business needs. EU and US law differ, the latter giving a greater surveillance power to employers, even if in a regime of good faith.[179] Conversely, in many European countries with strong labour protection practices similar to those outlined above, this reality would most likely be regarded as an unfair labour practice (at least in a formalised context). The problem is that the contractual ambiguities of many 'new' work arrangements pose additional hurdles to the exercise and protection of collective rights. In short, trade unions are often largely absent in these workplaces and even preliminary attempts at coalition can be suffocated by digitalisation.

Scoring, yet another activity outsourced to users, is now ubiquitous – it is present in airport toilets, restaurants, universities, shopping centres and even public administration offices. The implication is that the customer's opinion is taken into great consideration, the result is the creation of a regime of suspicion – since ratings are now generalised. Only by securing the highest possible scores (stars, smiles, little hearts or whatever) will the risk of disciplinary consequences or adverse responses from colleagues be ruled out. Any '4 out of 5' or below review risks being read as a sign of poor performance. In a certain sense, surveillance technologies are helping to project 'a quantified version of oneself', as political economist Phoebe Moore put it, in her book describing new forms of monitoring and control.[180]

In general, it is the triumph of the assumption that the customer is always right, under the guise of creating experiences increasingly in line with the typical expectations of those who choose our services (according to typical press releases launching these tools). Services, activities, interactions and products can be evaluated by the customer, who writes reviews that are often inaccurate and biased, especially in customer service sectors such as hospitality, restaurants, or at any counter where workers are required to smile, indulge, appease and ingratiate. Not to mention the risks of abusive treatment or sexual harassment caused by the imbalance of power – there are dozens of stories of workers who have been subjected to some version of blackmail, under the Damocles' sword of a negative review.[181]

Public awareness on these matters is almost non-existent. Unmindful of the fact that a thumbs down may exclude some low-wage worker from future rosters, who knows how many times each of us went along with these nerve-wracking exercises, by simply answering with no hesitation to questions like 'would you recommend this place to a friend?', 'how do you rate the cleanliness of these premises?', 'do you plan to visit us again in the future?'. In this 'scored society', as scholars

Danielle Citron and Frank Pasquale label it,[182] perceptions are transformed into data, the data becomes scores, the scores make up the rankings, and the rankings have repercussions. The tyranny of metrics is bolstered by our complacency.[183]

B. Working under the Algorithmic Boss

Whenever we ponder on the consequences of digital automation, we should keep it real and look around us. In a way, paradoxically, modern technologies deployed for hiring, scheduling, promoting and firing workers are both enhancing the role of decision-makers and discouraging them from coming to conclusions, thus diluting liabilities and muddying responsibilities. Technology, we must admit, is not born in a perfect society,[184] and history is full of unintended consequences. Yet, power augmentation efforts are 'less attention grabbing than full job automation',[185] as they cause repetitive, uneven shifts to internal processes and job quality. This recent development has been so far considered from a limited, external perspective.[186] Conversely, we aim at examining the full digitisation of managerial powers thanks to technological tools. It is possible that, before 'stealing' our jobs, technologies have taken over our bosses' tasks.[187]

Is this nothing new under the sun? Despite wishful thinking to 'be your own boss' – no shifts, no supervisors, no rules – many workers, also in the most tech intensive sectors, have to deal with a rigid system of constraints, incentives and sanctions. A devious system, based on immaterial and, therefore, often invisible management, yet unable to be stopped. As argued above, this form of monitoring often feeds on potentially sensitive latent personal data, frequently generated by those who record and share whatever they do, contributing to their own profiling[188] ('How many steps have I fast walked today?', 'Let me add a tag to remind myself where I parked', 'I must leave my contact details so I won't miss the next discounts').[189] Even worse, data are also collected without the person who generates them being aware of it. Anticipatory conformity is encouraged.[190] Performance standards are unclear and their application often impossible to understand, to encourage workers to live up to the perceived expectations of the 'digital bosses' and avoid harmful consequences.[191]

There are many cases of company rules memorised as a mantra, which are used to disseminate internal guidelines and influence conduct discretely. This is a great example of 'soft' (or not so soft) power! The mechanism works by word of mouth between colleagues, putting together a doctrine of good practices to which it is 'convenient' to adhere in order to avoid excommunication, or being seen as slackers, good-for-nothings or troublemakers. Downstream we have conducts that are all too human, while upstream there are 'intelligent' and yet unintelligible algorithms, or an AI, often based on machine learning, with a licence to command, on its own and on behalf of third parties.

'Management by algorithms' designates organisational practices that are carried out totally or partially by non-human agents, including applied mathematical formulas.[192] Although these processes aim to increase competitiveness, they often end up being implemented arbitrarily and irresponsibly, undermining workers' rights.[193] Today, these methods aimed at running a business in an efficient and data-driven way, epitomise new evidence-based human resources practices, which can be boiled down to the expression '*boss ex machina*',[194] an adaptation from the Latin phrase '*deus ex machina*' (a god from the machine) describing a theatrical trick used in Greek and Roman theatre whereby a divine creature abruptly entered the scene via a mechanical crane to provide an artificial solution to a problem in the story, by altering the plot of events or even rewriting the fate of the protagonists, often against all logic. In short, a simple mechanical arm enabled a superior intelligence to take decisions on behalf of the main characters, much to the surprise of the audience.

We should ask whether the authority and prerogatives exercised by employers today are really the same as those of the past or whether the stockpiling of new forms of control has not led to a qualitative leap compared to what was practised in the pre-digital era, on which the main regulatory and contractual instruments have been gauged. Employment law has been designed to address and curb the managerial prerogative by means of mandatory provisions, co-negotiated limits or collectively taken countermeasures, in an attempt to promote human dignity.[195] The employment relationship is indeed a two-way organisational platform aimed at reconciling conflicting interests, but these new practices call into question its capability, role and significance.

While literature has recently prospered in the field of AI-enabled employee monitoring, it would be deceptive to consider these practices as a mere threat to privacy. Something more complicated is happening. This amounts to a genetic variation, an uncontrolled increase in forms and methods, for which existing standards protecting equality and non-discrimination, health and safety, data protection and collective rights are poorly equipped. Surveillance, deeply ingrained in all workplaces,[196] is only one of its many complex jigsaw pieces. It is instrumental in allocating automated or semi-automated decision-making prerogatives to separate agents, either human or mechanic – thus reducing workers' autonomy. At the same time, monitoring informs the imposition of sanctions and benefits. Whatever the means used to wield them, such powers are strictly intertwined and should be seen as a continuum: they operate in a cooperative fashion and pursue the goals of efficient coordination of economic factors.[197]

Platform workers have witnessed a large-scale experimentation of these techniques.[198] Uber has been reported to monitor the smartphones of its drivers to map how they were using the pedals and identify good and bad acceleration and braking practices. The *Worksmart Productivity Tool* allowed people to keep an eye on remote workers by capturing screenshots of their desktops or taking photos via the webcam at pre-set 10-minute intervals.[199]

However, we are not just talking about the brave new world of the gig-economy. Major retail companies and restaurant chains have been using these methods for a while, having internalised and updated the lessons learned from human resources management: compartmentalise, measure, optimise, correct. Thanks to barcodes, photocells, optical readers and QR code guns, it is possible to intensify work performance. All it takes is a flashing light to signal to the worker how many pieces remain to be completed in order to reach a target, or an alarm clock that beeps every time a maintenance worker takes longer than expected to make an inspection, a sensor on a chair to detect the level of stress and map musculoskeletal disorders, a flashing icon of a cup of coffee to remind the call centre operator to be more lively and empathetic, or a medal in the company chat awarded after closing a contract with a new customer.[200] They are unacceptable 'digital whips', as a US trade unionist has branded them, which all too often end up increasing injury and illness.[201]

Scheduling technologies have been around for three decades now. In the beginning they were only used to forecast customer presence and generate shifts to match, by using sale maximisation per worker's hour as an objective. Today, software can 'factor in variables like weather or nearby sporting events [resulting in the request for] staff in 15-minute increments'.[202] In trade and services, shifts and rest periods are already organised using software launched by companies such as Kronos, Onshift and Dayforce.[203] Algorithms are watching over hotel house-keepers, telling them which room to clean and tracking their speed.[204] Advertising materials swear that these tools serve to reduce labour costs by means of accurate workload and assignments forecasts. They are presented as being more effective than human-based processes as they combine historical series, weather reports, seasonal trends, past sales and customers' propensity to spend.

The reservoir of collected information is used to update code strings which will take on managerial roles. Much more commonly, algorithms – from basic ones, comparable to decision trees, to more advanced tools capable of self-perfecting over time – suggest 'optimal' decisions over which managers may have the last word. It is also possible to blankly delegate the management, control and disci-plinary functions to a host of applications that act by approximation or by trial and error. After all, even if managers are nominally given the discretion to disre-gard a decision suggested by an algorithm, put yourself in their shoes – would you really contradict at your own risk a technology that was introduced with great fanfare, and most likely cost a fortune? People presented with the suggestion of automated tools are prone to preconceptions whereby they defer to the system without paying it any kind of scrutiny.[205] Rather than automation, it is an augmen-tation of managerial powers and prerogatives. What links this field to the adjacent area of workforce analytics is the risk – or rather the certainty – of an unrestrained expansion of employers' powers, a reduction of workers' autonomy and, therefore, an intensification of the state of subordination at work.

By way of illustration, during the pandemic, both frontline and behind-the-scenes workers had to follow precautionary measures.[206] According to a tech-solutionist narrative,[207] there was an app for that.[208] Several companies reinvented themself to offer what they touted as new 'biometric solutions for safer spaces' of questionable usefulness. The inventory of these gadgets included ultrasonic bracelets beeping every time a blue-collar worker in the UK automotive industry or a docker in a Belgian port were within virus catching distance of a co-worker and a camera connected to the thermal scanner to release a green light in public offices. Other companies introduced alerts giving notice of sanitation shifts around the clock, hand-washing stations connected with smartphones, GPS-integrated applications tracking employees' every moves or enforcing hygiene guidelines, RFIDs measuring and optimising the occupancy rate of the spaces (employing a software to track time attendance and ensure group rotation), SMSs urging compliance with good practices. All in all, such normalisation of what we call 'panopticon' technologies has also resulted in shifting accountability to workers.[209]

Power is thus changing its face. In this uncertain context, a broad spectrum of reactions takes place, ranging from indignation to self-indulgence. We veer from outrage, partly justified by the uncontrollability of these models, partly increased by the lack of transparency, to a sort of acceptance, while convincing ourselves that no, we would never end up dealing with an omnipresent and omniscient algorithmic boss. The second reaction risks being the most dangerous, since it paves the way for surrender and capitulation.

This is not science fiction. 'Workforce analytics' and 'management by algorithms' are well-established realities able to make the fortune of tech tycoons. They are not 'niche' things. There are handbooks, tutorials and podcasts based on setting up an organisation entirely managed by IT-based systems, promising access to unmissable opportunities for 'amplification', 'optimisation' 'customisation' and 'product differentiation'.[210]

And yet, although the race against time to develop prototypes and pilot projects has been underway for a while now, very scant attention has been paid to how the employer's key functions were so far clumsily artificialised, intensified and augmented by the applications we have described above,.[211] This is a micromanagement system without a manager. In order to appeal against arbitrary decisions, workers have to resort to the equivalent of 'customer service'. Unfortunately, most of the time they have to be content with imprecise solutions that refer to internet pages, limiting interaction with managers to a minimum. The effect of these cumbersome processes is clearly to discourage complaints and nip disputes in the bud – yet another bureaucratisation of our discontent.

Informed by principles of transparency, equal treatment, due process, accountability, valid reasons for termination and effective remedy, many legal frameworks constrict how managers can go about taking workplace decisions.[212] Nevertheless, the nature of the new computerised tools involved and the possibility of developing capabilities essentially 'differ from the traditional management structures around which employment law has been designed'.[213] This causes an enlargement of the managerial prerogative upon which labour regulation is premised. The historical boundaries to managerial powers were conceived when the potential of current technology was unthinkable, at a time when command was exercised by humans in a more direct, physical manner, not cloaked in software code.

In 2021, California lawmakers passed a pioneering bill to crack down on the unclear algorithm-led decision-making in fulfilment centres run by retail giant Amazon. The text aims at bringing transparency regarding quotas and work speed metrics to employees and government agencies. It would also ban 'time off task' (TOT) penalties that have a negative impact on health and safety, and would prohibit retaliation against workers who complain.[214] Bizarre though it may sound, California had to introduce *new* legislation to ensure workers would not be penalised when they take a bathroom or water break. Recently, lawsuits were filed in the Netherlands by former Uber and Ola drivers claiming that algorithms automatically determined which drivers should be 'deactivated' from the platform in a non-transparent way and with no meaningful human intervention, thus breaching notification obligations under Articles 13 and 14, access rights under Article 15 and safeguards set forth under Article 22 of the GDPR.[215] In some of these cases, however, based on the information provided by the defendants, the simple intervention of some limited human scrutiny was interpreted by the Dutch court as a justification not to apply the ban on solely automated processing. In the case of only one applicant, the court decided that deductions from driver earnings amounted to an automated decision lacking human intervention, thus triggering the right to demand human intervention, to express their point of view and to appeal such decisions.[216]

Notably, an important aim of the newly proposed EU Directive on platform work is to promote 'transparency, fairness and accountability in algorithmic management in platform work and by improving transparency in platform work'.[217] The information duties regard digital surveillance tools and automated decision-making. In the former case, workers must be informed about the adoption of such instruments and 'the categories of actions monitored, supervised or evaluated [...], including evaluation by the [clients]'.[218] In the latter case, besides the notification of the introduction, workers shall be informed about the categories of decisions made, the parameters considered and their relative weight and the motivation behind a decision to 'restrict, suspend or terminate the platform worker's account, to refuse the remuneration for work performed [...], on the platform worker's contractual status or any decision with similar effects'.

The text strengthens the gold standard set in the GDPR. It explicitly provides for a right to an explanation for a decision taken – even only supported – by automated systems which significantly affects working conditions such as access to tasks, earnings, occupational health and safety, working time, promotion, suspension or termination. All decisions upheld by data-driven instruments would have to be presented in an accessible way, so as to allow workers to challenge them. The processing of data regarding the mental and emotional states of workers is banned as well as the collection of data regarding their health or their private conversations, including with their workers' representatives. This debunks many myths as to 'algorithmic impenetrability' – where a lack of transparency is often cited as an excuse for undermining legibility and contestability – and would guarantee a pre-emptive right for workers to understand the consequences of certain conducts.

A 'workplace due process' model is envisaged, in line with obligations applying to conventional employers.

Having said that, protection under this proposal still needs strengthening. The draft Directive still takes for granted that algorithmic management should, in principle, be allowed, provided that it meets the Directive's requirements. Arguably, however, algorithmic management should not be assumed as a 'given'; its very introduction should be – at the very least – a matter for negotiation with the social partners. This has been the approach taken in the past by some European national legislation concerning the use of technology that may allow monitoring the work performance. It is hard to see why algorithmic management, which relies on technologies that could be much more invasive than those more severely scrutinised in the past, should be held to lower regulatory standards.

Blamed as a source of dishonesty and arbitrariness, human flexibility is soon to be simplified by complex sequences of infallible codes. This ignores the promotion of 'virtues of human discretion, judgement and agency, which have long been recognised [...] as vital in overcoming the inevitable imperfection associated with legal rules'.[219] Granted: human bosses are far from perfect; however, modern legal systems have a wealth of experience in confronting flaws in human decision making.[220] The rise of '*bosses ex machina*' fundamentally unsettles the existing mechanisms. Without compassion or mercy, digital tools are less controllable when they embed developers' explicit or implicit biases, shutting the door on 'intersubjective negotiation of meaning in favor of objectification'.[221] What could be the most suitable legal strategies to counter autonomous decision-making processes at the workplace? How can prior authorisation and codetermination procedures be fulfilled when workers freely give their consent to gamification tools to collect data to surreptitiously assess them? What role can dismissal regulation play when non-standard workers can be simply 'discontinued' by not receiving tasks due to negative feedback left by disappointed customers?[222] How can we streamline the burden of proof when access to data is not routinely granted to alleged victims of harms? What if data controllers are uncooperative and take advantage when information is unevenly distributed?

Under the veneer of innovation, code-based governance systems are too rigid to depart from predetermined solutions and less adaptable than human flexibility. In addition, technology-coded authority is far less open-minded than human hierarchies, as it optimises previous and current disparities arranged into granular datasets, bringing them to a debatable level of verifiability that may also limit the effectiveness of existing legal remedies.[223] Given their obscure nature, they end up impeding the understanding of strategies, jeopardising contestation thanks to a powerful chilling effect on industrial action. Their 'accuracy', 'precision', 'comprehensiveness', 'completeness' and 'impartiality' guarantee hidden flaws, avoiding the possibility of feedback.[224] Advocating the application of these principles as fixes to current problems is a way of sleepwalking into defective, yet statistically correct outcomes.

The routinisation of all the functions of management, whilst evoking an air of infallibility, also represents a challenge for businesses and tech providers, especially large-scale companies where chains of command are sophisticated. From a legal perspective, the unpredictability of often difficult to explain executive choices cannot excuse employers from meeting their responsibilities. Paradoxically, the impossibility of reverse-engineering, explaining or documenting the concrete steps of decision-making processes exaggerates the vulnerability of bosses' position in court,[225] especially in jurisdictions where presumptions may be in force in fields such as equality and non-discrimination law or in cases of unlawful dismissal.

Algorithmic management also benefits from 'gamification' practices. To give an example, *MissionRacer* is a software that allows people working in Amazon warehouses to be assigned an avatar and engage in a heart-pounding race against their colleagues to reduce the boredom of overly tiring and repetitive jobs (they can choose between dragons and toy cars).[226] While the order picker is running between the shelves, the worker's digital projection is wiggling on a monitor to win a few pats on the shoulder, or at most credits to spend on company merchandising. Thanks to unwritten rules and design features, a seemingly gentle version of authority here produces 'nimble, unobtrusive and highly potent' persuasion,[227] the subtlest version of coercion.[228] Literally, a full-blown race to the bottom, an effective system of incentives based on dopamine, the neurotransmitter at the heart of motivation. The aspiration is to 'infantilise' the workforce. Making a physical effort through apparently fun activities is the easiest way to push workers over the limits in package preparation, by recommending actions to be taken and setting the results to be achieved.

As illustrated by Karen Yeung, a professor of law, ethics and informatics at the University of Birmingham,[229] decision-making choice contexts are 'intentionally designed in ways that systematically influence human decision-making in particular directions'. Perhaps it is again time to ask ourselves whether we should not be rejecting a given technology when the risks to society are too high. More often than not, technologies unduly compromise the space for autonomy, thus devaluing work.[230] In warehouses, fulfilments centres,[231] logistic hubs, fast food and kitchen chains, cleaning and maintenance services, when new practices or digital tools replacing bosses are introduced with the purposes of cost reduction, reception of these technologies can be negative, which adversely affects the worker's skills and commitment to the organisation. On the contrary, when technologies are adopted to improve the overall work experience and enhance well-being, those methods have been well-received and have had a positive effect on workplaces. This shifts the power from institutions to individuals, who are consequently empowered to own their actions and choices. When accompanied by training and proper resources, providing workers with the ability to make their own decisions correlates with successful performances[232] in an 'autonomy-supportive context'.[233]

Since algorithmic management systems are becoming very affordable and easy to use, it can be expected that their adoption will multiply, with a ripple effect. We cannot abandon attempts to limit the most deranged and invasive aspects of these practices. It is, as always, up to us to decide whether the '*boss ex machina*' shall be used to automate the all-encompassing spectrum of HR management functions, from pre-hiring screening to the filtering of applications, from the issuing of directives to the evaluation of performance and the termination of workers. If we think that we should not be bossed around by the algorithms, and their programmers and masters, we should start questioning unilateral decisions to introduce these alienating tools in work environments.[234]

C. Beating AI at its Own Game

Rest assured, if the 'gig-economy' has been the buzzword for the last decade, 'artificial intelligence' (AI) will be one of the most recurrent terms in the years to come.[235] Many people are jumping on the bandwagon. Barkers, entrepreneurs, enthusiasts, they all swear that they have 'the next big thing' on their hands. One cannot help being wary of these claims, since 'next big things' do not normally need to be advertised. In any case, the mystique of AI is attracting a remarkable amount of attention. 'AI' designates an algorithmic system of analysis that, thanks to large amounts of data, is able to extract patterns and make predictions by mimicking functions that humans associate with their own intelligence, as we read in one of the first documents issued by the group of experts on AI set up by the European Commission in June 2018.[236]

There are several angles from which this trend could be explored. First of all, there is already so much AI in all of our private and professional lives. What exists today is the 'weak' or 'narrow' version – as experts call it – to distinguish it from the 'strong' or 'general' version, capable of understanding and interacting as a human being would, which only exists on paper.[237] You can find AI in everyday activities and tools, from spam filters in email boxes to the 'Recommended for you' sections of online shopping sites, from weather forecasts to stock performance calculations, from dynamic pricing on booking websites to popular vocal assistants, from subtitles in online videos to instant translation programmes. The playlist suggested on the basis of personal musical tastes, Twitter's 'While you were away' and Facebook's 'People You May Know' features, the proposal of a good hotel in the middle of a trip (or too often, once the trip is over), and even the spell checker on your smartphone are the result of the use of AI-powered applications.

In order to develop a healthy relationship with this innovation, we should start to consider it not as a stand-alone object, but as a component embedded in different physical or digital tools. In the two previous sections, we described different uses and abuses related to the organisation and monitoring of the workforce. There is, therefore, much anticipation, and perhaps even hope, of understanding next moves. Contrary to popular belief, however, AI has deep roots and, after initial enthusiasm,[238] it has experienced a long period of hibernation ('the winter of AI', as the those in the know say). Its future, therefore, depends not only on multiple investments, but above all on the tasks that will be entrusted to this general-purpose technological 'platform'.[239]

It is perhaps not a bad thing that bombastic statements have stimulated a certain excitement, even if they were usually disproved by the facts. Popular interest may have the merit of paving the way for intelligent uses of AI. Institutions such as the OECD and the European Union, as well as national governments, are working hard to bring about the long-awaited AI spring.[240] Given the economic resources involved, it is logical that governments are willing to reap the economic benefits that come from this breakthrough.

In amongst all the expectation,[241] there is a perspective on the phenomenon that is still perhaps little explored. If it were not for the fact that, in a moment of unusual honesty, Jeff Bezos himself named one of his signature creations after it, the anecdote we are about to report would count as an addition to the ranks of a fictitious neoluddite army.[242] The story has already been told many times, including by some brilliant colleagues of ours,[243] but it never ceases to 'amaze'.

In 1769, at the time of Maria Theresa of Austria, the wealthy scientist Johann Wolfgang Ritter von Kempelen took up the challenge launched by the Empress – to emulate the inventions of a certain Frenchman who amazed the royal family with spectacular demonstrations halfway between science and circus. A year passes and Kempelen proclaimed himself the inventor of the first device capable of playing chess, and even winning, against human champions. It was known as the Mechanical Turk, a wooden cabinet that houses the life-size puppet of a man, wearing a turban and an oriental tunic similar to those worn by the necromancers of the time. Its eyes were fixed on a wooden chessboard, its right hand holding a pipe and its left hand ready to move the pawns. The accounts of the time recall that at each performance the inventor made an effort to reassure the audience that there were no tricks involved. Opening the cabinet, he revealed to spectators an intricate mechanism of wheels, gears, levers and springs. The show included the lighting of a candle to illuminate the inside of the automaton and convince the audience of the full legitimacy of the invention. Once the inspection phase was over, it was time to see the Turk in action. It demonstrated its ability to manoeuvre chess with its gloved hand and, after a move capable of challenging its opponent, it gloated in amusement. It would also shake its head to show disappointment if the other player tried to cheat.

For about 15 years, the attraction travelled across half of Europe. Most of the time it won without too much difficulty, even though the reports are silent on the level of the opponents, nor do they inform us if the novelty was a source of entertainment for them. Kempelen was always around, but kept himself at a safe distance from the Turk to stress the total 'autonomy' of his automaton. In 1785 the inventor sent his creature into retirement. A few decades later, a Turk reappeared at the court of Napoleon Bonaparte. The emperor was even disqualified for having tried some unauthorised moves. The prodigious fame of the device spread rapidly. The entrepreneur and music boxes producer, Johann Nepomuk Maelzel, who had organised the match between the Turk and Napoleon, displayed the device in various places. Even Edgar Allan Poe was so impressed that he wrote a ponderous essay, 'Maelzel's Chess Player', making some hypotheses about the operation of the wondrous machine.

The whole scheme was remarkable. Unfortunately, it goes without saying, there was nothing technological about it, aside from mock cogs and clockwork machinery. The movements of the puppet were operated by a man hidden inside the cabin, who interacted with the outside through an apparatus of magnets, mirrors and tie rods. The trick is rather disconcerting in its banality, as a *New York Times* journalist reviewing an illustrated book recalling the history of the Turk noted.[244] The person who had built the structure was an illusionist, not an inventor, having created a show to divert viewers' attention from the secret. Behind the gears, behind the coveted mannequin there was a man. And there is no better example to illustrate the theme that this section deals with. The Turk is prophetic. A telling example of humans usurping robots' labour in activities such as content moderation, programming and audio/video transcription.[245] Even more ironically, workers are allocated the most awkward parts of these projects, since computers can only function with refined files and clean tracks.[246]

Jeff Bezos not only named the micro-work platform he launched 15 years ago after the Turk, but also proudly made it a manifesto. The internet is full of flesh and blood handymen, engaged in a sophisticated ensemble of digital levers aimed at producing the impression of a perfect automatic mechanism. This is the philosophy behind the numerous crowdwork apps. What, you may ask, links workforce analytics and algorithmic governance to the Mechanical Turk, both the original one and the one Bezos conceived? They both make human labour invisible by hiding behind a technological smokescreen. The modern Turk's fortune lies in the vast amount of data generated and collected. It is raw, confused, often superfluous data.[247] Platforms such as the Amazon Mechanical Turk (AMT), originally created as intranet platforms within Amazon itself for cataloguing items on sale, do exactly that – they use humans to clean up, organise and make sense of otherwise useless information. Other humans, on different platforms, are given the tasks of moderating content, deleting pirated files or excluding materials that do not meet 'community standards'. Some others sift through social networks to extrapolate feelings, reactions and trends.

The circularity of these practices is striking. Data are extracted to efficiently organise the workforce, and manage it from hiring to dismissal, and, to reduce their chaos, numerical series are entrusted to 'downloadable digital workers' or 'data janitors'.[248] Do not forget that the AMT has a long list of imitators. Scholars speak of 'heteromation' (a neologism that is the antonym of 'automation') whenever someone extracts value from someone else's work, especially when the latter's contribution is low-cost, unpaid, or even concealed behind a techy façade.[249] 'Artificial' AI can be described in this way: a myriad of very small activities completed by unsuspecting or, worse, underpaid contributors.[250]

It also encompasses our endeavours, when we are asked to prove on Google reCAPTCHA that we are not a robot, by identifying objects such as cars, crosswalks, traffic lights and buses to feed image recognition software databases. There is, in fact, something ironic about the so-called user-generated content, a form of work touted as a playful pastime. In his book on digital work, sociologist Antonio Casilli wrote that humans steal machines' jobs, not the other way around.[251] It is true. Once, to download a document or to subscribe to a newsletter, you were forced to interpret and copy letters and figures crumpled, dilated or lying on one side. A computer would never have succeeded in doing so accurately. Therefore, we filled up (free of charge) the archives of software to make manuscripts digital. Each of us contributed to digitising texts for Google Books, a seemingly automated service. Today the system has evolved, the tasks consist in recognising pictures of bridges, bicycles, signals or hydrants. We are training the AI that is struggling to drive an autonomous car and are enriching the collection of tagged images that will in turn improve other services (including facial recognition – an ever more controversial issue normalised by Apple Face ID).

Who gets their hands dirty completing these untraceable, free and non-documented activities? Behind the prodigious coverup of pretend AI, there is a global contingent of labourers. By using chess and the lesser-known game of Go – both fascinating and dazzlingly complex activities – IBM (with the Deep Blue chess-playing expert system) and Google (with AlphaGo) have designed their own AI applications. Invisibility, however, describes the different phases of a slow and perhaps permanent process of work transformation, thanks to the maze of contractual formulas, designed in response to provisional needs and devised to circumvent the full suite of labour protection. In today's workplaces, people are working as an 'extension' of the machines or behind AI-enabled tools and algorithms.[252] The 'behind the façade' of an IT-tool is an inaccessible warehouse in which, thanks to the contribution of service design, it is possible to apply standardised legal rules. Even unassailable professions are at risk – *Axiom Law* gets you low-priced legal advice;[253] *Innocentive* allows you to outsource research and open innovation development activities; thanks to *AmWell* you no longer need to sit in your doctor's waiting room; and *Business Talent Group* dispatch managers to solve business problems.

Mounting evidence reveals a widespread trend towards workforce homogenisation and, in turn, de-skilling, which can be considered enabling factors in introducing automated decision-making systems.[254] This causes a process of simultaneous regimentation, parcellisation and uniformisation of work, compounded by the risk of individual harm, partially disproving popular theories according to which automation should remove highly demanding and psychosocially dangerous jobs.[255] While skill specialisation has been often designated as the foundation of modern economic growth,[256] workers are increasingly forced to comply with standardised rules in unchangeable environments.[257] In this perverse cycle, once work is stripped of its abstract and creative components, it rapidly becomes outsourceable alternatively to individuals without extensive training or to dysfunctional machines, in their turn, fed by invisible workers. In the second case, human intervention is often confined to tasks such as supervising algorithms, fixing errors, handling exceptions or even impersonating machines.[258] This is a both a prelude to, and an incentive for, broader substitution.

Lilly Irani was among the first to deal with the phenomenon, beginning by working on Google's innovative projects and then as a scholar.[259] She described the advent of the 'dirty work of the web' since its inception, bringing to light the vast outsourcing schemes of digital behemoths – informal contracts, essential in keeping countless services up and running. This is yet another example of 'work at the service of technology', as digital services constantly need to be reconfigured, gauged and adjusted. The case of AMT's workers is only the tip of the iceberg of a system that sits on invisible work – from maintenance engineers in automated factories to traumatised moderators who analyse reports of violent content. Beyond the surface, there are ghost workers, often marginalised on the basis of gender and ethnicity. Even worse, the digital interface offers a get out clause to clients and consumers at the expense of workers,[260] who now begin to react and make themselves visible, reclaiming their protections and denouncing stress, discrimination, trauma and job insecurity.

In *RealLife*, a magazine critical of technology, Jathan Sadowski talked about some innovations, both analogical and digital, like a big battleship Potemkin.[261] According to a legend spread by his detractors, the Russian minister Potemkin embarked on the construction of several fake villages in order to impress Empress Catherine II. Behind his illusive papier-mâché setting a much less glittering reality was hidden. A thread of trickery and hoax links various services that we commonly use and are kept together by an army of ghost workers, even if from the outside they appear to be based on software and algorithms. Most of the time, workers are required to masquerade as robotic devices, to disguise themselves as AI, and even to imitate common mistakes made by machines. A photograph of a technician concealed as a seat at the wheel of a driverless car has been widely circulated.[262] Less awkwardly than in this borderline case of 'AI washing', many pretend automated vehicles are driven (or overseen) remotely by human hands, as is the case with underground trains in many cities today.

It has also emerged that, in order to refine spam email filters and personalised messaging products, people have been employed by platform companies to read the content of email messages to improve computational language software.[263] Other audio transcription services marketed as automatic actually used translators. Closer to home, every time we resort to Google's translator and correct its paradoxical results, we are working two times for Mountain View, first when we fill its gigantic database with new texts, and secondly when we develop it with our corrections. A case of workers in the backroom of the digital assistants that many of us have in our living rooms demonstrates this.[264] Even more disturbing, these applications have proved to be perfect channels for theft of sensitive passwords. Before that, Facebook was testing an exceedingly effective virtual assistant – and indeed a real-life team was behind it.[265] The same was true for Facebook's trending topic column, whose human-powered operation has been lately disclosed.[266] In the meantime, who knows how many investors and clients will have fallen for the claims of digital snake oil salespersons who travel around tech fairs to advertise new Mechanical Turks.

Although the debate on work transformation is largely focused on 'front-line' workers in urban gig-economies, empirical research on hidden digital work has flourished in recent years. Amazon has found a way to monetise this deception by offering 'humans as a service' (this definition is courtesy of Jeff Bezos) with a very simple formula: a virtual billboard where companies and individuals hire workers that are spread all over the world. In contrast with platforms operating in defined physical locations, these activities can easily be outsourced to places where labour costs per unit of product are much lower. Payment is, at best, a few cents, or otherwise in credits to spend on the Amazon website. The labour force, mainly American and Indian (the latter until recently made up 40 per cent of the platform's workforce),[267] guarantees a massive coverage, that does not know about time zone limitations. Describing the 'new class of workers [who] stands opposite the coding elite', sociologists Jenna Burrell and Marion Fourcade wrote that 'what stands beneath the fetish of AI is a global digital assembly line of silent, invisible men and women, often laboring in precarious conditions, many in postcolonies of the Global South'.[268]

AMT is a pilot project, and was never fully developed. At the same time, it is the prototype of the platform that makes it possible to recruit 'providers', according to its internal terminology, to perform low value-added activities. These are routine chores ('Human Intelligence Task'), which no algorithm is able to complete: tagging photos, reporting data, unravelling audio, rewriting invoices, completing surveys, translating short texts, tracking down errors, editing articles, correcting drafts, searching addresses, participating in market research, recognising violence. Practices that are so boring that even computers refuse to discharge them, one might say. This is why humans are used, by splitting up the orders into infinitesimal tasks. There is scant knowledge regarding workers who resort to digital platforms to perform tasks online, without any face-to-face interaction. This approach, with a few exceptions, is reflected in the regulatory measures adopted, in case law and in most of the social partners' initiatives.

It's hard to make a business assessment of the prodigious AMT. Little is known about the real number of the 'Turkers', as workers on the AMT are called, but we know about their living conditions after the publication of extensive research. They are mainly young people, often highly educated, and aware of their choice to be engaged online through the API ('application programming interface'). They frequently manage several accounts, in contravention of the terms and conditions, in order to earn a small income for relatives and friends. Sometimes they complete tasks during periods of inactivity, such as during a commute. In other scenarios, they are crammed by the dozens into so-called click-farms, actual digital sweatshops. An internet connection is enough to have some micro tasks assigned to them by a company operating on the other side of the world – there is also a strong concentration on the part of clients, since almost all the requests are published by a small number of companies. The system is deliberately indifferent to requests for improvements that would make money transfers less complicated.

Jeff Bezos, a few Christmases ago, was the target of an email-bombing campaign set up by workers. 'We are people, not avatars', they wrote, calling for adjustments that were never made. The signatories of the appeal broke through the veil of silence that was surrounding these forms of work; some idiosyncrasies of online work make the matter very elusive, including the invisibility of workers and the conflict of laws and jurisdictions if someone works online for a platform that is based in a different country. More recently, stories of refugees in shattered camps have emerged. Caged in a virtual assembly line, they may be working to maintain AI-powered tools that could be used for war operations against them. These activities are safer and more lucrative than other informal jobs, but replicate some schemes of unfree labour, sometimes in airless spaces. Similar arrangements have been extended to incarcerated people as part of their sentence.[269]

This model marks an unquestionably dramatic paradigm shift: in the future, a large slice of middle-class jobs could be outsourced to a worldwide crowd of underpaid freelancers, heralding the arrival of the human infrastructure of automation.[270]

---

[1] P Holland and A Bardoel, 'The impact of technology on work in the twenty-first century: exploring the smart and dark side' (2016) 27(21) *The International Journal of Human Resource Management* 2579–80.

[2] GS Lowe, *The Quality of Work: A People-Centred Agenda* (Oxford, Oxford University Press, 2000).

[3] E Brynjolfsson and A McAfee, *The Second Machine Age: Work, Progress, and Prosperity in a Time of Brilliant Technologies* (New York, WW Norton & Company, 2014).

[4] C Estlund, 'What Should We Do after Work: Automation and Employment' (2018) 128(2) *Yale Law Journal* 257–326.

[5] B Merchant, 'Amazon's first fully automated factory is anything but' *The New York Times* (21 October 2019) www.nytimes.com/2019/10/21/opinion/future-amazon-automation.html.

[6] B Rogers, *Data and democracy* (Cambridge MA, MIT Press, 2022). See also N Scheiber, 'Inside an Amazon Warehouse, Robots' Ways Rub Off on Humans' *The New York Times* (3 July 2019) www.nytimes.com/2019/07/03/business/economy/amazon-warehouse-labor-robots.html.

[7] See, for instance, B Heater and K Korosec, 'Walmart reportedly ends contract with inventory robotics startup Bossa Nova' (*TechCrunch*, 3 November 2020) https://techcrunch.com/2020/11/02/walmart-reportedly-ends-contract-with-inventory-robotics-startup-bossa-nova/.

[8] A Mateescu and MC Elish, 'AI in context, the labor of integrating new technologies' (*Data & Society*, 2019) https://datasociety.net/wp-content/uploads/2019/01/DataandSociety_AIinContext.pdf at 36.

[9] B Merchant, 'There's an automation crisis underway right now, it's just mostly invisible' (*Gizmodo*, 11 October 2019) https://gizmodo.com/the-trickle-down-disaster-of-automation-1838974516.

[10] Algorithm Watch, 'Automating Society Report' (October 2020) automatingsociety.algorithmwatch.org.

[11] T Lamont, 'The student and the algorithm: how the exam results fiasco threatened one pupil's future' *The Guardian* (18 February 2021) www.theguardian.com/education/2021/feb/18/the-student-and-the-algorithm-how-the-exam-results-fiasco-threatened-one-pupils-future.

[12] DK Citron, 'Technological Due Process' (2007) 85 *Washington University Law Review*, 1249–1313.

[13] F Pasquale, *New Laws of Robotics* (Cambridge MA, Harvard University Press, 2020).

[14] E Di Nicola, *La dissolvenza del lavoro* (Roma, Ediesse, 2019).

[15] V De Stefano, A Aloisi and N Countouris, 'The Metaverse is a labour issue' (*Social Europe*, 1 February 2022) https://socialeurope.eu/the-metaverse-is-a-labour-issue.

[16] K Schwab, *The Fourth Industrial Revolution* (Geneva, World Economic Forum, 2016).

[17] G Leonhard, *Technology vs. Humanity: The coming clash between man and machine* (Kent, UK, Fast Future Publishing, 2016). See also A Azhar, *Exponential: How Accelerating Technology Is Leaving Us Behind and What to Do About It* (London, Random House, 2021).

[18] G Vardaro, 'Tecnica, tecnologia e ideologia della tecnica nel diritto del lavoro' in L Gaeta, AR Marchitiello and P Pascucci (eds), *Itinerari* (Milano, Franco Angeli, 1989) 231–308 (presenting entrepreneurship as the 'domination over technology').

[19] JY Chen and JL Qiu, 'Digital Utility: Datafication, Regulation, Labor, and DiDi's Platformization of Urban Transport in China' (2019) 12(3) *Chinese Journal of Communication* 274–89. See also N Srnicek, 'The Only Way to Rein in Big Tech Is to Treat Them as a Public Service' *The Guardian* (23 April 2019) www.theguardian.com/commentisfree/2019/apr/23/big-tech-google-facebook-unions-public-ownership.

[20] A Toffler, *Future shock* (New York, Random House, 1970). See also EG Popkova, YV Ragulina and AV Bogoviz, 'Fundamental Differences of Transition to Industry 4.0 from Previous Industrial Revolutions' in *Industry 4.0: Industrial Revolution of the 21st Century* (Cham, Springer, 2019) 21.

[21] Art 4(1), Regulation (EU) 2016/679 of 27 April 2016 on the protection of natural persons with regard to the processing of personal data and on the free movement of such data (GDPR). See H Schildt, *The Data Imperative: How Digitalization is Reshaping Management, Organizing, and Work* (Oxford, Oxford University Press, 2020).

[22] PV Moore and J Woodcock (eds), *Augmented Exploitation: Artificial Intelligence, Automation, and Work* (London, Pluto Press, 2021). S Adler-Bell and M Miller, 'The datafication of employment, Report on surveillance and privacy' (*The Century Foundation*, 19 December 2018) https://tcf.org/content/report/datafication-employment-surveillance-capitalism-shaping-workers-futures-without-knowledge.

[23] S Zuboff, *In the Age of the Smart Machine: The Future of Work and Power* (New York, Basic Books, 1988). See also V Mayer-Schönberger and K Cukier, *Big Data: A Revolution That Will Transform How we Live, Work, and Think* (Boston MA, Houghton Mifflin Harcourt, 2013).

[24] S Zuboff, 'Big other: Surveillance capitalism and the prospects of an information civilization' (2015) 30(1) *Journal of Information Technology* 75–89. See also J Cheney-Lippold, *We Are Data: Algorithms and the Making of Our Digital Selves* (New York, New York University Press, 2017).

[25] See generally R Milkman, *Farewell to the Factory* (Berkeley, University of California Press, 1997); A Goldstein, *Janesville: An American Story* (New York, Simon and Schuster, 2017).

[26] J Russo and S Lee Linkon, 'The social costs of deindustrialization' (2009) *Manufacturing a better future for America* 183–216.

[27] A Benanav, *Automation and the Future of Work* (London, Verso, 2020).

[28] Eurostat, 'Three jobs out of four in services' (2019) https://ec.europa.eu/eurostat/web/products-eurostat-news/-/wdn-20190612-1.

[29] Eurofound, *The future of manufacturing in Europe* (Luxembourg, Publications Office of the European Union, 2019).

[30] S Helper, E Reynolds, D Traficonte and A Singh, *Factories of the Future: Technology, Skills, and Digital Innovation at Large Manufacturing Firms* (MIT Work of the Future Research Brief, 2021).

[31] Eurofound, *Game changing technologies: Exploring the impact on production processes and work* (Luxembourg, Publications Office of the European Union, 2018).

[32] R Baldwin, *The Globotics Upheaval: Globalization, Robotics, and the Future of Work* (Oxford, Oxford University Press, 2019).

[33] In 2021, however, obstacles in the interdependent global supply chain and surge in demand caused a shortage in computer chips, which threatened to reduce the availability of electronic devices.

[34] A Merkel, 'Speech by Federal Chancellor Angela Merkel to the OECD Conference' (2014), available at www.bundesregierung.de/breg-en/chancellor/speech-by-federal-chancellor-angela-merkel-to-the-oecd-conference-477432.

[35] Gartner, 'Forecasts Global Spending on Wearable Devices to Total $81.5 Billion in 2021' (*Gartner*, 12 January 2021) www.gartner.com/en/newsroom/press-releases/2021-01-11-gartner-forecasts-global-spending-on-wearable-devices-to-total-81-5-billion-in-2021.

[36] B Gutelius and N Theodore, 'The future of warehouse work: technological change in the U.S. Logistics Industry' (UC Berkeley Labor Center-Working Partnerships USA); G Winant, 'Life under the algorithm' (*The New Republic*, 4 December 2019) https://newrepublic.com/article/155666/life-algorithm.

[37] C Mims, *Arriving Today: From Factory to Front Door – Why Everything Has Changed About How and What We Buy* (London, Harper Collins, 2021); A MacGillis, *Fulfillment: Winning and Losing in One-Click America* (New York, Farrar, Straus and Giroux, 2021).

[38] S O'Connor, 'Amazon unpacked' *Financial Times* (8 February 2013) www.ft.com/content/ed6a985c-70bd-11e2-85d0-00144feab49a.

[39] K Votavova, 'In Central Europe, Concern Over Toll, Fairness of Amazon Algorithms' (*Balkan Insight*, 13 September 2021) https://balkaninsight.com/2021/09/13/in-central-europe-concern-over-toll-fairness-of-amazon-algorithms/.

[40] SOC, 'Primed for Pain: Amazon's Epidemic of Workplace Injuries', https://thesoc.org/amazon-primed-for-pain/.

[41] S O'Connor, 'Why I was wrong to be optimistic about robots' *Financial Times* (9 April 2021) www.ft.com/content/087fce16-3924-4348-8390-235b435c53b2. See also S Soper, 'Amazon Delivery Partners Rage Against the Machines: "We Were Treated Like Robots"' (*Bloomberg*, 7 October 2021) www.bloomberg.com/news/features/2021-10-07/amazon-delivery-partners-claim-treated-like-robots-by-algorithms.

[42] W Evans, 'How Amazon hid its safety crisis' (*Real News*, 29 Sumpter 2020) https://revealnews.org/article/how-amazon-hid-its-safety-crisis/. The gruelling working conditions are not confined to warehouses, see D Politi, 'Amazon Admits Drivers Sometimes Have to Pee in Bottles While on the Job' (*Slate*, 4 April 2021) https://slate.com/news-and-politics/2021/04/amazon-admits-drivers-pee-bottles-pocan.html.

[43] C O'Neil and others, 'Burnout by design? Warehouse and shipping workers pay the hidden cost of the holiday season' (*The Conversation*, 29 November 2021) https://theconversation.com/burnout-by-design-warehouse-and-shipping-workers-pay-the-hidden-cost-of-the-holiday-season-172157.

[44] MC Carrozza, *The Robot and Us. An 'antidisciplinary' perspective on the scientific and social impacts of robotic* (Cham, Springer, 2019).

[45] V Maio, 'Il diritto del lavoro e le nuove sfide della rivoluzione robotica' (2018) 6 *Argomenti di Diritto del Lavoro* 1414–54. The author warns that machines will be 'at the top of the chain of command, in a position above the human controller of artificial intelligence'.

[46] The imperfect, quasi-human features of many of the new robots are also illustrated by a theorem, the so-called 'uncanny valley', according to which the sensation of pleasantness in contact with a robot rises to a maximum point, beyond which too perfect a resemblance generates a sense of repulsion and disgust.

[47] Recital n. 1, Civil Law Rules on Robotics, European Parliament resolution of 16 February 2017 with recommendations to the Commission on Civil Law Rules on Robotics (2015/2103(INL)) (2018/C 252/25).

[48] B Ng, 'Could Robots From Boston Dynamics Beat Me in a Fight?' (*The New York Time Magazine*, 8 September 2021) www.nytimes.com/2021/09/08/magazine/boston-dynamics-robots.html?smid=url-share.

[49] HR Ekbia, *Artificial dreams: The quest for non-biological intelligence* (Cambridge, Cambridge University Press, 2008).

[50] We discussed about which personal pronoun to use for Sophia. Sophia is not a person or an animal, it is a robot. We use 'it', reserved for things, rejecting any 'humanisation' of this android. To pretend that it could have a gender would be another concession to the dangerous rhetoric of its inventors.

[51] UNDP Asia and Pacific, 'UNDP in Asia and the Pacific appoints world's first non-human innovation champion' (2017).

[52] The company has also announced plans to begin mass-producing Sophia, to combat pandemic-related loneliness, while the newly launched robot doctor assistant Grace will enter (and revolutionise) the healthcare sector. M Hennessy, 'Makers of Sophia the robot plan mass rollout amid pandemic' (*Reuters*, 25 January 2021) www.reuters.com/article/us-hongkong-robot-idUSKBN29U03X.

[53] Civil Law Rules on Robotics, European Parliament resolution of 16 February 2017 with recommendations to the Commission on Civil Law Rules on Robotics (2015/2103(INL)) (2018/C 252/25).

[54] See generally J Turner, *Robot rules: regulating artificial intelligence* (Cham, Palgrave Macmillan, 2018); DJ Gunkel, *Robot Rights* (Cambridge, MIT Press, 2018).

[55] J Vincent, 'Pretending to give a robot citizenship helps no one' (*The Verge*, 30 October 2017) www.theverge.com/2017/10/30/16552006/robot-rights-citizenship-saudi-arabia-sophia. See also JJ Bryson, 'Patience is not a virtue: The design of intelligent systems and systems of ethics (2018) 20 *Ethics and Information Technology* 15–26.

[56] A group of independent experts consulted by the European Commission pointed out that 'there is currently no need to give a legal personality to emerging digital technologies. Harm caused by even fully autonomous technologies is generally reducible to risks attributable to natural persons or existing categories of legal persons, and where this is not the case, new laws directed at individuals are a better response than creating a new category of legal person. Any sort of legal personality for emerging digital technologies may raise a number of ethical issues …', Expert Group on 'Liability and New Technologies,

Liability for Artificial Intelligence and other emerging digital technologies' (Luxembourg, Publications Office of the European Union, 2019). Report from the Commission to the European Parliament, the Council and the European Economic and Social Committee Report on the safety and liability implications of Artificial Intelligence, the Internet of Things and robotics COM/2020/64 final ('The Union product safety legislation takes into account the complexity of the value chains, imposing obligations to several economic operators following the principle of 'shared responsibility').

[57] E Guendelsberger, *On The Clock: What Low-Wage Work Did to Me and How It Drives America Insane* (Boston, Little, Brown and Company, 2019).

[58] B Veneziani, 'Le nuove forme di lavoro' in R Blanpain and M Biagi (eds), *Diritto del lavoro e relazioni industriali nei Paesi industrializzati ad economia di mercato. Profili comparati, I. Diritto del lavoro* (Rimini, Maggioli, 1991) 107–39.

[59] ILO, *Teleworking During the COVID-19 Pandemic and Beyond: A Practical Guide* (Geneva, International Labour Office, 2020). See also C Warzel and AH Petersen, *Out of Office: The Big Problem and Bigger Promise of Working from Home* (New York, Knopf Publishing Group, 2021).

[60] According to Eurofound, in July 2020 34% of respondents were solely working from home. Just 3.2% of employees in the EU-27 usually worked from home – a share that had remained stable since 2008. Eurofound, *Employee Monitoring and Surveillance: The Challenges of Digitalization* (Luxembourg, Publications Office of the European Union, 2020). It is early to say whether the shift will be permanent, initial data suggests a gradual throwback. Eurofound, *Workers want to telework but long working hours, isolation and inadequate equipment must be tackled* (Luxembourg, Publications Office of the European Union, 2021).

[61] Article 2, ETUC, BusinessEurope, CEEP and UEAPME (2002), 'Framework agreement on telework' ('a form of organising and/or performing work, using information technology, in the context of an employment contract/relationship, where work, which could also be performed at the employers premises, is carried out away from those premises on a regular basis').

[62] J Crary, *24/7: Late capitalism and the ends of sleep* (London-New York, Verso, 2013).

[63] T Makimoto and D Manners, *Digital nomad* (Chichester, Wiley, 1997).

[64] G Mari, *Libertà nel lavoro. La sfida della rivoluzione digitale* (Bologna, Il Mulino, 2019). See also AJ Martin, JM Wellen and MR Grimmer, 'An eye on your work: How empowerment affects the relationship between electronic surveillance and counterproductive work behaviours' (2016) 27(21) *The International Journal of Human Resource Management* 2635–51.

[65] Eurofound and International Labour Office, 'Working anytime, anywhere: The effects on the world of work' (Luxembourg, Publications Office of the European Union and Geneva, International Labour Office, 2017).

[66] Several countries have witnessed an increase in the number of returnees reversing the brain drain. See, for instance, the project 'South Working' at southworking.org/ (the promoters intend to reduce the economic, social and territorial gap by enabling people and businesses to work from less developed provinces and small villages). See D Ghiglione and V Romei, 'Italian returnees seize on pandemic to stop Mezzogiorno brain drain' *Financial Times* (6 April 2021) www.ft.com/content/2c8f6ff9-ee12-4f0c-a7b2-fe2ac4469c11.

[67] T Alon, Titan, M Doepke, J Olmstead-Rumsey and M Tertilt, 'The impact of the coronavirus pandemic on gender equality' (2020) 4 *Covid Economics Vetted and Real-Time Papers* 62–85.

[68] ETUC, Business Europe, CEEP and UEAPME (2002), 'Framework agreement on telework'.

[69] E DeFilippis, SM Impink, M Singell, JT Polzer and R Sadun, 'Collaborating During Coronavirus: The Impact of COVID-19 on the Nature of Work'. No. w27612. *National Bureau of Economic Research* (2020).

[70] Eurofound and Cedefop, *European Company Survey 2019: Workplace practices unlocking employee potential* (Luxembourg, Publications Office of the European Union, 2020).

[71] This section also draws upon A Aloisi and V De Stefano, 'Essential jobs, remote work and digital surveillance. Addressing the Covid19 pandemic panopticon' (2022) 161(2) *International Labour Review*.

[72] *The Economist*, 'Covid-19 Has Forced a Radical Shift in Working Habits' (*The Economist*, 12 September 2020) www.economist.com/briefing/2020/09/12/covid-19-has-forced-a-radical-shift-in-working-habits.

[73] D Thompson, 'Hard Work Isn't the Point of the Office' (*The Atlantic*, 21 September 2021) www.theatlantic.com/ideas/archive/2021/09/offices-microsoft-study-out-group-connections/620137/.

[74] JM Jensen and JL Raver, 'When Self-Management and Surveillance Collide: Consequences for Employees' Organizational Citizenship and Counterproductive Work Behaviors' (2012) 37(3) *Group*

& Organization Management 336–38; PJ Holland, B Cooper and R Hecker, 'Electronic monitoring and surveillance in the workplace: The effects on trust in management, and the moderating role of occupational type' (2015) 44(1) *Personnel Review* 170–71.

[75] E Hafermalz, 'Out of the Panopticon and Into Exile: Visibility and Control in Distributed New Culture Organizations' (2020) 42(5) *Organization Studies* 697–717. GF Delfino and B Van Der Kolk, 'Remote Working, Management Control Changes and Employee Responses During the COVID-19 Crisis' (2021) 34(6) *Accounting Auditing & Accountability Journal* 1376–87.

[76] The expression 'panopticon' has been firstly adopted by Foucault who borrowed it from Bentham. It was originally used to identify a prison design, where a watch tower is located in the centre of spherical prison and the wall-less cells face inwards, resulting in a regime of permanent visibility and coerced discipline. See OH Gandy Jr, *The Panoptic Sort: A Political Economy of Personal Information* (Oxford, Oxford University Press, 2021).

[77] S Migliano, 'Employee Surveillance Software Demand up 51% Since Start of Pandemic' (*Top10VPN*, 18 November 2020) www.top10vpn.com/research/covid-employee-surveillance/.

[78] TUC, 'Technology Managing People – The Worker Experience' (TUC, 2020); R Allen QC and D Masters, 'Technology Managing People – The Legal Implications' (TUC, 2021).

[79] D Abril and D Harwell, 'Keystroke tracking, screenshots, and facial recognition: The boss may be watching long after the pandemic ends' (*The Washington Post*, 24 September 2021) www.washingtonpost.com/technology/2021/09/24/remote-work-from-home-surveillance/; D Harwell, 'Contract lawyers face a growing invasion of surveillance programs that monitor their work' (*The Washington Post*, 11 November 2021) www.washingtonpost.com/technology/2021/11/11/lawyer-facial-recognition-monitoring/.

[80] D Harwell, 'Managers turn to surveillance software, always-on webcams to ensure employees are (really) working from home' (*The Washington Post*, 30 April 2020) www.washingtonpost.com/technology/2020/04/30/work-from-home-surveillance/.

[81] See https://docs.microsoft.com/en-us/viva/insights/ and https://workspace.google.com/products/workinsights/.

[82] B Cyphers and K Gullo, 'Inside the Invasive, Secretive "Bossware" Tracking Workers' (*EFF*, 30 June 2020) www.eff.org/it/deeplinks/2020/06/inside-invasive-secretive-bossware-tracking-workers.

[83] A Nguyen, 'On the Clock and at Home: Post-COVID-19 Employee Monitoring in the Workplace' (*SHRM*, Summer 2020) www.shrm.org/executive/resources/people-strategy-journal/summer2020/Pages/feature-nguyen.aspx/.

[84] C Tucker, 'Privacy, Algorithms, and Artificial Intelligence' in A Agrawal, J Gans and A Goldfarb, *The Economics of Artificial Intelligence: An Agenda* (Chicago, University of Chicago Press, 2018).

[85] Eurofound, *Right to disconnect: Exploring company practices* (Luxembourg, Publications Office of the European Union, 2021).

[86] T Bateman, 'Portugal makes it illegal for your boss to text you after work in "game changer" remote work law' (*EuroNews*, 11 November 2021) www.euronews.com/next/2021/11/08/portugal-makes-it-illegal-for-your-boss-to-text-you-after-work. See also A Kersley, 'Portugal's Home Working Laws Are a Model for the Post-Pandemic World' (*Tribune*, 20 November 2021) https://tribunemag.co.uk/2021/11/portugal-remote-working-laws-bosses-right-to-disconnect-covid.

[87] Case C-266/14 *Federación de Servicios Privados del sindicato Comisiones obreras (CC.OO.) v Tyco Integrated Security SL and Tyco Integrated Fire & Security Corporation Servicios SA* [2016] 1 C.M.L.R. 22.

[88] S Jaffe, *Work Won't Love You Back: How Devotion to Our Jobs Keeps Us Exploited, Exhausted, and Alone* (New York, Bold Type Books, 2021). See also RA Ventura, *Teoria della classe disagiata* (Rome, minimum fax, 2017); S Lorusso, *Entreprecariat* (Brescia, Krisis Publishing, 2018).

[89] L Widdicombe, 'The WeWork Documentary Explores a Decade of Delusion' (*The New Yorker*, 5 April 2021) www.newyorker.com/culture/culture-desk/the-wework-documentary-explores-a-decade-of-delusion. See also M Isaac, *Super Pumped, The Battle for Uber* (New York, W. W. Norton, 2019).

[90] KL Miller, '"Micromanaged and disrespected": Top reasons workers are quitting their jobs in "The Great Resignation"' (*The Washington Post*, 7 October 2021) www.washingtonpost.com/business/2021/10/07/top-reasons-great-resignation-workers-quitting/ (identifying increased workloads and unrealistic manager expectations, along with health concerns, are the key drivers behind the mass resignation trend).

[91] S Lund, A Madgavkar, J Manyika, S Smit, K Ellingrud, M Meaney and O Robinson, *The future of work after COVID-19* (McKinsey Global Institute, 2021).

[92] I Ajunwa, 'The Algorithmic Capture of Employment and The Tertius Bifrons' (*LPE Project*, 10 May 2020) https://lpeproject.org/blog/the-algorithmic-capture-of-employment-and-the-tertius-bifrons/. See also S Zuboff, *The Age of Surveillance Capitalism: The Fight for a Human Future at the New Frontier of Power* (London, Profile Books, 2019). But see R Morozov, 'Capitalism's New Clothes' (*The Baffler*, 4 February 2019) https://thebaffler.com/latest/capitalisms-new-clothes-morozov. See also SE Merry, 'Controlling Numbers: How Quantification Shapes the World' in C Besteman and H Gusterson (eds), *Life by Algorithms* (Chicago, University of Chicago Press, 2019) 145–64.

[93] I Ajunwa. 'The "black box" at work' (2020) 2 *Big Data & Society* 7. See also P Kim, 'Manipulating Opportunity' (2020) 106 *Virginia Law Review* 867–935.

[94] AE Waldman, 'Power, Process, and Automated Decision-Making' (2019) 88(2) *Fordham Law Review* 613–32.

[95] A Aneesh, 'Global Labor: Algocratic Modes of Organization' (2009) 27(4) *Sociological Theory* 347–70; J Danaher, 'The threat of algocracy: Reality, resistance and accommodation' (2016) 29(3) *Philosophy & Technology* 245–68.

[96] AlgorithmWatch, 'People analytics in the workplace – how to effectively enforce labor rights', https://algorithmwatch.org/en/auto-hr/.

[97] M Bogen and A Rieke, 'Help wanted: An examination of hiring algorithms, equity, and bias' (2018).

[98] C O'Neil, *Weapons of math destruction: how big data increases inequality and threatens democracy* (New York, Crown, 2016). See also AE Waldman, *Industry Unbound: The Inside Story of Privacy, Data, and Corporate Power* (Cambridge, Cambridge University Press, 2021).

[99] I Ajunwa, 'Beware of Automated Hiring' *The New York Times* (8 October 2019) www.nytimes.com/2019/10/08/opinion/ai-hiring-discrimination.html, I Ajunwa, 'The paradox of automation as anti-bias intervention' (2019) 41(5) *Cardozo Law Review* 1671–1742. See also P Kim and S Scott, 'Discrimination in Online Employment Recruiting' (2018) 63(1) *St. Louis University Law Journal* 93–118.

[100] J Dastin, 'Amazon scraps secret AI recruiting tool that showed bias against women' (*Reuters*, 11 October 2018) www.reuters.com/article/us-amazon-com-jobs-automation-insight/amazon-scraps-secret-ai-recruiting-tool-that-showed-bias-against-women-idUSKCN1MK08G; M Oppenheim, 'Amazon scraps "sexist AI" recruitment tool' *Independent* (11 October 2018) www.independent.co.uk/life-style/gadgets-and-tech/amazon-ai-sexist-recruitment-tool-algorithm-a8579161.html.

[101] A Agrawal, J Gans and A Goldfarb, *Prediction Machines: The Simple Economics of Artificial Intelligence* (Brighton MA, Harvard Business Press, 2018); G Resta, 'Governare l'innovazione tecnologica: decisioni algoritmiche, diritti digitali e principio di uguaglianza' (Rome, Forum Disuguaglianze e Diversità, 2019).

[102] R Xenidis, 'Tuning EU equality law to algorithmic discrimination: Three pathways to resilience' (2020) 27(6) *Maastricht Journal of European and Comparative Law* 736–58.

[103] For a similar EU case based on gender, see Case C-236/09 *Association belge des Consommateurs Test-Achats ASBL and Others v Conseil des ministres* [2011] ECR I-00773.

[104] J Walker, 'Meet the New Boss: Big Data' (*The Wall Street Journal*, 20 September 2012) www.wsj.com/articles/SB10000872396390443890304578006252019616768.

[105] See generally R Benjamin, *Race After Technology: Abolitionist Tools for the New Jim Code* (Cambridge, Polity, 2019); S Skinner-Thompson, *Privacy at the Margins* (Cambridge, Cambridge University Press, 2020).

[106] SU Noble, *Algorithms of oppression* (New York, New York University Press, 2018). See also B Harcourt, *Against Prediction: Profiling, Policing and Punishing in the Actuarial Age* (Chicago, University of Chicago Press, 2006).

[107] V Eubanks, *Automating Inequality. How High-Tech Tools Profile, Police and Punish the Poor* (London, St. Martin's Press, 2018).

[108] A Murad, 'The computers rejecting your job application' (*BBC*, 8 February 2021) www.bbc.co.uk/news/business-55932977.

[109] J Fuller, M Raman, E Sage-Gavin and K Hines et al, *Hidden Workers: Untapped Talent* Harvard Business School Project on Managing the Future of Work and Accenture (September 2021); N Lewis and J Marc, 'Want to work for L'Oreal? Get ready to chat with an AI bot' (*CNN Business*, 29 April 2019) https://edition.cnn.com/2019/04/29/tech/ai-recruitment-loreal/index.html.

[110] See the MIT podcast about the automation of everything: https://forms.technologyreview.com/in-machines-we-trust/; B Waber, *People Analytics: How Social Sensing Technology Will Transform Business and What it Tells us About the Future of Work* (Upper Saddle River, FT Press, 2013).

[111] LF Barrett, R Adolphs, S Marsella, AM Martinez and SD Pollak, 'Emotional Expressions Reconsidered: Challenges to Inferring Emotion From Human Facial Movements' (2019) 20(1) *Psychological Science in the Public Interest* 1–68.

[112] D Harwell, 'A face-scanning algorithm increasingly decides whether you deserve the job' (*The Washington Post*, 6 November 2019) www.washingtonpost.com/technology/2019/10/22/ai-hiring-face-scanning-algorithm-increasingly-decides-whether-you-deserve-job/.

[113] L Zuloaga. 'Industry leadership: New audit results and decision on visual analysis' (*Hire Vue Blog*, 12 January 2021) www.hirevue.com/blog/hiring/industry-leadership-new-audit-results-and-decision-on-visual-analysis.

[114] M Murgia, 'Emotion recognition: can AI detect human feelings from a face?' *Financial Times* (12 May 2021) www.ft.com/content/c0b03d1d-f72f-48a8-b342-b4a926109452.

[115] L Graham, A Gilbert, J Simons and A Thomas, *Artificial intelligence in hiring, Assessing impacts on equality* (Institute for the Future of Work) www.ifow.org/publications/artificial-intelligence-in-hiring-assessing-impacts-on-equality.

[116] Independent EU Advisory Body on Data Protection and Privacy (Art. 29 Working Party, 'WP29'), Opinion 2/2017 on data protection at work, adopted in June 2017 and aimed at complementing the Opinion 08/2001 on the processing of personal data in the employment context. Independent EU Advisory Body on Data Protection and Privacy (Article 29 Working Party, 'WP29'), Working document on the surveillance of electronic communications in the workplace, U.N. Doc. 5401/01/EN/Final; Guidelines on Automated individual decision-making and Profiling for the purposes of Regulation 2016/679 (wp251rev.01).

[117] Regulation (EU) 2016/679 of the European Parliament and of the Council of 27 April 2016 on the protection of natural persons with regard to the processing of personal data and on the free movement of such data, and repealing Directive 95/46/EC (General Data Protection Regulation).

[118] Council of Europe, The protection of individuals with regard to automatic processing of personal data in the context of profiling Recommendation CM/Rec(2010)13 adopted by the Committee of Ministers of the Council of Europe on 23 November 2010 and explanatory memorandum.

[119] Article 4(4) defines 'profiling' – a relatively novel concept in European data protection law – as 'any form of automated processing of personal data consisting of the use of personal data to evaluate certain personal aspects relating to a natural person, in particular to analyse or predict aspects concerning that natural person's performance at work, economic situation, health, personal preferences, interests, reliability, behaviour, location or movements'. A concrete example of this practice would be e-recruiting (Recital 71). See M Hildebrandt, 'Defining Profiling: A New Type of Knowledge?' in M Hildebrandt and S Gutwirth (eds), *Profiling the European Citizen* (Cham, Springer, 2008).

[120] ME Kaminski and G Malgieri, 'Algorithmic Impact Assessments under the GDPR: Producing Multi-layered Explanations' (2021) 11(2) *International Data Privacy Law* 125–44.

[121] M Veale and L Edwards, 'Clarity, surprises, and further questions in the Article 29 Working Party draft guidance on automated decision-making and profiling' (2018) 34(2) *Computer Law & Security Review* 398–404.

[122] D Kamarinou, C Millard and J Singh, 'Machine Learning with Personal Data' in R Leenes et al (eds), *Data Protection and Privacy: The Age of Intelligent Machines* (Oxford, Hart Publishing, 2020) 89–114.

[123] AD Selbst and J Powles, 'Meaningful Information and the Right to Explanation' (2017) 7(4) *International Data Privacy Law* 233–42. Interestingly, the draft directive on platform work seems to respond to these uncertainties in a purposive and systematic way, by providing for the right to obtain an explanation 'for any decision taken or supported by an automated decision-making system that significantly affects the platform worker's working conditions' (Article 8).

[124] EDPB, Guidelines 05/2020 on consent under Regulation 2016/679.

[125] See also Article 9 of the revised Council of Europe's Convention for the Protection of Individuals with regard to Automatic Processing of Personal Data concerning the right not to be subject to automated decision-making without human intervention.

[126] A model of 'municipal sovereignty' is that of the Coalition of Cities for Digital Rights promoted by Amsterdam, Barcelona and New York City with the aim of protecting, promoting and monitoring the personal data of citizens and visitors by 'opening up' the shared management of information generated by public services. L Dencik, 'Towards Data Justice Unionism? A Labour Perspective on AI Governance' in P Verdegem (ed), *AI for Everyone? Critical Perspectives* (London, University of Westminster Press, 2021) 267–84.

[127] In June 2020, the European social partners signed a landmark framework agreement. While acknowledging the significant contribution in terms of security, health and safety and efficiency, the agreement stresses the risk of deterioration of working conditions and well-being of workers and calls for 'data minimisation and transparency along with clear rules on the processing of personal data limits

the risk of intrusive monitoring and misuse of personal data'. Interestingly, it advocates for worker representative's involvement to address issues related to consent, privacy protection and surveillance. Available at www.etuc.org/en/document/eu-social-partners-agreement-digitalisation.

[128] S Wachter, B Mittelstadt and C Russell, 'Counterfactual explanations without opening the black box: Automated decisions and the GDPR' (2018) 31(2) *Harvard Journal of Law & Technology* 841–87. See also S Wachter, Sandra, B Mittelstadt and L Floridi, 'Why a right to explanation of automated decision-making does not exist in the general data protection regulation' (2017) 7(2) *International Data Privacy Law* 76–99.

[129] G Buttarelli, *Privacy 2030*, available at https://iapp.org/media/pdf/resource_center/giovanni_manifesto.pdf.

[130] T Bucher, *If … then: Algorithmic power and politics* (Oxford, Oxford University Press, 2018).

[131] Judgment of 14 March 2017, Case C-188/15 *Asma Bougnaoui et Association de défense des droits de l'homme (ADDH) contre Micropole SA* [2018] ICR 139. See R Ducato, M Kullmann and M Rocca. 'European Legal Perspectives on Customer Ratings and Discrimination' in T Addabbo, E Ales, Y Curzi, T Fabbri, O Rymkevich and I Senatori (eds), *Performance Appraisal in Modern Employment Relations* (Palgrave Macmillan, Cham, 2020) 225–51.

[132] R Xenidis and L Senden, 'EU non-discrimination law in the era of artificial intelligence: Mapping the challenges of algorithmic discrimination' in U Bernitz et al (eds), *General Principles of EU law and the EU Digital Order* (Alphen aan den Rijn, Kluwer Law International, 2020) 151–82; L Grozdanovski, 'In search of effectiveness and fairness in proving algorithmic discrimination in EU law' (2021) 58(1) *Common Market Law Review* 99–136.

[133] Or much more disturbingly and seriously, S Curtis, 'Google Photos Labels Black People as "Gorillas"' *The Telegraph* (4 May 2017) www.telegraph.co.uk/technology/google/11710136/Google-Photos-assigns-gorilla-tag-to-photos-of-black-people.html. See generally M Broussard, *Artificial unintelligence: How computers misunderstand the world* (Cambridge, MIT Press, 2018).

[134] See generally L DeNardis, *The Internet in Everything* (New Haven, Yale University Press, 2020).

[135] M Hildebrandt, *Smart Technologies and the End(s) of Law: Novel Entanglements of Law and Technology* (Cheltenham, Edward Elgar, 2016); C Véliz, *Privacy is Power. Why and How You Should Take Back Control of Your Data* (London, Penguin Books, 2020); FN David, *Forces of production: A social history of industrial automation* (New York, Routledge, 2017).

[136] A Gorz, 'La personne devient une entreprise. Note sur le travail de production de soi', (2001) 18 *Revue du Mauss* 61–66.

[137] M Hirsch, 'Future Work' (2020) *University of Illinois Law Review* 889–958.

[138] M Palm, *Technologies of Consumer Labor: A History of Self-Service* (New York, Routledge, 2016). See also I Bogost, 'Hyperemployment, or the Exhausting Work of the Technology User' (*The Atlantic*, 8 November 2013) www.theatlantic.com/technology/archive/2013/11/hyperemployment-or-the-exhausting-work-of-the-technology-user/281149/.

[139] L Lurtis, 'Apple locked me out of its walled garden. It was a nightmare' (*Quartz*, 13 August 2019) https://qz.com/1683460/what-happens-to-your-itunes-account-when-apple-says-youve-committed-fraud/.

[140] I Manokha, 'The Implications of Digital Employee Monitoring and People Analytics for Power Relations in the Workplace' (2020) 18(4) *Surveillance & Society* 540–54.

[141] S Adler-Bell and M Miller, *The datafication of employment. How surveillance and capitalism are shaping workers' futures without their knowledge* (The Century Foundation, 2018).

[142] I Bogost, 'Welcome to the age of privacy nihilism' (*The Atlantic*, 23 August 2018) www.theatlantic.com/technology/archive/2018/08/the-age-of-privacy-nihilism-is-here/568198/. See also M Sacasas, 'Personal Panopticons' (*Real Life Mag*, 5 November 2018) https://reallifemag.com/personal-panopticons/.

[143] See also S Marassi and P Collins, 'Is That Lawful? Data Privacy and Fitness Trackers in the Workplace' (2021) 37(1) *International Journal of Comparative Labour Law and Industrial Relations* 65–94.

[144] S Brayne, *Predict and Surveil: Data, Discretion, and the Future of Policing* (Oxford, Oxford University Press, 2020).

[145] D Lyon, *The Culture of Surveillance: Watching as a Way of Life* (Hoboken, New Jersey, John Wiley & Sons, 2018).

[146] Trades Union Congress (TUC), 'Technology managing people, The worker experience' (2021).

[147] S Zuboff, 'You Are the Object of a Secret Extraction Operation' *The New York Times* (23 November 2021) www.nytimes.com/2021/11/12/opinion/facebook-privacy.html. See also C Gilliard and D Golumbia, 'Luxury Surveillance' (*Real Life Mag*, 6 July 2021) https://reallifemag.com/luxury-surveillance/.

[148] G Marx, *Windows Into the Soul: Surveillance and Society in an Age of High Technology* (Chicago, University of Chicago Press, 2016).

[149] A Robin Q.C. and D Masters, 'Technology Managing People – the legal implications' (*AI Law*, 11 February 2021); M Tomprou and M Kyung Lee, 'Employment relationships in algorithmic management: A psychological contract perspective' (2022) 126 *Computers in Human Behavior* 1–12.

[150] RA Bales and KVW Stone, 'The Invisible Web at Work: Artificial Intelligence and Electronic Surveillance in the Workplace' (2020) 41(1) *Berkeley Journal of Employment & Labor Law* 1–60.

[151] T May and AC Chien, 'Slouch or Slack Off, This "Smart" Office Chair Cushion Will Record It' *The New York Times* (12 January 2021) www.nytimes.com/2021/01/12/world/asia/china-office-cushion-surveillance.html; J Jerome, 'Embedded Chip on Your Shoulder? Some Privacy and Security Considerations' (*Iapp Privacy Perspectives*, 1 August 2017) https://iapp.org/news/a/embedded-chip-on-your-shoulder-some-privacy-and-security-considerations/.

[152] M Otto, *The Right to Privacy in Employment: A Comparative Analysis* (Oxford, Hart Publishing, 2016); A Aloisi and E Gramano, 'Artificial Intelligence is Watching You at Work. Digital Surveillance, Employee Monitoring and Regulatory Issues in the EU Context' (2019) 41(1) *Comparative Labor Law and Policy Journal* 95–121; S Simitis, 'Reconsidering the Premises of Labour Law: Prolegomena to an EU Regulation on the Protection of Employees' Personal Data' (1999) 5(1) *European Law Journal* 45–62.

[153] A Kelly-Lyth, 'Challenging Biased Hiring Algorithms' (2021) 41(4) *Oxford Journal of Legal Studies* 899–928.

[154] C Hinkle, 'The Modern Lie Detector: AI-Powered Affect Screening and the Employee Polygraph Protection Act (EPPA)' (2020) 109(5) *Georgetown Law Journal* 1201–62.

[155] V De Stefano, 'Neuro-surveillance and the right to be human at work' (*OnLabor*, 15 February 2020) https://onlabor.org/neuro-surveillance-and-the-right-to-be-humans-at-work/.

[156] H de Romree, B Fecheyr-Lippens and B Schaninger, 'People analytics reveals three things HR may be getting wrong' (2016) *McKinsey Quarterly*. See also N Newman, 'Reengineering Workplace Bargaining: How Big Data Drives Lower Wages and How Reframing Labor Law Can Restore Information Equality in the Workplace' (2017) 85 *University of Cincinnati Law Review* 693–760.

[157] FZ Borgesius and J Poort, 'Online price discrimination and EU data privacy law' (2017) 40(3) *Journal of Consumer Policy* 347–66.

[158] Graham, Gilbert, Simons and Thomas (n 115) at 9. See also A Jean, *De l'autre côté de la machine: voyage d'une scientifique au pays des algorithmes* (Éditions de l'Observatoire, 2019).

[159] FS Lane, *The Naked Employee: How Technology is Compromising Workplace Privacy* (AMACOM Div American Mgmt Assn., 2003). Or 'transparent' in the sense of being looked through by managers, see M Hildebrandt, *Smart Technologies and the End(s) of Law: Novel Entanglements of Law and Technology* (Cheltenham, Edward Elgar Publishing, 2015).

[160] D Harwell, 'Contract lawyers face a growing invasion of surveillance programs that monitor their work' (*The Washington Post*, 11 November 2021) www.washingtonpost.com/technology/2021/11/11/lawyer-facial-recognition-monitoring/; R Boot, 'UK businesses using artificial intelligence to monitor staff activity' *The Guardian* (7 April 2019) www.theguardian.com/technology/2019/apr/07/uk-businesses-using-artifical-intelligence-to-monitor-staff-activity.

[161] This section also draws upon A Aloisi, 'Automation, autonomy, augmentation: labour regulation and the technological transformation of managerial prerogatives' in T Gyulávári and E Menegatti (eds), *Decent work in the digital age: European and Comparative Perspectives* (Oxford, Hart Publishing, 2022).

[162] KC Kellogg, MA Valentine and A Christin, 'Algorithms at Work: The New Contested Terrain of Control' (2020) 14(1) *Academy of Management Annals* 366–410. See also K Levy and S Barocas, 'Refractive Surveillance: Monitoring Customers to Manage Workers' (2018) 12 *International Journal of Communication* 1166–88.

[163] A Gilbert and A Thomas, 'The Amazonian Era: How Algorithmic Systems are Eroding Good Work' (IFOW, 13 May 2021).

[164] J Meijerink, M Boons, A Keegan and J Marler, 'Algorithmic Human Resource Management: Synthesizing Developments and Cross-Disciplinary Insights on Digital HRM' (2021) 32(12) *The International Journal of Human Resource Management* 2545–62.

[165] PT Kim, 'Manipulating opportunity' (2020) 106(1) *Virginia Law Review* 867–935.

[166] Aneesh (n 95) 347.

[167] MK Lee, D Kusbit, E Metsky and L Dabbish, 'Working with Machines: The Impact of Algorithmic and Data-Driven Management on Human Workers' (2015) *Proceedings of the 33rd Annual ACM Conference on Human Factors in Computing Systems* 1603–12; P Fleming, 'Robots and organization studies: Why robots might not want to steal your job' (2019) 40(1) *Organization Studies* 23–38.

[168] F Pasquale, *The Black Box Society: The Secret Algorithms That Control Money and Information* (Cambridge MA-London, Harvard University Press, 2015); BD Mittelstad et al, 'The ethics of algorithms: Mapping the debate' (2016) 3(1) *Big Data & Society* 1–12 (arguing that parameters are 'configured by users with desired outcomes in mind that privilege some values and interests over others').

[169] T Prasanna, P Cappelli and V Yakubovich, 'Artificial intelligence in human resources management: Challenges and a path forward' (2019) 61(4) *California Management Review* 17.

[170] T Elmer, K Chaitanya, P Purwar and C Stadtfeld, 'The validity of RFID badges measuring face-to-face interactions' (2019) 51(5) *Behavior Research Methods* 2120–38.

[171] https://humanyze.com/privacy-policy.

[172] Week Staff, 'The rise of workplace spying' (*The Week*, 5 July 2015) https://theweek.com/articles/564263/rise-workplace-spying.

[173] V Doellgast and S O'Brady, 'Making Call Center Jobs Better: The Relationship between Management Practices and Worker Stress', ILR School, Cornell University and DeGroote School of Business, McMaster University (2020).

[174] P Mosendz and A Melin, 'Bosses panic-buy spy software to keep tabs on remote workers. Phones are ringing off the hook at companies providing a bit of big brother' (*Bloomberg*, 27 March 2020) www.bloomberg.com/news/features/2020-03-27/bosses-panic-buy-spy-software-to-keep-tabs-on-remote-workers. S Morrison, 'Just because you're working from home doesn't mean your boss isn't watching you' (*Vox Recode*, 2 April 2020) www.vox.com/recode/2020/4/2/21195584/coronavirus-remote-work-from-home-employee-monitoring.

[175] C Lecher, 'How Amazon automatically tracks and fires warehouse workers for "productivity"' (*The Verge*, 25 April 2019) www.theverge.com/2019/4/25/18516004/amazon-warehouse-fulfillment-centers-productivity-firing-terminations.

[176] J Peters, 'Whole Foods is reportedly using a heat map to track stores at risk of unionization' (*The Verge*, 20 April 2020) www.theverge.com/2020/4/20/21228324/amazon-whole-foods-unionization-heat-map-union. See also J Logan, 'The Union Avoidance Industry in the United States' (2006) 44(4) *British Journal of Industrial Relations* 651–76.

[177] L Fang, 'Facebook pitched new tool allowing employers to suppress words like "Unionize" in workplace chat product' (*The Intercept*, 12 June 2020) https://theintercept.com/2020/06/11/facebook-workplace-unionize/; H Peterson, 'Amazon-owned Whole Foods is quietly tracking its employees with a heat map tool that ranks which stores are most at risk of unionizing' (*Business Insider*, 20 April 2020) www.businessinsider.com/whole-foods-tracks-unionization-risk-with-heat-map-2020-1?IR=T.

[178] C O'Donovan, 'An invisible rating system at your favorite chain restaurant is costing your server' (*BuzzFeed*, 21 June 2018) www.buzzfeednews.com/article/carolineodonovan/ziosk-presto-tabletop-tablet-restaurant-rating-servers#.nuLMmQWgL.

[179] See references in RE Kidwell and R Sprague 'Electronic Surveillance in the Global Workplace: Laws, Ethics, Research and Practice' (2009) 24(2) *New Technology, Work and Employment* 194–208; M Finkin, 'Chapter 7: Privacy and Autonomy' (2017) 21(2) *Employee Rights and Employment Policy Journal* 589–621; BI Sachs, 'Privacy as Sphere Autonomy' (2014) 88 *Bulletin of Comparative Industrial Relations* (Alphen aan den Rijn, Kluwer Law International, 2019).

[180] PV Moore, *The Quantified Self in Precarity: Work, Technology and What Counts* (New York, Routledge, 2017). G Lindsay, 'HR Meets Data: How Your Boss Will Monitor You To Create The Quantified Workplace' (*Fast Company*, 21 September 2015) www.fastcompany.com/3051275/hr-meets-data-how-your-boss-will-monitor-you-to-create-the-quantified-workplace.

[181] A Rosenblat, K Levy, S Barocas and T Tim Hwang, 'Discriminating Tastes: Customer Ratings as Vehicles for Bias' (*Data & Society*, October 2016). See generally E Albin, 'Customer Domination at Work: A New Paradigm for the Sexual Harassment of Employees by Customers' (2018) 24(2) *Michigan Journal of Gender and Law* 167–220.

[182] DK Citron and F Pasquale, 'The scored society' (2014) 89(1) *Washington Law Review* 1–33.

[183] JZ Muller, *The Tyranny of Metrics* (Princeton, Princeton University Press 2018). See also S Barocas and AD Selbst, 'Big Data's Disparate Impact' (2016) 104 *California Law Review* 671–732.

[184] I Manokha, 'Facial analysis AI is being used in job interviews – it will probably reinforce inequality' (*The Conversation*, 7 October 2019) https://theconversation.com/facial-analysis-ai-is-being-used-in-job-interviews-it-will-probably-reinforce-inequality-124790.

[185] B Rogers, 'The Law and Political Economy of Workplace Technological Change' (2020) 55 *Harvard Civil Rights-Civil Liberties Law Review* 531–84.

[186] Human actions can be 'supported with augmenting technologies that are related to perceiving, affecting, or cognitively processing the world and information around the user'. See R Raisamo, I Rakkolainen, P Majaranta, K Salminen, J Rantala and A Farooq, 'Human Augmentation: Past, Present and Future' (2019) 131 *International Journal of Human-Computer Studies* 131–43. The formula 'augmentation' was originally adopted in the tech design field and then imported to 'describe mediated communication processes which incorporate both the affordances of digital tech and the established feature of face-to-face interaction'.

[187] S Kessler, 'Robots are replacing managers, too' (*Quartz*, 31 July 2017) https://qz.com/1039981/robots-are-replacing-managers-too/.

[188] M Swan, 'The quantified self: Fundamental disruption in big data science and biological discovery' (2013) 1(2) *Big Data* 85–99. L Edwards and M Veale, 'Slave to the algorithm: Why a right to an explanation is probably not the remedy you are looking for' (2017) 16 *Duke Law & Technology Review* 18–84.

[189] G Neff and D Nafus, *Self-tracking* (Cambridge, MIT Press, 2016).

[190] EL Bucher, PK Schou and M Waldkirch, 'Pacifying the algorithm – Anticipatory compliance in the face of algorithmic management in the gig economy' (2021) 28(1) *Organization* 44–67.

[191] K Ball, 'Workplace Surveillance: An Overview' (2010) 51(1) *Labor History* 87–106; I Ajunwa, K Crawfor and J Schultz, 'Limitless worker surveillance' (2017) 105 *California Law Review* 735–76. See also O Solon, 'Big Brother isn't just watching: Workplace surveillance can track your every move' *The Guardian* (6 November 2017) www.theguardian.com/world/2017/nov/06/workplace-surveillance-big-brother-technology.

[192] MT Bodie, MA Cherry, ML McCormick and J Tang, 'The law and policy of people analytics' (2016) 88 *University of Colorado Law Review* 2–79. See generally AJ Wood, 'Algorithmic management consequences for work organisation and working conditions' (JRC Working Papers Series on Labour, Education and Technology, WP No. 7, 2021).

[193] D Stark and I Pais, 'Algorithmic management in the platform economy' (2020) 14(3) *Sociologica* 47–72. See also MH Jarrahi, G Newlands, M Kyung Lee, CT Wolf, E Kinder and W Sutherland, 'Algorithmic management in a work context' (2021) 28(2) *Big Data & Society* 8.

[194] According to the Encyclopaedia Britannica, 'a person or thing that appears or is introduced into a situation suddenly and unexpectedly and provides an artificial or contrived solution to an apparently insoluble difficulty. The term was first used in ancient Greek and Roman drama, where it meant the timely appearance of a god to unravel and resolve the plot. The *deus ex machina* was named for the convention of the god's appearing in the sky, an effect achieved by means of a crane (Greek: *mēchanē*)'. See https://bossexmachina.ie.edu/.

[195] S Deakin and F Wilkinson, *The Law of the Labour Market: Industrialization, Employment and Legal Evolution* (Oxford, Oxford University Press 2005).

[196] A Nguyen, 'The Constant Boss: Work Under Digital Surveillance' (*APO*, 19 May 2021) https://apo.org.au/node/312352.

[197] L Tebano, *Lavoro, potere direttivo e trasformazioni organizzative* (Napoli, Editoriale Scientifica, 2020). M Persiani, *Contratto di lavoro e organizzazione* (Milan, Giuffrè, 1966).

[198] M Ivanova, J Bronowicka, E Kocher, A Degner, 'The app as a boss? Control and autonomy in application-based management' (2018) Europa-Universität Viadrina Frankfurt ArbeitGrenze-Fluss 2.

[199] www.crossover.com/people-at-crossover/worksmart.

[200] K Roose, 'A machine may not take your job, but one could become your boss' *The New York Times* (2019) www.nytimes.com/2019/06/23/technology/artificial-intelligence-ai-workplace.html?smid=nytcore-ios-share.

[201] V Gabrielle, 'The dark side of gamifying work' (*FastCompany*, 11 January 2018) www.fastcompany.com/90260703/the-dark-side-of-gamifying-work. See also S Lopez, 'Disneyland workers answer to "electronic whip"' *Los Angeles Times* (19 October 2011) www.latimes.com/health/la-xpm-2011-oct-19-la-me-1019-lopez-disney-20111018-story.html.

[202] J Dzieza, 'How Hard Will The Robots Make Us Work?' (*The Verge*, 27 February 2020) www.theverge.com/2020/2/27/21155254/automation-robots-unemployment-jobs-vs-human-google-amazon.

[203] A Mateescu and A Nguyen, 'Algorithmic management in the workplace, Data & Society' (2019).

[204] J Feliciano Reyes, 'Hotel housekeeping on demand: Marriott cleaners say this app makes their job harder' *The Philadelphia Enquirer* (2 July 2018) www.inquirer.com/philly/news/hotel-housekeepers-schedules-app-marriott-union-hotsos-20180702.html.

[205] B Green and A Kak, 'The False Comfort of Human Oversight as an Antidote to A.I. Harm' (*Slate*, 15 June 2021) https://slate.com/technology/2021/06/human-oversight-artificial-intelligence-laws.html.

[206] See generally E Press, *Dirty Work. Essential Jobs and the Hidden Toll of Inequality in America* (New York, Farrar, Straus and Giroux, 2021).

[207] E Morozov, *To Save Everything, Click Here: Technology, Solutionism, and the Urge to Fix Problems That Don't Exist* (London, Penguin, 2014).

[208] MT Bodie and M McMahon, 'Employee Testing, Tracing, and Disclosure as a Response to the Coronavirus Pandemic' (2020) 64 *Washington University Journal of Law & Policy*.

[209] Crucially, almost all tools also permit private contact tracing. A Ponce Del Castillo, 'Covid-19 Contact-Tracing Apps: How to Prevent Privacy from Becoming the Next Victim' (2020) 5 *ETUI Policy Brief* 1–5; A Zarra, S Favalli and M Ceron, 'Algorithms and prejudice? Covid-19, contact tracing and digital surveillance in the EU' (2021) 56 *Biblioteca delle Libertà* 1–32. See also A Nguyen, 'Watching the Watchers: The New Privacy and Surveillance Under COVID-19' (2020) *Surveillance & Privacy*.

[210] Pew Research Center, 'Artificial intelligence and the future of humans' (2018); T Fountaine, B McCarthy and T Saleh, 'Building the AI-Powered organization' (2019) *Harvard Business Review* 63–73.

[211] Moore and Woodcock (n 22).

[212] P Tambe, P Cappelli and V Yakubovich. 'Artificial intelligence in human resources management: Challenges and a path forward' (2019) 61(4) *California Management Review* 15–42.

[213] J Adams-Prassl, 'What if your boss was an algorithm? Economic Incentives, Legal Challenges, and the Rise of Artificial Intelligence at Work' (2019) 41(1) *Comparative Labor Law and Policy Journal* 123–46.

[214] E Caroli and M Godard, 'Does Job Insecurity Deteriorate Health?' (2016) 25 *Health Economics* 131. M Roosevelt, '"The algorithm fired me": California bill takes on Amazon's notorious work culture' *Los Angeles Times* (31 August 2021) www.latimes.com/business/story/2021-08-31/la-fi-amazon-warehouse-injuries-ab701-bill-calosha.

[215] P Sawers, 'Uber Drivers Union Asks EU Court to Overrule "Robo-Firing" by Algorithm' (*VentureBeat*, 26 October 2020) https://venturebeat.com/2020/10/26/uber-drivers-union-asks-eu-court-to-overrule-robo-firing-by-algorithm/. N Lomas, 'Dutch Court Rejects Uber Drivers "Robo-Firing" Charge But Tells Ola to Explain Algo-Deductions' (*TechCrunch*, 21 March 2021) https://techcrunch.com/2021/03/12/dutch-court-rejects-uber-drivers-robo-firing-charge-but-tells-ola-to-explain-algo-deductions/; N Lomas, 'Uber hit with default "robo-firing" ruling after another EU labor rights GDPR challenge' (*TechCrunch*, 14 April 2021) https://techcrunch.com/2021/04/14/uber-hit-with-default-robo-firing-ruling-after-another-eu-labor-rights-gdpr-challenge/. For a detailed analysis, see R English, 'The Providers of "Ride Hailing Apps" and their Drivers: Another Judgment from Amsterdam' (*UK Human Rights Blog*, 19 March 2021) https://ukhumanrightsblog.com/2021/03/19/the-providers-of-ride-hailing-apps-and-their-drivers-another-judgment-from-amsterdam/.

[216] A Ekker, 'Dutch court rules on data transparency for Uber and Ola drivers' (*Ekker.legal*) https://ekker.legal/en/2021/03/13/dutch-court-rules-on-data-transparency-for-uber-and-ola-drivers/; A Ekker, 'The contribution of the GDPR to protect platform workers' rights', presentation at the ETUI workshop 'Labour rights & the digital transition' (Brussels, 28–29 October 2021). See also R Gellert, M Van Bekkum and F Zuiderveen Borgesius, 'The Ola & Uber judgments: for the first time a court recognises a GDPR right to an explanation for algorithmic decision-making' (*EU Law Analysis*, 28 April 2021, http://eulawanalysis.blogspot.com/2021/04/the-ola-uber-judgments-for-first-time.html.

[217] Article 1, Proposal for a Directive of the European Parliament and of the Council on improving working conditions in platform work COM(2021) 762 final 2021/0414 (COD).

[218] Article 6(2), Proposal for a Directive of the European Parliament and of the Council on improving working conditions in platform work COM(2021) 762 final 2021/0414 (COD).

[219] K Yeung, 'Why Worry about Decision-Making by Machine?' in K Yeung and M Lodge (eds), *Algorithmic Regulation* (Oxford, Oxford University Press, 2019) 21.

[220] ibid.

[221] FA Pasquale, 'The Resilient Fragility of Law' in Deakin S and C Markou, *Is Law Computable? Critical Perspectives on Law and Artificial Intelligence* (Oxford, Hart Publishing, 2021).

[222] P Collins, 'Automated Dismissal Decisions, Data Protection and The Law of Unfair Dismissal' (*UK Labour Law Blog*, 19 October 2021) https://uklabourlawblog.com/2021/10/19/automated-dismissal-decisions-data-protection-and-the-law-of-unfair-dismissal-by-philippa-collins/.

[223] P Collins and J Atkinson, 'Labour Rights, Labour Values and Technology at Work' (manuscript presented at the LLRN5 conference, June 2021).

[224] RE Kidwell and R Sprague, 'Electronic Surveillance in the Global Workplace: Laws, Ethics, Research and Practice' (2009) 24(2) *New Technology, Work and Employment* 194–208. See also V Dignum, 'The Myth of Complete AI-Fairness' in *International Conference on Artificial Intelligence in Medicine* (Cham, Springer, 2021) 3–8.

[225] ME Kaminski, 'The Right to Explanation, Explained' (2019) 34 *Berkeley Tech. L.J.* 189–218. Presenting facts from which it can be implied a lack of compliance with equal treatment rules has occurred or is likely to occur would be enough to trigger evidentiary simplifications for the benefit of the victim. See also G Gaudio, 'Algorithmic Bosses Can't Lie! How to Foster Transparency and Limit Abuses of the New Algorithmic Managers' (forthcoming) *Comparative Labor Law & Policy Journal*.

[226] G Beninger, '"MissionRacer": How Amazon is addressing the tedium of warehouse work' *The Washington Post* (21 March 2019) www.washingtonpost.com/technology/2019/05/21/missionracer-how-amazon-turned-tedium-warehouse-work-into-game/?noredirect=on.

[227] K Yeung, '"Hypernudge": Big Data as a Mode of Regulation by Design' (2017) 20(1) *Information, Communication & Society* 122.

[228] B Callaci, 'Puppet Entrepreneurship: Technology and Control in Franchised Industries' (2021) *Data & Society*. See also J-H Hoepman, *Privacy Is Hard and Seven Other Myths: Achieving Privacy Through Careful Design* (Cambridge, MIT Press, 2021) on how to use technology to protect our privacy, when we apply 'privacy by design' rules.

[229] Yeung (n 227) 120. See also RH Thaler and CR Sunstein, *Nudge: Improving Decisions about Health, Wealth, and Happiness* (New Haven, Yale University Press, 2008).

[230] H Schildt, *The Data Imperative: How Digitalization is Reshaping Management, Organizing, and Work* (Oxford, Oxford University Press, 2020).

[231] A Delfanti, *The Warehouse. Workers and Robots at Amazon* (London, Pluto Press, 2021).

[232] L Manganelli, A Thibault-Landry, J Forest and J Carpentier, 'Self-Determination Theory Can Help You Generate Performance and Well-Being in the Workplace: A Review of the Literature' (2018) 20(2) *Advances in Developing Human Resources* 227–40; C Rosengren and M Ottosson, 'Employee monitoring in a digital context' (2016) *Digital Sociologies* 181–94; ON Godart, H Görg and A Hanley, 'Trust-based work time and innovation: Evidence from firm-level data' (2017) 70(4) *ILR Review* 894–918; A Weibel, DN Den Hartog, N Gillespie, R Searle, F Six and D Skinner, 'How do controls impact employee trust in the employer?' (2016) 55(3) *Human Resource Management* 437–62.

[233] SC Rigby and RM Ryan, 'Self-Determination Theory in Human Resource Development: New Directions and Practical Considerations' (2018) 20(2) *Advances in Developing Human Resources* 133–47; S Viete and D Erdsiek, 'Mobile Information Technologies and Firm Performance: The Role of Employee Autonomy' (2020) 51 *Information Economics and Policy* 1–17.

[234] A Delfanti, 'Machinic dispossession and augmented despotism: Digital work in an Amazon warehouse' (2021) 23(1) *New Media & Society* 39–55.

[235] AI HLEG, *A Definition of AI: Main Capabilities and Scientific Disciplines* (Brussels, High-Level Expert Group on Artificial Intelligence, European Commission, 2019). In 2018 the European Commission presented a strategy aimed at stimulating investment (public and private) of 20 billion euros per year for the next 10 years. See also AI HLEG, *Ethics guidelines for trustworthy AI. High-level expert group on artificial intelligence* (Brussels, High-Level Expert Group on Artificial Intelligence, European Commission, 2019).

[236] See also J Kaplan, *Artificial Intelligence: What Everyone Needs to Know* (Oxford, Oxford University Press, 2016).

[237] MA Boden, *Artificial intelligence: A Very Short Introduction* (Oxford, Oxford University Press, 2018); G Marcus and E Davis, *Rebooting AI: Building Artificial Intelligence We Can Trust* (New York, Penguin Random House, 2019). For a comprehensive overview, see P McCorduck, *Machines Who Think, A Personal Inquiry into the History and Prospects of Artificial Intelligence*, 2nd edn (Natick, MA, A K Peters/CRC Press, 2004).

[238] The term was coined at Dartmouth College, New Hampshire, in 1956. See J Mccarthy, M Minsky, N Rochester and CE Shannon, *A Proposal for the Dartmouth Summer Research Project on Artificial Intelligence* (1955).

[239] Daron Acemoglu, 'Harms of AI', NBER Working Paper Series 29247. See also White Paper on Artificial Intelligence – A European approach to excellence and trust, COM(2020) 65 final.

[240] H Nowotny, *In AI We Trust: Power, Illusion and Control of Predictive Algorithms* (Hoboken, New Jersey, John Wiley & Sons, 2021).

[241] N Smuha, 'Beyond the individual: governing AI's societal harm' (2021) 10(3) *Internet Policy Review*.

[242] G Mueller, *Breaking Things at Work: The Luddites Are Right About Why You Hate Your Job* (London, Verso Books, 2021).

[243] J Prassl, *Humans as a Service: The Promise and Perils of Work in the Gig Economy* (Oxford, Oxford University Press, 2018); AA Casilli, *En attendant les robots. Enquête sur le travail du clic* (Paris, Seuil, 2019).

[244] D Teresi, 'Turkish Gambit' *The New York Times* (2 June 2002) www.nytimes.com/2002/06/02/books/turkish-gambit.html.

[245] J Zittrain, 'Ubiquitous human computing' (2008) 366(1881) *Philosophical Transactions of the Royal Society A: Mathematical, Physical and Engineering Sciences* 3813–21.

[246] C Thompson, *Coders: The Making of a New Tribe and the Remaking of the World* (London, Penguin Books, 2020). See also P Olson, 'Much "Artificial Intelligence" Is Still People Behind a Screen' (*Bloomberg*, 13 October 2021) www.bloomberg.com/opinion/articles/2021-10-13/how-good-is-ai-much-artificial-intelligence-is-still-people-behind-a-screen (explaining that 'the practice of hiding human input in AI systems still remains an open secret among those who work in machine learning and AI').

[247] L Gitelman (ed), *Raw Data is an Oxymoron* (Cambridge, MIT Press, 2013).

[248] K Roose, *Futureproof: 9 Rules for Humans in the Age of Automation* (London, Hachette UK, 2021).

[249] H Ekbia and B Nardi, 'Heteromation and its (dis) contents: The invisible division of labor between humans and machines' (2014) 19(6) *First Monday*; D Mindell, *Our Robots, Ourselves: Robotics and the myths of autonomy* (New York, Penguin, 2015).

[250] P Tubaro, AA Casilli and M Coville, 'The Trainer, the Verifier, the Imitator: Three Ways in Which Human Platform Workers Support Artificial Intelligence' (2020) 7(1) *Big Data and Society* 1–12.

[251] Casilli (n 243).

[252] A Taylor, 'The Automation Charade' (*Logic*, 1 August 2018) https://logicmag.io/failure/the-automation-charade/.

[253] D Remus and F Levy, 'Can Robots Be Lawyers? Computers, Lawyers, and the Practice of Law' (2017) 30(3) *Georgetown Journal of Legal Ethics* 501–58.

[254] JG Harris and TH Davenport, 'Automated Decision Making Comes of Age' (2005) 4 *MIT Sloan Management Review* 46. See also P Domingos, *The Master Algorithm: How the Quest for the Ultimate Learning Machine Will Remake Our World* (New York, Basic Books, 2015).

[255] A Gilbert and A Thomas, 'The Amazonian Era: How Algorithmic Systems are Eroding Good Work' (*IFOW*, 13 May 2021).

[256] A Smith, *The Wealth of Nations* (London, W. Strahan and T. Cadell, 1776).

[257] M Crowley, D Tope, LJ Chamberlain and R Hodson, 'Neo-Taylorism at Work: Occupational Change in the Post-Fordist Era' (2010) 57(3) *Social Problems* 421–47.

[258] J Smids, S Nyholm and H Berkers, 'Robots in the Workplace: A Threat to – or Opportunity for – Meaningful Work?' (2020) 33(3) *Philosophy & Technology* 503–22.

[259] L Irani, 'Justice for "data janitors"' (*Public Books*, 15 January 2015) www.publicbooks.org/justice-for-data-janitors/.

[260] MC Elish and danah boyd, 'Situating methods in the magic of Big Data and AI' (2018) 85(1) *Communication Monographs* 57–80.

[261] J Sadowski, 'Potemkin AI' (*Real Life Mag*, 6 August 2018) https://reallifemag.com/potemkin-ai/.

[262] D Etherington, 'Ford disguised a man as a car seat to research self-driving' (*TechCrunch*, 13 September 2017) https://techcrunch.com/2017/09/13/ford-disguised-a-man-as-a-car-seat-to-research-autonomous-driving/.

[263] D MacMillan, 'Tech's "dirty secret": The app developers sifting through your Gmail' (*The Wall Street Journal*, 2 July 2018) www.wsj.com/articles/techs-dirty-secret-the-app-developers-sifting-through-your-gmail-1530544442.

[264] D Goodin, 'Alexa and Google Home abused to eavesdrop and phish passwords' (*ArsTechnica*, 21 October 2019) https://arstechnica.com/information-technology/2019/10/alexa-and-google-home-abused-to-eavesdrop-and-phish-passwords/.

[265] K Wagner, 'Facebook's virtual assistant "M" is super smart. It's also probably a human' (*ReCode*, 3 November 2015) www.vox.com/2015/11/3/11620286/facebooks-virtual-assistant-m-is-super-smart-its-also-probably-a-human.

[266] C Kang and S Frenkel, *An Ugly Truth: Inside Facebook's Battle for Domination* (London, HarperCollins, 2021).

[267] P Guest and Y Zhou, 'The gig workers index: Mixed emotions, dim prospects' (*Rest of World*, 21 September 2021) https://restofworld.org/2021/global-gig-workers-index-mixed-emotions-dim-prospects/.

[268] J Burrell and M Fourcade 'The Society of Algorithms' (2021) *Annual Review of Sociology* 47; see also M Graham et al, *The Risks and Rewards of Online Gig Work At The Global Margins* (Oxford, Oxford Internet Institute, 2017).

[269] P Jones, *Work Without the Worker: Labour in the Age of Platform Capitalism* (London, Verso Books, 2021); A Chan, CT Okolo, Z Terner and A Wang 'The Limits of Global Inclusion in AI Development' (2021).

[270] A Mateescu and MC Elish, 'AI in context, the labor of integrating new technologies' (2019) *Data & Society*. See also M Altenried, *The Digital Factory: The Human Labor of Automation* (Chicago, University of Chicago Press, 2022); M Iansiti and KR Lakhani, *Competing in the Age of AI: Strategy and Leadership When Algorithms and Networks Run the World* (Brighton MA, Harvard Business Press, 2020); P Briône, *Mind over machines: New technology and employment relations* (London, ACAS, 2017).

3

Social Rights in the Digital Age

I. What We Talk About When We Talk About 'Platform Work' (And Why Do We Talk About it So Much?)

At first glance, both algorithmic bosses and the advent of 'pseudo artificial intelligence' may seem to be isolated cases.[1] However, if we look at a part of the labour market where these technology-enabled practices are already working overtime, we should examine platform work,[2] an employment form which has galvanised public interest and inspired heated debates.

The frenzied attention so far devoted to the gig-economy and its social implications is justified by the fact that workers mediated and managed by digital labour platforms experience at first hand the most clear contradictions of this fast-growing sector. The most extreme inventions tested in this arena are indicators of a much broader change sweeping across our economies. Importantly, the platforms' business model should be seen as an ongoing experiment. The many critical aspects of this form of employment such as automated profiling, algorithmic management, opaque evaluation, piecework micropayments or bogus self-employment can easily be applied to other contexts, defining a dominant organisational paradigm.[3] This is already happening in regard to PedidosYa's riders, Uber drivers, Fiverr freelancers, GoPillar architects, software developers on Upwork, Helpling domestic workers and TaskRabbit hodmen, who are the linchpins of a new task-based corporate organisation, made up of micro-chores and mini-rewards.[4] The most recurrent model is based on the fragmentation of jobs into small, sporadic assignments, which can be distributed to legions of arms-length workers who are constantly available, often in excessive numbers and always temporary. At the other end of the scale, high levels of authority are coupled with light employer responsibilities through a variety of legal stratagems.

In its original design, the system does not feature any workers' entitlements, such as overtime, sickness payments, paid leave, compensation for wrongful termination, severance payments and statutory (or collectively negotiated) minimum wages. Workers also face legal and practical obstacles in exercising fundamental rights, such as freedom of association, collective bargaining or protection against discrimination. On top of their ambiguous employment status, workers have to deal with lack of transparency in their responsibilities regarding tax and social security.[5]

The neverending discussion on this matter has given rise to kneejerk reactions, which overlook the deep differences existing between the sub-segments of the platform workforce and minimise the extent of this paradigm shift. This super-ficiality can be traced back to the tendency to pre-emptively adhere to long-held beliefs, be they an *a priori* opposition to technology, a blind faith in innovation, whataboutism, and business-friendly paternalism, always keen on turning a blind eye when a handful of powerful companies exert enough pressure.[6]

The strength of this phenomenon undoubtedly lies in its form: diverse and variable, while at the same time paradigmatic. Reflecting on the side effects of this type of work allows us to describe the negative effects of tech on labour, inspiring intense interest from academia, policymakers, social partners and the public. It is difficult to assess with certainty why this topic has rapidly become so central to the socioeconomic agenda. There are several elements that have ensured its high prominence. First of all, the emergence of a visible and recognisable workforce (partly because of the fluorescent clothes they wear), mostly consisting of young people and migrants, and the powerful claims they raised before management, and also for the 'newsworthiness' of their initiatives.

Secondly, platform work is solidly grounded on a persistent process of precari-sation, fragmentation and casualisation of work relations. This is yet another stage in the race for outsourcing, restructuring and downsizing that has been unfolding for decades. We have been emphasising that the forms of work that are lumped together under the expression 'gig-economy' share many characteristics with temporary work and bogus self-employment.[7] Many workers in various sectors face the ominous consequences of the inefficiency of labour standards resulting from deliberate attempts to evade employment legislation with the aim of cost-cutting. Although platforms cannot be blamed for having disintegrated the welfare state, their contributory role cannot be denied.

For some years, city streets have been crowded with delivery couriers equipped with voluminous coloured backpacks riding around on bicycles or, more rarely, on mopeds and in cars.[8] Simultaneously, smartphones were packed with new apps designed for a wide range of services: not only for ordering food, groceries and booze deliveries, minor maintenance work, small household errands, but also the possibility of 'renting' cooks and bartenders at home, babysitters, translators, proof readers, graphic designers and all sorts of consultants and freelancers. While the first promotional campaigns were launched in Europe – in newspapers, with leaf-lets in areas most populated with young consumers, thanks to multiple discount codes and with dozens of riders dressed in flashy colours sent around towns just to promote new brands – in the US the first disputes over the classification of gig workers had already reached their final stage. Although most of them were closed through arbitration and out-of-court settlements whose content is often bound by secrecy, the preliminary court documents speak for themselves. Just to name two of the most striking cases, Californian judges Chen and Chhabria dissected the business model of two urban transportation giants, Uber and its competitor

Lyft, disproving that they were simply intermediaries not involved in transport activities.[9]

Turning now to the magnitude of this phenomenon, the most reliable estimates suggest that employment in platform work accounts for around 1 per cent to 3 per cent of total employment.[10] Approximately 1.5 per cent of the working-age population (16–74 years) state that platform work is their main occupation;[11] some researchers estimate that 11 per cent of adults have earned income from platform work at some point in time (over 28 million people's activities in the EU are mediated by platforms).[12] Many studies also show that, for a large portion of workers, these activities represent their main source of income at a time of economic malaise, as revealed by a survey of workers using two of the main operators.[13] The market size in the EU has grown almost fivefold from an estimated EUR 3 billion in 2016 to about EUR 14 billion in 2020.[14]

These figures are neither astronomical nor microscopic, but they show a constant growth – they have increased more than six times compared to 2017 figures. According to the International Labour Organization, the number of taxi and delivery platforms has soared 10-fold worldwide in the last 10 years.[15] However, it is necessary to briefly discuss the 'elephant in the data room', namely the issues of methodology and replicability. Any reliable mapping of platform work is a rather complex matter, partly due to the high turnover of staff, but above all due to lack of reporting and transparency. All this sounds quite paradoxical. In the midst of an abundance of information, company numbers regarding platform workers remain taboo. On the contrary, with the exception of a handful of surveys conducted by international institutions, the few quantitative studies that exist are those that have benefited from an endowment of data by the platforms themselves.

It is hard to disagree with those who complain that the results of these studies often end up corroborating the message of their promotors. Several major issues remain unsolved, as researchers Janine Berg and Hannah Johnston pointed out regarding a very popular paper brandished by Uber to persuade policymakers.[16] First, the fact that the data are not shared by the platforms that own them, nor by the researchers who handle them, makes any verification or replication of information impossible, diminishing the scientific nature of the contributions. Secondly, some of the publications that use first-hand information see the participation, sometimes even as co-authors, of employees of the same companies; more commonly, these papers are the result of consultancy or are directly sponsored by the companies surveyed. A touch of scepticism towards these studies is required. As economist Luigi Zingales wrote, as long as this fog hangs in the air, Sherlock Holmes' intuitive conclusions are valid: if the dog did not bark, it must be because it knew the thief.[17]

Moreover, the questions in these surveys are often formulated in a leading or biased manner, habitually putting respondents in a position of giving predictable answers. Similarly, in many questionnaires, the options, almost always presented as binary, are deliberately misleading, not to mention the low rate of participation or the fact that there is no doubt the workers involved choose to answer favourably in order to avert unpleasant consequences or refrain from answering because they think that their opinion will not be taken into account.

For instance, a questionnaire given to Italian food-delivery riders asked: 'would you accept to work for your platform under an employment contract if this meant that: (i) your net income would be reduced; (ii) you would answer to a boss who tells you how, where, how much and when to work?'. A scene in Roberto Benigni's *Life is Beautiful* comes to mind immediately. It is late at night in a restaurant and the kitchen is closed, but an important customer arrives, one who cannot be sent away. The sole remaining food is a salmon dish, left uneaten by another client. The customer asks for something light and, to steer him towards the only available option Benigni starts proposing: 'A nice heavy steak, lamb, kidneys, some greasy breaded liver … Otherwise a nice fatty turbot, or eel stuffed with fatty sausage and greased with Grand Marnier …. Or some lean salmon!' – 'The salmon, thank you!' is the answer. And no contract of employment, thanks all the same.

Unfortunately, the difficulty of mapping the breadth and dynamics of this sector makes any legislative intervention regarding platform workers a gamble, all the more justified by opposing societal pressures than by a lucid and neutral analysis of the phenomenon. As useful as they may be, surveys are often incomplete: there is no watertight system of statistics to map platform workers. Moreover, the relative novelty of this mapping means that even platform workers find it difficult to identify themselves as part of the sector.[18] Many workers, especially in care, logistics, or catering services, are in fact engaged in the same activities as they were before the advent of apps; others still do not perceive themselves as workers at all – which leads them not to tick that box in surveys. Furthermore, a number of these workers have another main occupation and thus appear in the statistics, but under a different label. Finally, the same questions never cover all the subtleties of contractual formulas (that workers often ignore), let alone social security or tax aspects.

While no agreed-upon definition exists, the term 'platform work' has the merit of unifying very different activities, focusing on the channel through which they are exchanged, organised and remunerated. At the same time, it must be acknowledged that this label covers various types of economic activities that have very different social implications, even if they share a significant number of characteristics. In short, as scholars Koen Frenken and Juliet Schor commented, the umbrella definition has become a very large 'tent'. Referring to platform work as a large, powerful and indivisible phenomenon would therefore be inaccurate and deceptive;[19] a number of variables need to be considered, and this variation exceeds similarities.[20]

To cut to the chase, and leave behind the pretence of producing a definition on which everyone agrees, we borrow the formula adopted by Eurofound, the European Union agency whose objective is promoting the improvement of living and working conditions.[21] An early report on which we collaborated identifies 'platform work' as one of the nine new non-standard forms of work that have emerged in Europe since the early years of the new millennium.[22] 'Platform work is a form of employment that uses an online platform to enable organisations or individuals [workers] to access other organisations or individuals [clients] to solve problems or to provide services in exchange for payment.' It follows that, from a labour law standpoint, the most problematic and significant digital platforms are those that exchange temporary work activities and coordinate such an exchange between the worker and the client, and where online and offline activities are distributed through either open calls or individual task assignment. Three chief groups of economic actors are involved: (i) workers or 'service providers' on a casual (amateur or professional) basis; (ii) customers (also called users or 'requesters', these may be individuals, households or businesses); and (iii) businesses that use software to match the demand and supply of work and services and to organise their performance.[23]

The consensus is to classify platform work into two main categories, activities performed remotely and those performed on location. The two categories have been referred to as 'crowdwork' and 'work on demand via app', respectively.[24] They are both based on mobilising an unstable and dispersed workforce, the former being mainly based on task offers addressed to a large audience of workers potentially connected from all over the world, the latter relying on people available within a few kilometres. They differ in the place of performance. Much more attention has been deservedly paid to on-location work, even though crowdwork features risks that should not be underestimated.[25]

The common denominator is a strained version of work, whereby social protection is renounced in exchange for peanuts, to the benefit of digital giants wanting fast and cheap results. They invade a sector and undercut fees artificially, subsidised by venture capital in a money-squandering attempt to dominate the market in the longer run. This is all done under the strange assumption that innovation is only genuine if it asks for forgiveness, not permission.

II. 'What is Mine is Yours'. Doublespeak and the Mythology of Sharing

In the beginning was the drill. In 2014 or so, the image of this tool stood out boldly in every presentation on the latest inventions that – according to their supporters – were soon to revolutionise our lifestyles, rewrite the rules of the market, and even (brace yourselves) put capitalism out of business. Once upon a time, therefore, it was all about the sharing economy.

The message conveyed through this metaphor was quite simple and straightforward. 'You just need a hole in the wall, or at most to assemble a bunch of drawers, you do not need a drill. What's the point of owning your own drill if you're going to be using it for an average of six to twenty minutes?' At its world debut, the religion of the 'sharing economy' built around the sharing of resources relied on this suggestive parable to champion the enlightenment of membership over the dark ages of ownership. The first commandment sounded simple: 'What is mine is yours'. Coveting other people's possessions was not only allowed, but encouraged. Renting would guarantee the salvation, if not of souls, at least of wallets. The dogma dictated the sharing of unutilised or underused resources. A principle that is acceptable when it comes to exploiting the use of carpentry devices otherwise destined to rot in a basement, but rather awkward when the paradigm of the drill is applied to the global workforce.[26]

In spite of the absurdity of this idea, the gospel of 'sharing' spread, on the viral wave of a handful of messianic videos in perfect TED talk style.[27] The worship found its preachers in storytellers and managers co-opted by the platform companies that were colonising urban areas all over the world. The app for finding a cheap room in Paris, the one for getting a lift to the airport, the one for getting sushi delivered instantly to your home on a rainy Sunday, the one for booking a maths tutoring session, the one for getting someone to queue up at the drugstore for you. Many believed in them,[28] comforted by the illusion of entering an Eden of low-cost privileges, and enticed by the opportunity to operate as small-scale suppliers (of beds, rides, tools, time, or talents).

To give an account of the collaborative ethos, some ventured into discussions about the collapse of trust in public institutions, a failure that would be remedied by mutualism among strangers, facilitated by a few small tricks cleverly devised by the platforms – first and foremost consumer-sourced reviews. These discussions partially reflected genuine changes in the tastes and attitudes of the new consumer generation. Subsequent studies, freed from the near-evangelical enthusiasm of the early days, have identified the aftermath of the 2008 financial crisis as one of the factors behind the success of the naïve, and sometimes disingenuous, rhetoric of peer-to-peer exchange. On the one hand, even affording a few minimal luxuries had suddenly become impossible for many, especially millennials, who were grappling with hectic professional hours and frustrated by the difficulty of balancing personal budgets; on the other hand, the idea of earning pocket money to help round out their meagre salaries seemed like a godsend in the absence of more stable alternatives. In reality, what passed for salvation would soon turn out to be penance.[29]

After a decade of smoke and mirrors, our gently mocking tone is motivated by the need to warn against scams.[30] Now that the miracles promised have been universally acknowledged as hype, to reveal the truth we will try to condense years of overexcitement. Before focusing on the legal aspects, we consider the evolution of the labels with which the phenomenon has been christened, to map how the attitudes of jurists, sociologists, economists and decision-makers have changed.

Given the volatility of this part of the economy, several institutions have tried to sketch out their own taxonomy and entire book chapters have been spent distinguishing between synonyms and 'false friends'. Until recently, it was very difficult to find one's way through this maze. Over time, as we made clear in the introductory paragraph, the neutral expression 'platform work' has become the most accepted. However, it is worth exploring an anthology of the many claims in defence of the platforms, a series of clichés that are still quoted today when it is time to face up to responsibilities. The catalogue is rich and includes arguments on both ends of the scale, depending on the circumstances. However, it should not be overlooked that definitions, and the ideas they encapsulate, influence general perception and social impact as much as regulatory interventions do. Words can carry considerable weight.

A vast and collective debunking operation became necessary to counter the prevailing false narrative trap. Simultaneously, although on a case-by-case basis, courts across the world have taken up the task of disproving certain misrepresentations. Following a sort of chronological order, the first myth to dispel is that we are dealing with some new and amateurish type of relationship. Someone simply picks up and deliver parcels from one end of the city to the other, another person transports people in her car, others perform repetitive tasks on their computer, someone else completes remote consultancies. These tasks are all performed for remuneration, however small. It is only work, not recognising it as such is ridiculous. Among other things, the lack of recognition of these activities as work is a repetition of what has happened in the past in sectors such as temporary employment agencies, and playing down the value of women in part-time work.[31]

Jeremias Adams-Prassl at the University of Oxford rightly talks about a 'doublespeak' of gig companies.[32] Platform work has been disguised as 'favour', 'task', 'partnership', 'help' or even 'game'; workers have been referred to by dozens of labels verging on the farcical, from 'ninjas' to 'peers', from 'gorillas' to 'rabbits', from 'partners' to 'friends'.[33] There have been attempts to distinguish genuinely altruistic mutual practices from the lexical expropriation that has taken place for the benefit of staffing business giants: but it was too late. The internal vocabulary prepared by the apps, unveiled by journalistic investigations and documents leaked by whistle-blowers, aimed at creating a parallel reality where 'independent suppliers' work 'with' the platform (not 'for' it!), they 'onboard' after signing a 'supplier agreement' (don't say 'hire'), they offer their 'availability' (they are not assigned a shift). They wear 'branded clothing' (not a uniform) and are part of a 'community'. They 'log in' at the beginning of their shift in a 'chosen area', receive a 'fee' (not a wage) after invoices are processed and, if service delivery standards are not met (do not say 'performance review'), their account is 'terminated' (which is basically a code word for 'they are dismissed').[34]

Next came the formulas 'on-demand economy' and 'just-in-time workforce'. Seemingly drab, they both emphasise instant performance and the fragmented nature of a workforce, borrowing the terminology of assembly line work in a lean production model. Also in this case, the emphasis is on the speed of the service, a 'hit and run' model aimed at catering to the client's insatiable appetite for convenience. 'On demand', 'on call', 'on tap' are insincere euphemisms that conceal an underlying hypocrisy,[35] according to which platforms operate in a universe where exceptions are the norm. Imagine if waiters in a café, in the name of an 'on demand' format, were only paid every time they pick up an order and move from table to bar to pull a pint, and not for all the hours they put on their aprons and make themselves available to customers. It would be absurd! It does, however, show the excessive tolerance with which a shrewd exercise of reality warping has been treated.

Any other business in traditional industries would not have survived such hypocrisy. And yet, years after the launch of these 'start-ups', we are still being forced to respond to the assertion that in low value-added sectors, complying with the rules would mean depriving many vulnerable workers of their living or forcing them into undeclared work. Enforcing current regulations would dampen the creativity of entrepreneurs who are allergic to formalities. Let's instead keep this 'formalised informal economy' and be happy with it. How this adds to an already too widespread culture of commodifying and depreciating work is evident. Thanks to unyielding 'regulatory entrepreneurship',[36] a modest version of innovation has proliferated, one according to which existing rules should be disregarded because they are the legacy of a black-and-white world, or shadow-economies and illegal alternatives are used as a yardstick for comparing the validity of debatable business models.

It is appropriate to state for the record the remark of a manager of a food-delivery platform, according to whom 'Foodora is not a job to make ends meet, but an opportunity for those who love to ride bikes, earning a small salary'.[37] In short, it is claimed it is a 'gift' for bike lovers, or the opportunity to make a profit from the very popular obsession of racing round the cobblestones of city centres on rainy nights. A wellness exercise for free.

Even today, managers continue to play the 'leisure activity' card, even in parliamentary hearings, without anyone raising an eyebrow. From a legal point of view, though, it does not matter whether people do a job to survive, to earn extra money or for pleasure. No one would ever argue that someone who inherited a fortune and still works 'for passion', even if they could afford to be idle, is not entitled to employment protection – its coverage does not depend on the recipient's motivation for work. The reasons for engaging in a certain activity are completely irrelevant when it comes to classifying work arrangements and identifying which rules apply to them. Nor can the casual nature of certain activities lead us to consider them as good neighbourly relations.

This *nouvelle vague* also includes the term 'gig economy', borrowed from the world of live performances in the entertainment sector. It conveys the idea of a casual arrangement, whereby a musician is recruited to perform a show in exchange for a small reward (free drinks or, at best, a percentage of the tickets sold). If the audience is cheerful, the performer gets another date, otherwise thank you and goodbye. The term perpetuates a flippant interpretation, which has contributed to a trivialisation of the phenomenon. Why bother regulating something that is by nature short-lived? This trite argument ends up justifying avoiding existing rules and, in an unending vicious circle, increases the number of those who are placed in a legal no man's land. What is more, the busted mythology of 'odd jobs' clashes with an argument often used by platforms' advocates: self-entrepreneurship. One the one hand, there is the image of an amateur activity. On the other hand, strengthened by cycling under inclement weather conditions, an ingenious business idea will germinate in the souls of platform workers, and will soon be ready to be listed on the stock exchange. The (mostly phony) hagiographies of CEOs who started out delivering pizzas as scrappy, penniless students are also part of this narrative of 'entrepreneurial renaissance'.[38]

Emphasising grassroots self-entrepreneurship is a common rhetorical trick of many players. It sends three main messages. The first, whereby the app acts as a mere point of contact between customers and third-party suppliers, was already refuted by the Court of Justice of the European Union. The second purports to justify the adoption of self-employment arrangements before the courts – not exactly a watertight strategy, given how many platform workers have been reclassified as employees. The third is even more surreal, according to which any different legal classification, including employment status, would make a stricter control on the workforce mandatory, with the result of leaving no room for flexibility.[39] None of these arguments makes sense.

Simply put, nothing could be further from the notion of entrepreneurship than services of a predominantly personal nature, often rendered under exclusivity clauses (with the practical impossibility of being replaced), coupled with constant tracking through GPS, the need to rent uniforms and company equipment out of one's own pocket, while putting up with inconveniences caused by malfunctioning technology.[40] People who are obliged to respect deadlines, shifts and instructions imposed by others to avoid being excluded from the platform are hardly their own boss.[41] Advertising campaigns started glorifying professional martyrdom, presented as an alternative to the boredom of working for an over-demanding boss. An outrageous ad for Fiverr hit the headlines, capturing the spirit of the times. 'You eat a coffee for lunch', it proclaimed. 'You follow through on your follow through. Sleep deprivation is your drug of choice. You might be a doer.'[42] Sure!

In the words of the Court of Justice of the European Union, an economic unit is not an undertaking if it is unable to determine independently its own conduct on the market,[43] but is entirely dependent on its principal, for instance because it must passively accept the pricing policies decided by the platforms. Similarly, a service that does not have direct access to markets and a client base does not qualify as genuine self-employment. The judges of the London Employment Tribunal branded as 'faintly ridiculous' the notion that 'Uber in London is a mosaic of 30,000 small businesses linked by a common "platform"'.[44] If this were the case, each client would be free to negotiate rates and fees directly with the workers (as is the case whenever you use a freelancer, be it for a consultancy or a leaky tap). After all, when you ask who is at your door the answer you get is: 'Glovo', not 'Tony, the rider'.

Likewise, as we discuss below, it is blatantly false that adopting a model based on regular employment would negate any margin of flexibility. Moreover – as we learned during the lockdowns, when we almost started cheering platforms, instead of healthcare workers – the platform business would not be viable without the contribution of the workers who are central to the business model: the labour factor is much more important than machinery and capitals.[45]

Now that the initial buzz is over, and extensive research has revealed the harsh reality, the propaganda is stalling. Claiming that food delivery drivers are all university students eager to earn a quick buck is at odds with the results of surveys (and with what anyone can see in plain sight). Platform workers may also sometimes be highly educated, but their average age is going up (in 2018 it was 33.9 years), and the bulk of the workforce is engaged for dozens of hours a week (more than 60).[46] As can be seen on the streets or on suburban trains (especially at the end of the shift), and as shown by judicial investigations, some delivery platforms contracted legions of migrant workers through a tortuous pattern of elusive practices. Unfamiliarity with the local language, combined with the fear linked to migrant statuses and the need to scrape together resources to avoid starvation, leads to abuses, silence and subjugation – sweatshops run through smartphones. Accidents are not reported for fear of retaliation or exposure, and complaints are nipped in the bud because removing troublemakers is too easy.

Meanwhile, the health crisis and the resulting state of exception have provided a golden opportunity for many platforms.[47] On the one hand, there were draconian measures imposing social distancing on millions of citizens, on the other, the forced shutdown of many businesses was mitigated by the possibility of operating as delivery-only concepts. In between, platforms were able to seize this unexpected state of affairs to consolidate their position as critical societal infrastructures, by controlling and monetising a large volume of critical data flows.

They could take advantage of this situation to stimulate the consumers' appetite,[48] subsidise the business with artificially low prices[49] and generous incentives and keep investors off their backs, forcing the latter to accept balance sheets in the red by forking out huge recapitalisations, in the hopes of wiping out brick-and-mortar rivals. We should not underestimate how much data the platforms are able to collect with a single call and then sell or use: such as what time we eat, what we eat, where drivers take us and when, how much we are willing to pay etc. Not to mention how easy it is to cash in on the data collected – platforms often sell traffic data back to public transport authorities or use it to develop other projects, such as self-driving cars. It is this huge amount of capital that makes companies that often burn huge piles of money attractive to venture capitalists.

It would then be easy to raise prices, lower costs and reap the benefits of this scheme by elbowing out competitors.[50] Only then would we see plainly that that the new clothes of the digital emperors, which had made them invisible to the eyes of the regulator, are the same ones once worn by the most aggressive protagonists of the Gilded Age. Some CEOs have openly admitted that the long-term goal is to become an 'operating system for everyone's entire lives',[51] in order to set up monopolies or, at most, an oligopoly. This may be the only way to make a struggling entrepreneurial adventure sustainable. There would then be little point in the crocodile tears of a society that would realise it had been flattered and deceived by a handful of anti-competitive discount codes.

This is a serious issue, and marketing charades certainly do not help. It's why it is imperative to clear the field of all semantic traps. To do so, let us begin once and for all to tell it like it is. The solution to the problem starts here.

A. Workers on Tap and Untapped Appetites

This section contains a review of the ways in which work is organised by platforms. For the sake of simplicity, we outline the features of an almost prototypic but nevertheless realistic pilot, and account for divergences from it. There is a great deal of available information. While in the past it was limited to the legal notes published on the companies' websites, over time detailed studies, court rulings, media investigations and revelations from workers have complemented, and sometimes debunked, it.

Each platform is a case in point, but the vast bulk of them engage with providers who are almost invariably classified as self-employed workers (including schemes of 'dependent self-employment', where they exist, which we will analyse below). While avoiding the obligations and costs associated with direct employment, many platforms, as we will see, still wield some degree of managerial prerogatives, albeit in a sophisticated and misleading manner.

Notably, labour regulation around the world has developed effective 'antibodies' to cure the inconsistency between contractual labels and reality. Simply put, a work arrangement cannot be given a legal classification that contradicts the actual nature of the work performance.[52] If this happens, and the parties of a self-employment arrangement behave as if an employment relationship was in place, with the principal exerting control on the work performance and the worker being dependent on that hiring entity, courts or labour authorities can rectify this situation by reclassifying the work arrangement as an employment contract or relationship. This is also known as 'primacy of fact'. In its various and multifaceted form, it is a widely established and applied principle or practice in a vast number of countries and legal systems around the world. This allows disregarding contractual (mis)classifications by giving priority to substance over form.

It is also recognised by a specialised instrument of the International Labour Organization, the Employment Relationship Recommendation, 2006 (No. 198), which stipulates: 'the determination of the existence of [an employment relationship] should be guided primarily by the facts relating to the performance of work and the remuneration of the worker, notwithstanding how the relationship is characterised in any contrary arrangement, contractual or otherwise, that may have been agreed between the parties'.[53] The newly proposed EU Directive on platform work adopts the very same language, also mentioning the need to 'tak[e] into account the use of algorithms in the organisation of platform work, irrespective of how the relationship is classified' by the parties.[54] Boilerplate clauses which classify workers as independent contractors, but which are omitted in practice or do not correspond to the reality of the work performed cannot deprive workers of employment status and its accompanying protections.

There is, therefore, a broad international consensus on the primacy of fact principle both in general and with regard to platform work, as shown in a recent study of the University of Leuven commissioned by the ILO.[55] The study mapped litigation and legislation on the employment status of platform workers around the world and found that, in general, courts were often ready to reclassify platform workers as employees when platforms behaved as ordinary employers, with notable exceptions in Russia and China and, after the ballot on Proposition 22, also in California. Consequently, our study is based on factual circumstances, notwithstanding any contrary arrangement agreed upon by the parties.

For the sake of simplicity, we begin with the registration and recruitment phase. All a worker needs to join a platform is a fast internet connection. There are no particular barriers to entry, mainly because the model needs a large pool of workers available around the clock to meet the volume of demand while keeping fees low. When candidates first sign up on the website of one of the many platforms, they find a mandatory route. Generally, a first step is dedicated to basic personal data, including a profile picture, as well as tax and financial details. A second page hosts a standardised form contract. After this stage, one can move on to agree on the unilaterally determined boilerplate terms and conditions.[56] The content of these clauses is deliberately ambiguous, barely comprehensible and, in most cases, it goes the extra mile to deny the existence of an employment relationship through a series of verbal acrobatics. The adhesion contracts, which are not static over time, often include dubiously enforceable waivers and arbitration clauses aimed at discouraging or preventing workers from claiming their rights in court.

In the fields of transport, delivery and handyman work, the recruitment and hiring phases may be followed by training sessions, either in person or via online tutorials. Rules of conduct are aggressively shared, they encompass cleanliness of vehicles, specific music genre recommendations, professional clothing, gadgets and assistance for customers.

Usually, it is the automated management system that matches workers to clients, either on the basis of specific requests (it is up to the client to establish the criteria to which the worker's profile must respond) or on the basis of geographical proximity recorded at regular intervals.[57] A bidding mechanism is also possible (but beware: again, it is the platform or the final user that set the key conditions). Many platforms – especially those exchanging creative activities – include competitive contest-based processes to win a gig, allowing room for self-promotion and, in rare cases, even direct contact with the clients.

Once recruited, workers are encouraged, and prompted, to accept all requests, on pain of being downgraded in the internal ranking. To that end, the apps themselves incorporate rather intrusive notification mechanisms that leave workers with no choice but to switch off the device permanently, exposing themselves to recalls and penalties of all kinds, or to be swamped with notifications. The couriers involved in door-to-door delivery services in last-mile logistics are in contact with the company through messaging applications, or through group chats. Workers are called in on the basis of anticipated deliveries, without much notice, and divided into shifts, and sometimes into zones of competence. They are allowed to cancel a shift within certain limits, late cancellations can lead to them being labelled as unreliable by the automated reputational system and excluded from new job offers. Compliance with data protection regulation is largely illusory. The platforms use sophisticated monitoring devices such as geo-localisation via GPS and precise data on online accesses of workers and customers as well as on the number of restaurants active at a given time. Yet, the address of the consumer or the destination of the trip are rarely revealed before acceptance – which can lead to long routes being taken.[58]

During the pandemic, many platform workers had no choice but to keep working to avoid financial hardship and not to see their ratings cancelled, while exposing themselves directly to the risk of infection and to being vectors of transmission within their families and communities.[59] What is more, with the aim of minimising misclassification claims, some platforms waited weeks before distributing personal protective equipment – lest this distribution be interpreted as something only employers would do – with workers being forced to pay for masks, hand sanitiser gel and gloves out of their own pockets.[60] In several countries, it took a court order to recognise the riders' right to basic safety equipment, regardless of their contractual classification.[61] The emergency has exposed people to hazard, heightened by the lack of information on the health status of both their fellow workers and their clients (to reassure customers 'contactless deliveries' were introduced). In addition, the long lockdowns were formidable opportunities for platforms to build customer loyalty. With restaurants and supermarkets restricted to home delivery, only a semi affluent elite, grappling with overloaded systems and in a constant battle with their neighbours to grab the few available time slots, was able to afford the privilege of quick and no-touch delivery.[62]

In sectors such as cleaning or, more generally, domestic work, many apps have specialised in booking household jobs and offering complementary services, from calculating rates to managing invoices, or even selling cleaning products. To avoid the risk that workers and clients build a personal bond that could bypass them, several companies impose non-circumvention clauses and penalties if anyone sidesteps the platform to negotiate deals. Arguably, given the nature of these services, the scope for monitoring workers in this context ought to be greatly reduced, because the surveillance is one-sided. Very few mechanisms are put in place to avoid opportunistic behaviour from household clients, particularly when it comes to ratings.

The profiling of workers and clients is now one of the core businesses for platforms' operators.[63] Internal reputation has a major influence on the remuneration of workers, particularly where exclusivity clauses channelling work through single platforms are present. The exercise of control and disciplinary powers is facilitated by non-transparent internal rating systems, which collect and factor into data the number of orders accepted and the proportion of deliveries completed or rejected upon receiving an order, availability rates in designated areas during the most inconvenient shifts, and the overall appreciation of customers. If workers fall behind, they are subject to disciplinary action, without any guarantee.[64] Recently, it has been found that the use of outsourcing and substitution chains could make the identification of the worker less and less reliable. But the platform-prescribed cure may be much worse than the disease. To prevent drivers from using phony documents and passengers from being at the mercy of 'unverified accounts', Uber is experimenting with facial recognition mechanisms, paving the way to intolerable mass surveillance practices and discriminatory results.

In 2019, a major trade union in Italy brought a legal action against Deliveroo. A year later, the court's decision was the first in the world that ruled against discriminatory algorithms at work. The order also uncovered the functioning of the model. Riders were ranked based on how reliable they were and how long they worked. The combination of these metrics determined their internal rankings, and the likelihood of them being called upon. Workers with the highest ratings were among the first to apply for jobs, those with the most orders, and had the opportunity to turn down jobs that were inconvenient. Some riders who returned from a period of absence were automatically downgraded and forced to start from scratch, even when they did not show up to work because they were on strike (or because they were sick, had a disability or had to assist a disabled person or a sick minor). This made the algorithm operate in an indirectly discriminatory way according to the court, as the system did not differentiate between people missing a shift for constitutionally protected reasons and other absent workers,[65] putting workers with a protected characteristic at a particular disadvantage.

Platforms have extensively argued that their workers are self-employed because they can 'switch off' the software or not log on to the app, thus being unavailable to take calls. However, many commentators and courts, including the Spanish and the French Supreme Courts,[66] have objected that making oneself available to work contributes, along with other factors, to defining the rating that by its very nature is very volatile and heavily depends on the customers' often arbitrary reviews, making personal scores highly unstable. This model results in a stressful subservience to both the platform and to the users, who are complimented with freebies and flattery.

Even though word of mouth has made it possible to develop a sort of code of conduct that satisfies the 'black box' (to give just a few examples: food couriers know that in order to be able to choose the best shifts they must have worked a certain number of hours, while drivers hand out water bottles and sweets as incentives for positive reviews from the client), many rules remain unclear. Over time, workers have done their best to be present and active on several platforms simultaneously to avoid downtime; but this trick is not always effective, and there is a great risk of being caught and sanctioned.[67] Additionally, the possibility of offering services to multiple third parties at the same time ('multihoming') can be used in court to defeat the claim of being included under the scope of employment protection.

Technology also allows for second-by-second monitoring of the worker's position and speed in performing a given task.[68] In online crowdwork, the client may assign the same task to several workers to check the quality of the performance, compensating only the best performer, or have access to the worker's screen in order to check if they are actually on the job at any given moment. After completion, work that does not meet the customer's expectations can be retained with no payment under a satisfaction clause found in many online freelancing platforms. As well as emphasising the forced compliance of workers, this approach can lead to opportunistic behaviour.[69] It is, after all, a sort of fickle 'lottery' in which the losers have to surrender their intellectual property rights over outputs.[70]

The compensation structure has been made public thanks to the controversy that has followed the cyclical and sudden changes to terms and conditions, which originally provided for an hourly wage while, more recently, remunerate each order with a few euros – it has been said, not without reason, that unoriginal forms of piecework on a 'pay-as-you-go' basis are making a spectacular comeback.[71] Very often hybrid formulas are used: a minimum hourly rate for certain time slots (a model later abandoned), payment per delivery, a few cents per mile travelled as the crow flies, pennies for every minute spent waiting at the restaurant or customer's premises. Increasingly, the payment has been decoupled from the cost of a service paid by the final client, with numerous incentives based on market and surge pricing. In the delivery industry, hybrid models coexist where – despite the attempts to link remuneration to collective agreements in comparable sectors – payment per delivery prevails, pushing workers into the risky practice of working long hours to ensure a decent salary. It is no coincidence that road accidents continue to rise year on year.[72] In summer 2019, a judge in Buenos Aires suspended major food-delivery platforms after a spike in the number of accidents. The *casus belli* was a viral tweet featuring the shameful interaction between an injured driver and a middle manager who, informed of an accident, insisted on asking for reassurance on the status of the order.[73] Aggressions against riders have also been reported in the media.[74]

The costs incurred for uniforms, equipment and vehicles (as well as fines, repairs and new purchases in case of stolen bikes, *ça va sans dire*) are entirely borne by the workers. The companies usually provide them, deducting the cost directly from pay. On average, the platform retains a hefty 25–30 per cent for each transaction. Only recently, many companies have agreed to the request to provide a tip button, but it was later discovered that the money was pocketed and used to pay the fee, providing yet another cost saving that most customers were unaware of.[75]

Platform work is a niche where extreme forms of deregulation by market players are permitted. The results are grim: unstable working hours and low earnings, well below the average wages of comparable industries (retail, logistics, services etc), no sick pay, holidays or overtime, limited room for collective bargaining and business risks passed on to the workers themselves. While creating new opportunities for some groups of workers, platforms impoverish labour markets and trigger downward pressure on prices. Their competitive edge derives from the ability to selectively disapply labour rules, and from the failure to comply with social security obligations. In practice, this unfair advantage is based on an avoidance formula whose adverse consequences end up being borne by societies at large (competitors, workers but also customers who cannot rely on clear rules on non-discrimination and vehicle safety).

It should be noted that, although for years the abandonment of invasive Ford-Taylorist models was unjustifiably celebrated, today we find ourselves dealing with ramped up versions on steroids. While the boundaries of the classical employment statuses are being abandoned, and the hypotheses that the employment relationship's model has an expansive force or, on the contrary, is experiencing a phase of eclipse are over-debated, some of the most characterising features of that hierarchical model are now widespread in every segment of the labour market, regardless of classifications. Paradoxically, the much-vaunted decoupling of labour measures from the standard employment relationship seems now to be achieved, not on the side of protection, but on the side of obligations and constraints for workers.

Thus, while the employment relationship has been gracefully de-standardised, the work performance is being routinised. At the end of the day, the dynamics of the glittering world of innovation are not too far removed from the ancient models with which nominally autonomous labourers were confronted decades ago.[76] If this is the future, the reaction (according to legend) of Gioachino Rossini to the composition of a fellow composer is still valid: 'I must confess that there is beauty and novelty in your work. Too bad, though, that while the beautiful is not new, the new is not beautiful!'.

B. The Platform Paradigm, Rethinking the Master–Server Dialectic

We often hear that digital companies such as Uber, Amazon and Deliveroo are to be considered as tech-forward organisations, hybrid structures at the cross-roads of classical institutional schemes.[77] It is often argued that the predominant Silicon Valley business model even transcends the traditional distinction between undertaking and market, 'make' and 'buy', vertical and horizontal, labour law and contract law.[78] This all too benevolent interpretation has helped to forge various rhetorical weapons through which platforms have presented themselves as mere brokers of connections – 'virtual Yellow Pages' that merely facilitate the matching of labour supply and demand, without interfering with the activities offered. To tell the truth, these same companies have invested quite a bit of energy in playing the role of (neo)intermediaries above the law, sensational 'Ebay for humans'. But are we sure that the 'uberisation' is revolutionising the notion of enterprise as we know it? Drawing insights from law and economics, we engage with the motivations and aims that now inform choices concerning corporate organisation and management of the firm, understood as a conglomerate of capital and labour – once compact and self-sufficient, now modular and interconnected.

At first glance, it might seem that platforms represent a living contradiction to the paradigm of the vertically integrated enterprise that emerged in the twentieth century and that, in turn, contributed to delivering the socio-economic development of industrialised countries.[79] This rebellious self-representation as rebellious players, accompanied by truly distasteful references to Rosa Parks and Gandhi, has inspired their claim to be operating in a legal vacuum, in a nascent market unconstrained by rules.[80] All these claims have turned out to be devious. For decades, economists and labour lawyers have tried to dissect the reasons why entrepreneurs find it convenient to directly manage ('internalise') the production factors and, consequently, to operate by means of a so-called vertically integrated structure.

Businesses grow by bringing activities within a firm to optimise transaction costs and exercise greater authority over the resources they own.[81] Today, instead, to quote a popular meme, 'Uber, the world's largest taxi company, owns no vehicles. Facebook, the world's most popular media owner, creates no content. Alibaba, the most valuable retailer, has no inventory. And Airbnb, the world's largest accommodation provider, owns no real estate. Something interesting is happening'.[82] Impressive, isn't it?

The classic distinction in business economics between 'make' (to do internally, by means of a hierarchical model) and 'buy' (to acquire from outside on the market, in horizontal and competitive conditions) is still useful today to describe the options on the map, as well as to draw the efficient boundaries of a given economic structure.[83] Of course, this binary option partly neglects more complex arrangements, first of all those established within networks – elastic business relations models of governance within a framework based on mutual preferences and relational contracts.[84] In networks, however, interdependence and integration among actors come into play, often thanks to idiosyncratic investments, which make relationships unbalanced even when they were conceived as being horizontal.[85] Think of the owner of a franchised shop who spent a lot of money to buy furniture, machines and software that they can only use by remaining within the same large chain; the franchisor can easily impose contractual conditions favourable to itself, and alter them when needed.

As early as the end of the 1980s, some scholars were already voicing their concern to propose a revision of classical theories, on the expectation that mass digitisation would reduce coordination costs, shifting the balance of convenience in favour of recourse to the market, or to interconnected value chains.[86] The fragmentation of the production landscape, the new tools for finding resources and the endless extra-legal possibilities of contract administration would have urged businesses to be sophisticated and flexible, able to adapt to changing market needs. This called for an upgrade of the strict make/buy distinction.[87] Regrettably, despite the validity of this insight, little energy has been devoted to investigating the ability of technology to reduce coordination costs even within a vertical structure.

Faced with these arrangements that fundamentally unsettle conventional categories, new questions emerge. Are platforms really the harbingers of a new economic order that rejects the distinction between making and buying and leads straight to the extinction of businesses as we know them? Will open interactions, based on distinctive elements and optimised by intelligent software, triumph, as argued by researchers Van Alstyne, Parker and Choudary in their book *Platform Revolution*?[88] In short: no. Instead of hailing the collapse of old categories to encourage innovation, we should understand the broader picture in which innovative firms are situated.

If we go beyond appearances, it becomes clear that the platforms' real strength lies in the formidable combination of basic AI, user-friendly interfaces, surge pricing and increasingly effective tools such as geo-localisation via GPS. Thus, information can be easily retrieved, taking into account distance, number of requests or even just the remaining battery charge level of the customer's phone. Likewise, the imposition of guidelines, recommendations and instructions – whose observance is easily monitored remotely – constitutes an invisible tool of command and, in cases of a breach, results in the deactivation of the worker's account.

This scenario has all the advantages of vertical models without the associated costs. All the privileges of horizontal contracting in the marketplace, without the associated shortcomings. In a single stroke, transaction costs are minimised. Like integrated enterprises, platforms rely on labour to extract value and adopt a command-and-control approach; like markets, platforms engage, dispatch and connect nominally independent actors; like networks, they combine and synchronise the supply and demand sides of goods or services. Like Cerberus, the mythological three-headed dog, platforms are versatile economic actors that continuously evolve from transaction enablers to participation gatekeepers.[89] The much-advertised idea of having set up a new generation business model, when tested in practice, turns out to be an illusion. The aim of platform companies is to grow at a loss by reaching a critical mass of users and then extracting profits from a dominant position. The result is an apparently 'win-win situation' in which firms control resources without owning them, rapidly adapting to downturns in the market.[90] Downsides for businesses are less evident. Platforms may find it difficult to deal with a segmented, uncommitted and inharmonious workforce, and with supervising isolated workers outside the firm's premises while meeting customers' needs.[91]

From the above analysis, it becomes clear that for online platforms it is much cheaper to orchestrate processes, solicit participants and interact fruitfully with the surrounding ecosystem than deal with owning and hiring.[92] On closer inspection, these centrifugal forces have existed for decades. The novelty lies in the penetration of the immaterial infrastructure that enables smoother exchanges, not to mention the effective collection of data that can bring about even more timely and successful functions. All this occurs at an extremely low cost, since the workers work for the same platform, even though they are classified as self-employed. Thus, platforms organise production inputs without incurring most of the costs associated with labour and social security protection. The chief costs to bear are, at most, those related to software, patents and a few other resources (investment in advertising, a good press office, a marketing department and strong compliance and lobbying teams).[93] When analysing platform work, therefore, Coase's classic theory of the firm, properly purged of its functionalist excesses, remains a compelling basis for describing the interrelationships between economic actors and justifying their organisational choices even in this era of shift from atoms to bits.[94]

At the end of 2017, however, the Court of Justice of the European Union took a clear stand when called on to rule on the nature of the service offered by the Uber platform following an appeal brought by a professional taxi drivers' association in Barcelona seeking a declaration that the activities of Uber Systems Spain amounted to misleading practices and acts of unfair competition. The platform's determination of many of the terms and conditions of the service (the driver's credential and performance, maximum fares, vehicle status and characteristics and working time) means that it cannot be qualified as a mere digital intermediary.[95] For the Court, in fact, Uber must be classified as 'a service in the field of transport' within the meaning of EU law precisely because of the direct and indirect influence it exerts on 'all relevant aspects' of the underlying service and on non-professional drivers. There is a huge difference between a website that merely compares the rates of a service (as is common for airline flights or insurance policies aggregators, and other mixed services where the electronic component prevails over the physical one) and a company that organises a mobility service in its entirety by operating in the highly regulated market. In short, Uber provides more than an intermediation service.

To put it another way, quoting an American ruling that has become a classic: unlike a technological enterprise, Uber 'does not simply sell software; it sells rides'.[96] It is, therefore, highly questionable that Uber has re-engineered the prototype of the enterprise. This was made clear by the Advocate General who reviewed the case with some extraordinarily clear passages: 'While [the platform's] control is not exercised in the context of a traditional employer-employee relationship, one should not be fooled by appearances. Indirect control such as that exercised by Uber, based on financial incentives and decentralised passenger-led ratings, with a scale effect, makes it possible to manage in a way that is just as – if not more – effective than management based on formal orders given by an employer to his employees and direct control over the carrying out of such orders'.[97]

While platforms operating in the last-mile logistics sector or exchanging back-office tasks have been accused of abandoning employer obligations and avoiding the associated costs, their legacy also rests on the intensification of authority and concentration of power. Platforms want to have it both ways: strong authority mechanisms and liquid obligations.[98] From rebels to mercenaries: with great power comes organised irresponsibility.[99] Therefore, they don't deserve any preferential treatment. Moreover, with the stabilisation of the industry, the use of vertically integrated models is growing. Consider that in the food-delivery sector, many platforms have moved from connecting restaurants and customers to owning and operating kitchens that prepare food exclusively for delivery – they call them 'dark' kitchens (at the same time, many platforms increasingly rely on 'dark stores' that cater primarily for online shopping 'within minutes').[100] Uber has also moved from transport services to food deliveries, bicycle rental and labour supply.

According to labour law scholar Brishen Rogers, examples from Amazon, Uber, McDonalds and Walmart emphasise the fact that fragmentation and consolidation reflect the same underlying logic.[101] This is not forecasting the future, but rather a question of industrial archaeology: it is the continuation of an eternal process of business disintegration by digital means. David Weil, who served as administrator of the Wage and Hour Division in the US Department of Labour during the Obama and Biden administrations, compiled a number of vignettes of a phenomenon he labelled 'fissured' work.[102] Borrowing from geological studies, Weil illustrated various situations that share one common denominator: the absence of a direct employment contract between the company and the worker, compounded by the ability to closely enforce standards on external suppliers thanks to the low costs of gathering information and digital monitoring. A cleaner hired by an external hotel management company that has a contract for the big hotel chain; cable installers – nominally self-employed business providers – working for years for the same installation company whose logo is on their uniform; a dock porter who unpacks, loads, and ships goods – temporarily staffed to a logistic company serving a large chain of grocery stores, but also (to update Weil's review)[103] riders wearing the backpacks of an app with whom they have at most a nominal freelancing relationship. In all cases there is an anomaly: a lot of control and a dearth of compliance, a perfect legal move to weaken worker rights.[104] While it is true that negotiating with suppliers on the market is undoubtedly more appropriate when it comes to acquiring technical skills that are peripheral to the core business, the acquisition of outside resources is often driven by the willingness to benefit from lower labour costs, given that the bargaining power of external providers is often weaker than that of internal personnel.

While we are busy shedding light on the demeaning working conditions of riders, cleaners and knowledge workers, we should not ignore the fact that the entire labour market runs the risk of facing a similar process of digitisation of management and platformisation, that is the replacement of stable relationships with instant, fragile contracts that are outside the scope of labour protection. This observation should induce us to treat the contractual arrangements typical of the gig-economy as pieces of the whole of non-standard forms of employment – without letting ourselves believe in platform work falling outside this definition.

C. The European Way: Strengthening the Social Dimension Step by Step

In the midst of the organisational gymnastics of these 'hyper weak superpowers', one might wonder how supranational institutions are trying to reinforce their imagined invincibility. More generally, what is the scope for intervention by governments and regulators?[105]

The usual dilemma applies. Are the rules already in place sufficient, or do we need specific measures to meet the new work-related challenges? This is no small matter. In the European Union, the fluid activism of its institutions, in particular the Commission and the Parliament (we have already reported on the clear position of the Court of Justice), should be noted. Recently, EU institutions have begun to give platform work the attention it deserves, by reassessing the regulatory fitness of all legislative measures aimed at reducing socioeconomic inequalities. Between 2016 and 2017, the 'European Pillar of Social Rights' (EPSR) has been launched to renew the European strategy to protect new forms of work while ensuring a proper functioning of the internal market.[106]

In the last five years, various instruments, including a communication on the collaborative economy, a Directive on 'transparent and predictable' working conditions, several Parliament resolutions and a Council recommendation on access to social protection, have reaffirmed the need to strengthen protection for all forms of work, including those enabled by digital tools.[107] This approach is very cautious, as it is assumed that, as far as possible, the existing legal toolbox should be used to the fullest extent possible to regulate situations that cannot be considered 'above and beyond' existing law.

At the end of 2019, the then newly appointed EU Commission President von der Leyen, in her letter of assignment sent to Labour Commissioner Nicolas Schmit, expressly mandated to 'monitor and promote the implementation of existing rules' and to 'improve working conditions for platform workers'.[108] Around the same time, Vice-President Margrethe Vestager, who was reappointed after a term as Competition Commissioner, challenged big platforms that abuse their data. The Commissioner also hinted that she would work on the issue of collective bargaining for platform workers (see below for more on this subject).

After a long period of neglect, there is growing engagement on the European 'social market economy' front. Although it mainly represents an amalgam of old and new principles, the EPSR, a document somewhere between a manifesto and a legal recommendation in the social field, responds to this logic – setting forth a charter of rights to counter the identity crisis of the European project by rebalancing the up till now visible tension between economic competitiveness and upward social convergence.[109] In this section, we will take stock of the latest initiatives while trying to imagine the direction that the Commission might take in the years to come.

Since the beginning of the 1990s, the EU has introduced legal instruments to legitimise and regulate non-standard forms of work. In particular, some EU Directives set out the principles of equal treatment between workers with fixed-term and permanent contracts, as well as between agency workers and those employed directly by the company. These regulatory instruments also required that part-time workers should not be treated less favourably than full-time workers. Labour lawyers have conflicting views on the interpretation of this 'chapter' of EU labour law. The objectives of the Directives are not perfectly aligned: while on the one hand, voluntary part-time work was encouraged, on the other hand, action was taken to limit abuses in the renewal of fixed-term contracts.[110] In spite of the difference in views, today, those non-standard forms of employment that are regulated at European level are considered 'the best of a bad job'.

Some critical issues have been mitigated by a compromise solution (so much so that temporary agencies, which have to meet a number of stringent financial and organisational criteria in order to operate, are alarmed by the unfair competition of digital labour platforms in their sector). One of the key limitations of this approach lies in the narrow and static personal scope of these instruments, which is inextricably linked to the existence of the employment relationship, as defined by the CJEU's case law.[111] Indeed, as recognised by professor Mark Bell, the risk is a stark polarisation between 'typified-atypical' workers and 'new' atypical working templates,[112] leaving too many aspects poorly regulated.[113] With a certain frustration, it must also be pointed out that after these Directives – in two cases the result of framework agreements between social partners – there has been a weakening of the momentum of social integration. The austerity programmes adopted in many EU countries during the early 2010s financial crisis and often channelled through international memorandums of understanding of dubious legal nature, have certainly not encouraged solidarity.[114]

The issue is all the more relevant if one considers that over the last 30 years, contrary to the myth about red tape imposed by the 'Brussels Eurocrats', it was also the EU that legitimised flexible formulas such as part-time, fixed-term and temporary work (and platform work, we will argue, is a peculiar combination of these models). At the time, the first reactions were harsh, and reflection on these measures has not yet been concluded. On the one hand, there are those who consider the so-called 'flexicurity' model to have failed in its implementation phase (only the flexibilisation part has been executed, to the detriment of the creation of quality jobs). On the other, there are those who recognise that atypical forms have contributed to ensuring a certain adaptability of the labour market in times of change. In any case, the 'integrated strategy' of flexicurity has only been partially realised.[115] Although the loosening of employment regulation has fostered a movement towards innovation in contractual formats, the strengthening of institutions responsible for providing unemployment benefits and facilitating transitions to new jobs has by no means counterbalanced it.

In June 2016, the Communication on the collaborative economy, a non-binding act of guidance with the aim of 'adapting and interpreting the existing regulatory framework', was published. Aware of the regulatory uncertainties that platforms have triggered, the Commission has reiterated its aim of creating a favourable environment for innovative economic initiatives and has sought to strengthen the rights and obligations of the players in this growing market. The text links the burden of prior authorisation for market access (licensing obligations or minimum quality requirements) to the nature of the activity carried out by the platform, ie to the 'underlying' service exchanged in addition to the IT service.

It is interesting to note that the Commission has identified the intensity of the 'influence' on the key terms and conditions of the service rendered and, more importantly, on the workers themselves as a key criterion for the classification as a service provider. In many legal systems, control is also a paramount criterion in the traditional assessment of the existence of the subordination of workers and, thus, of an employment relationship. It is, therefore, the addition of a classical employment law component into the toolbox of administrative and competition law.[116] Crucially, it is precisely the relationship between platforms and the workers that matters. The more intensively the former 'manage and organise the selection of the providers of the underlying services and the manner in which those underlying services are carried out – for example, by directly verifying and managing the quality of such services', the less likely it is that the company will be considered a mere technological intermediary.[117]

Addressing the question of worker classification, the Communication makes it clear that the existence of an employment relationship must be ascertained on a case-by-case basis, paying close attention to the manner in which the service is carried out, with regard to three cumulative indicators: 'the existence of a subordination link [something that corresponds generally to the control and economic reality tests of some common law jurisdictions]; the nature of work; and the presence of a remuneration'.[118] If the nature of the relationship between workers and platforms is key to defining the market in which they operate, the detection of an employment relationship ultimately drags platforms out of the ICT sector, removing them from the liberalised regime of the digital single market. For this reason, too, the Commission has urged Member States to assess the adequacy of their national rules.

The Parliament has repeatedly called on Member States to get ahead of the curve by modernising social security and collective bargaining legislation 'so as to stay abreast of technological developments while ensuring workers' protection'.[119] Although it contains declarations of intent on which there has been much negotiation, in some passages the parliamentary resolution seems light years ahead of the debate. First, it refers to the need to safeguard the right of workers to organise, and the right of collective bargaining and action. It then insists on a consideration that is taken for granted by labour law experts, but less so by the many, not disinterested factions, who praise the new business models: 'all workers in the [platform] economy are either employed or self-employed based on the primacy of facts and must be classified accordingly'.[120] *Tertium non datur.*

Despite some quibbles, the most concrete legislative result brought home by EU institutions is the Directive on transparent and predictable working conditions.[121] The history of this act is unusual in that it shows how the EU institutions seized the opportunity to update a Directive dating back to the 1990s to extend certain protections to new forms of work. To tell the truth, an atmosphere of excitement had surrounded this revision process, which ended up loading this instrument with expectations that were difficult to meet. Following lengthy negotiations, the final text ended up having a less than revolutionary scope. It should have been clear from the outset that a mere recasting of an instrument that, for the most part, merely imposed information obligations on the employing entities was unlikely to offer substantial answers to the multifaceted challenges posed by the digitalisation and casualisation of European labour markets. Therefore, before judging the legal intervention as too timid, it is necessary to contextualise its scope and accept the idea that correct, complete and timely information is an essential first step to improving working conditions. In practice, the Directive aims to fill some of the 'gaps in protection [that] have emerged for new forms of employment created as a result of labour market developments' in the last 30 years.[122]

To do so, it identifies from the outset certain categories of workers in need of protection because of their particular vulnerability: domestic workers, on-call workers, intermittent workers, voucher-based workers, platform workers, trainees and apprentices. The biggest criticism involves the subjective scope of the Directive – it concerns 'every worker in the Union who has an employment contract or employment relationship as defined by the law, collective agreements or practice in force in each Member State with consideration to the case law of the Court of Justice'.[123] Those who had hoped for a new and broader definition of 'worker' were confronted with an ambiguous formula. In short, despite the inclusive intentions, the least protected workers are likely to remain outside the scope of the Directive unless their employment status is recognised by a court. Sticking to traditional notions and interpretations of employment relationships may end up leaving outside the scope of protection legions of platform workers who will still be ostensibly classified as self-employed and will have to rely en masse on litigation to secure access to the full array of labour and employment rights.[124] Yet, a broad interpretation of its protective aims could lean towards the inclusion of non-standard workers in a deliberate way.[125] Once again, in this arena it will be necessary to sharpen our legal tools, especially in view of the transposition of the Directive (Members States have until August 2022 to implement the provisions in their domestic legislations).

What kind of information is required? Businesses with an entirely or mostly unpredictable organisation are obliged to inform the employee about the workforce management model, remuneration schemes and notice periods, so as to avoid the detrimental consequences of last-minute cancellations (this information can also be transmitted digitally). These provisions design a stable availability window, outside which workers cannot be penalised for refusing to show up and within which they must be compensated if a previously agreed slot is cancelled. The Directive also imposes restrictions on the use and, significantly, the duration of on-demand contracts. It even provides for the introduction of 'a rebuttable presumption of the existence of an employment contract with a minimum amount of paid hours based on the average hours worked during a given period' (Article 11). All in all, these are measures that could also improve the working conditions of platform workers. Therefore, it is to be hoped that, in the light of such clear and non-radical objectives, the Directive will be a good candidate for an extensive interpretation, in line with the measures implemented

by governments such as in Italy and Spain and the proposed Directive on platform work.

More specifically, in October 2020, the Commission adopted its 2021 Work
Programme, which includes a legislative proposal to improve the working conditions of platform workers and ensure adequate social protection.[126] Endorsed at
the Social Summit in Porto on 7 and 8 May 2021, The new 2021 'EPSR Action
Plan' includes two important legislative initiatives, notably on collective bargaining for autonomous workers who are in a vulnerable position, and on the working
conditions of platform workers.[127] In February 2021, the Commission began
consultations with the social partners in accordance with Article 154(2) of the
Treaty on the Functioning of the European Union (TFEU), requesting their opinion on the direction of EU action to improve the working conditions of those
working through digital labour platforms active in the EU. The second-stage
consultation was launched in June 2021, requesting European social partners to
submit their views on potential instruments for EU action.

In April 2021, a proposal for a Regulation on AI (AI Act) was presented.[128]
AI-systems 'used in employment, workers management and access to self-
employment, notably for the recruitment and selection of persons, for making
decisions on promotion and termination and for task allocation, monitoring or
evaluation of persons in work-related contractual relationships' are classified as
high-risk, 'since those systems may appreciably impact future career prospects
and livelihoods of these persons'.[129] These systems shall be subject to specific
transparency and oversight requirements toward the users of the systems with
the exception of non-professional persons entering into contact with the AI
tool. Disappointingly, the text of the proposal specifies that the assessment of the
conformity of these systems to existing rules will only be subject to an ex-ante self-
evaluation by the provider, with no 'involvement of a notified body'.

Worse still, the proposed Regulation seems to take for granted that if AI systems
used at work comply with the procedural requirements it sets forth, these systems
should be allowed. Such an approach is deeply debatable. Several EU national
legislations ban or severely limit the use of tech tools to monitor workers. The
draft Regulation risks prevailing over these more restrictive frameworks and triggering a deregulating landslide in labour and industrial relations systems around
Europe. While national rules often require involving the trade unions and works
councils before introducing tools allowing any form of tech-enabled surveillance,
the draft Regulation, instead, never specifically mentions any role of the social
partners in co-regulating AI systems at work. Consequently, considering that the
legal basis of the Regulation would be a liberalising one, aimed at harmonising
governance standards across the EU, the more protective national legislation risks
being overshadowed by this instrument that, in other words, could be functioning
as a 'ceiling' rather than a 'floor' for labour protection.

In September 2021, the Parliament approved a resolution calling for a European
framework to guarantee that people working for labour platforms have the same
level of social protection as standard workers of the same category.[130] This set of

rights should include social security contributions, responsibility for health and safety and the right to engage in collective bargaining to negotiate fair terms and conditions. Significantly, MEPs proposed a reversal of the burden of proof on the existence of an employment relationship: in case of litigation employers should prove there is no employment relationship. Moreover, the resolution lays down the right to transparent and non-discriminatory algorithms, ensuring the possibility of challenging automated decisions and asking to keep 'humans-in-the-loop'.

In December 2021, the European Commission proposed a new Directive on improving the conditions of platform workers. This instrument would principally apply to all platform workers, including domestic workers whose work is channelled via apps and, crucially, individuals who work for online platforms. The proposal extends full labour and employment protection to all platform workers who 'have, or who based on an assessment of facts may be deemed to have, an employment contract or employment relationship as defined by the law, collective agreements or practice in force in the Member States, with consideration to the case-law of the CJEU'.[131]

The proposed Directive provides a list of criteria to determine whether the platform asserts control. They encompass the determination of remuneration or key conditions of execution, supervision and assessment of the quality of performance, restriction of the freedom to organise one's work by preventing the refusal of task or use of substitutes and the limitation of the capacity to build a client base. If the platform fulfils at least two of those conditions, it is legally presumed to be an employer.[132] It is incumbent on platforms to prove that there is no employment relationship. While a presumption does not mean reclassification is always granted, the provision could be a game-changer in how employment status will be determined in court. Indeed, the set of indicators enshrines comparative jurisprudential *acquis* from the case law of several European countries, where courts have exposed the false nature of the self-employment status of platform workers and reclassified them as fully-fledged employees. The 'familiarity' of these elements should make reaching a political consensus around the proposal and transposing the Directive much smoother.

Nonetheless, there is still much room for improvement. Arguably, the current drafting of the indicators and the fact that at least two of them should be met to trigger the presumption risks making this provision scarcely operative, particularly for those workers, including online platform workers, who already face the most significant challenges in claiming employment status. For instance, 'supervising the performance of work' should already be sufficient for reclassification, as it already is the case under many domestic legislations. One can hardly see an improvement in the fact that this supervision should merely count as one of the indicators that would trigger a rebuttable presumption.

To complicate things further, Member States have started to intervene by regulating platform-mediated working arrangements. In Spain, Italy and France, where a binary distinction between employment and self-employment still applies (although the Italian and Spanish frameworks admit intermediate solutions such as 'quasi-subordinate' work and 'economically dependent self-employment', as we will see), policymakers have implemented diverse policy options. In Spain,[133] a specific, rebuttable presumption of the employment status for delivery riders was introduced in 2021, after a six-month process of tripartite social dialogue. Today, these riders fall within the scope of statutory labour protection, while platforms are engaged in heavy resistance, finding ways to flout the new rules.[134] Similarly, in 2015 and 2019, the Italian government expanded the full coverage of mandatory employment protection for self-employed workers whose work is organised by the principal, including through a digital platform.[135] Conversely, the 2016 French law defined a special regime: platforms must respect obligations relating to insurance and training for 'dependent' self-employed platform workers.[136] In the same vein, the 2019 French reform encouraged the adoption of codes of practice defining the rights and obligations of platform workers.

On the judicial front, platforms are embroiled in several lawsuits on the appropriate classification of workers. It is not possible to generalise specific judgments, as they are heavily fact dependent. However, while several decisions of lower instance courts produced mixed, and sometimes contradictory, outcomes, many higher courts across Europe moved towards determining the employment status of platform workers, or at least towards including them in the scope of labour protection.

Looking at the long catalogue of judicial parameters used by the courts in these judgments, some common threads emerge.[137] In particular, the idea that platform work is incompatible with employment status – a conviction that was very widespread among commentators and policymakers only a few years ago – has been thoroughly debunked in court, with arguments that also resonate with the CJEU case law.[138] Albeit unevenly, courts have refined the toolkit used to establish the existence of an employment relationship, interpreting in a modern way the classical criteria: employer's direction, organisational flexibility, economic reality, business integration, ownership of equipment and commercial risk. This has also allowed for a promising judicial dialogue both horizontally (among courts in different Member States) and vertically (between lower and higher courts within a country and at the comparative level).[139] Within this dialogue, a new social dimension could be developed that transcends domestic legal systems.[140] Domestic courts pay attention to what courts in other jurisdictions have concluded. This should not come as a surprise, seeing as in a very short time span there have been numerous judicial cases in various countries concerning the employment status of workers engaged and managed by the same multinational companies, applying analogous work conditions and replicating the same levels of business organisation.

Despite this, existing standards leave too much room for circumvention. In several jurisdictions, platform companies have reacted to negative legal outcomes by tweaking contractual terms or, more radically, refusing to comply with the relevant judgment under threat of leaving the local market.[141] Thus, it is now time to develop legislative solutions that offer more inclusive and innovative protections, not necessarily tailored to the new contractual models emerging from digitalisation, but sufficiently flexible to offer meaningful responses for all non-standard forms of work. Before doing so, however, it is critical to avoid any misconceptions about the ability of our regulatory frameworks to keep pace with change. We will discuss this issue in the next section.

III. Labour Law between Obsolescence and Resistance

Digital tools have profoundly altered the way work is carried out, and not always to the benefit of the workers' autonomy. There are too many cases in which 'progress' and technology have let us down. In many professional environments, workers are unfortunately confronted with top-down structures, tight schedules, intrusive methods and abuses of all kinds. It is also true that, traditionally, a good deal of workplaces are not particularly known for their contribution to people's agency, empowerment and wellbeing. Human power relations are hardly ever horizontal, even between co-workers, and are often fuelled by harassment, frustration and subjugation.[142] So why would it be the fault of hegemonic algorithms and platforms if human nature already seems prone to prevarication?

As we have previously attempted to argue, be careful not to fall into the trap of accepting 'that's the way it goes' for two main reasons. First, this isn't necessarily the case. 'Heterogony of ends' is a notion first described by German psychologist Wilhem Wundt in the late nineteenth century to caution against regarding goal-directed activities and frameworks that end up shaping motivations in ways that deviate from the original aims, and backfire. Many studies account for the unintended consequences that occur in highly authoritarian contexts.[143] Most of the time, the results obtained are the opposite of those intended – arbitrary systems may be responded to by the workforce through the development of a multifaceted system of avoiding impositions and conquering freedom,[144] combined with resistance movements that can lead to sabotage,[145] through an imperceptible yet inexorable divergence from top-down instructions. Literature shows how a context that supports personal autonomy – of action, and of judgement, too – is expected to increase the workers' responsibility, to foster their motivation, as well as to nurture new skills, fostered by the possibility of experimenting and diverging from conformism.[146] It has been proven that well-designed human resource management practices, inclusive and empathetic leadership models and a stimulating work environment have a significant impact on well-being and thus on relatedness, commitment and productivity.[147] Conversely, experts point out that when an instrument of domination turns into an end in itself, it ceases to be a good metric.[148] In simpler terms, if workers are obsessed with the idea of achieving a certain short-term result, in the manner described and within the timeframe imposed, the system quickly becomes distorted and unreliable for its inventors.

The second and much more relevant reason is that attempting to associate the failures of innovation with human error does not do justice either to technological development or to the achievements made over the centuries in mitigating the 'illiberal' structure of the employment relationship. Indeed, Hugh Collins observes that 'the contract of employment embraces an authoritarian structure that appears to be at odds with the commitment in liberal societies to values such as liberty, equal respect, and respect for privacy'.[149] The well-known analysis of Elisabeth Anderson conceptualises workplaces as undemocratic private governments.[150] Likewise, by reflecting on the workplace sovereignty of employers in the US, Gali Racabi likens their powers to those of kings.[151] It is undeniable that in the unique relationship between employers and workers authoritarian elements prevail in a one directional sense both before and during the course of the relationship – this is one of the many startling peculiarities of employment law, which makes this an exception in the field of contract law, However, various institutions, first and foremost those set forth by labour and employment regulation, have historically tried to counterbalance the dominant position of bosses and supervisors with a series of individual and collective countervailing factors.

In short, employers may exercise their prerogatives to organise, control and discipline the workforce, but in almost all legal systems they may not do so in an abusive or discriminatory manner. Process-based law is a shared trend in all EU countries' legal orders. For instance, redefining the tasks for which a worker has been hired is permitted, but regulation in many countries aims at avoiding that this results in harming their professionalism through demotion practices. Remote monitoring and data collection may be allowed, but many European countries do so only provided that works councils have been informed of the means of surveillance and that the most invasive forms of monitoring are banned. It may be lawful to unilaterally dismiss a worker, but never, at least in principle, on a whim. In most jurisdictions, the US being a conspicuous outlier here, it is essential to demonstrate that the reasons given to justify such a measure are genuine and effective or a reasonable notice of termination must be granted.

Despite the inevitable simplifications, an essential fact emerges. There is no doubt as to the allocation of powers. Most legal systems place the employers in a superior hierarchical position, legitimise their authority (which is extraordinary in a relationship between private individuals) and, at the same time, they constitutionalise and humanise it by tempering its excesses. On closer inspection, the endless discussions on the correct employment status under which to classify new work arrangements (including those mediated by digital platforms) are about this very recognition: the employment contract is a stunning organisational tool that generates an environment of efficient flexibility. The notions of control and subordination, which constitute common paramount indicators of the very existence of an employment relationship, are the 'gateway' for accessing labour rights and duties. Even before offering economic and employment security to workers, however, labour and employment regulation authorise sizeable managerial powers. In addition to this, in many industrialised countries checks and balances were put in place to avoid workplaces becoming an ecosystem bowing to the demands of the employer.

By its very nature, labour regulation has undergone major changes and does not lack adaptability. Thanks to its elastic nature, it provides instruments in line with the demands and needs of the productive system, even in highly unstable times such as the current ones.[152] Now we come to the point. A widespread awareness that employment regulation has a complex and multifaceted role is progressively emerging. This regulation is a field where contractual forces are tentatively brought to a delicate, dynamic equilibrium, in search of continuous compromises between freedom and equality, risk and solidarity, efficiency and protection. But it is also, and above all, a lens through which to observe the major transformations in society. It is therefore essential to establish a dialogue between the socio-economic reality and the existing regulatory systems, in order to test the robustness and future-proofing nature of the latter. It is here that a battle is being fought 'between the advocates of the emancipatory nature of the new organisational models and the assertors of their oppressive and commodifying character'.[153]

In this section, we focus on the resilience of labour regulation. It is worth noting that labour regulations were never aimed exclusively at workers in large vertically integrated firms. This is all the more so because the very first beneficiaries, employed in the construction or agricultural sectors, had nothing to do with blue- and white-collar workers. Labour regulation is only partially involved with industrial work, contrary to what is commonly believed. And even if those who allege the symbiosis between early twentieth-century industrial production models and social institutions were right, it would not make any sense to assume the obsolescence of labour regulation, given that many 'new' business models represent a digital revamping of very archaic schemes, typical of the proto-industrial putting-out system,[154] with one major difference: the current potential for control was unimaginable in that context.

NYU Law Professor Cinthia Estlund has observed that the hallmarks of the employment relationship, namely the possibility of dictating terms, appraising compliance and sanctioning wrongdoing, are now shared features in several professional contexts, challenging traditional assumptions that employees are preferred to external suppliers on the grounds of the wide managerial latitude afforded by this legal template.[155] The boss-worker pyramid embedded in centralised organisations is now spreading all over the labour market, without the corresponding entitlements compensating for the lack of agency that are enshrined in employment laws.[156] This power aggrandisement distorts the already weakened boundaries between legal categories. In the current discussions on the scope and extension of employment regulation, the use of digital technology as a tool to exaggerate tyrannical approaches cannot be neglected, as it can undermine the very foundations on which a broad set of protections are premised.[157]

While the canons of the classic employment relationship are being 'loosened', to borrow an expression from labour lawyer Riccardo Del Punta,[158] the possibilities of intensifying and multiplying that traditional bond of subjugation and control are increasing. Thanks to technology, the traditional parameters of work organisation are crumbling, and new highly hierarchical models are developing. While the employment relationship is 'pronounced dead' by many tech-enthusiasts and business lobbyists, its main hierarchical features are spilling beyond the borders of employment contracts. Many of the needs for protection enshrined in the wealth of rules that have come to shape and regulate work during the twentieth century remain valid; if at all, protection must be adapted to be much more inclusive as too many workers, and particularly women and minorities, were far too often ignored in the presumed 'golden era' of labour regulation. But the need for protection is more urgent than ever today when we are witnessing the revival of organisational templates, contractual arrangements and working conditions typical of past eras. It is also possible to be at the cutting edge in a sustainable way, as we argue in the next section.

A. Regulation, Flexibility and the 'Spirit' of Innovation

In an old episode of the *Wine for Normal People* podcast, Gaia Gaja – one of Italy's most iconic wine producers – shared a revealing anecdote about the secret of her wine's long-standing success.[159] In the middle of the last century, her grandfather Giovanni was obsessed with the idea of developing a superior Barbaresco wine by using high-quality raw materials. He would spend time walking through the vineyard getting rid of imperfect grapes with his pruning shears. In a time of austerity, just after the war, this practice was perceived as a sacrilege in the eponymous village of Barbaresco, in the district of Langhe, a hilly area at the foot of the western Alps. The *mezzadri*, the independent sharecroppers who tended the lands owned by the Gajas in exchange for a percentage of the harvest, believed that it was a true crime against Nature. Giovanni, however, was so fixated with excellence that he accepted the risk of producing less to raise the quality of his wine by adopting new techniques and experimenting with innovative processes. Still, the sharecroppers were dependent on volume, since their income depended on the quantity of grapes that they could collect: the more, the better.[160] Understandably, they were sceptical about this wasteful approach. To reassure them, but also to get them to follow his instructions, Giovanni decided to hire them as employees. As a result, they could work without worrying about the harvest. More importantly, they had to tolerate the landowner's eccentricities, and do as he said – even those who probably still disagreed with him.

You are probably wondering what this has to do with platform work, labour and tech. The story of the winery, which in 2019 celebrated its first 160 years in business and is now a global benchmark, is most certainly relevant. We have not written it down whilst under the influence of Giovanni's wine (not least because we cannot afford it). His approach is one that best illustrates the spirit of innovative enterprises. The story tells us a lot about the relationship between regulation, flexibility and innovation. It is a good example of mutualising business risk, integrating the production chain, making production more efficient, investing in long-term work relationships, aligning incentives between capital and labour and, last but not least, paying for organisational flexibility. The story of Gaja and the sharecroppers perfectly illustrates the argument we now intend to develop further.

Conventional wisdom often presents the relationship between regulation and innovation as a trade-off. However, contrary to predictions of the imminent demise of the standard employment relationship in the wake of technological disruptions and the rise of alternative business models, existing social institutions, in particular wage employment and its set of protections, can coexist well with the most advanced modernisation, even in the era of smart factories, hyper-digital systems and platform work. These long-established social institutions can act as true facilitators of innovation,[161] since they offer sustainable legal solutions to the needs of experimenting enterprises, thus easing impediments to investment and growth.

This case exemplifies a 'primordial' exchange between social protection and hierarchical organisational models. This arrangement (security in exchange for command) is crucial for companies, because it allows employers and managers to convey instructions to the workforce, to supervise their implementation and to evaluate the final result.[162] It can be seen as an essential tool for enabling rapid adjustment of production processes to new business needs or market demands, and results in a noteworthy combination of uniformity, speed and adaptability. When it comes to pursuing innovative strategies, flexibility and involvement of the workforce are indispensable – the employment relationship and employment regulation are the main vehicles that the legal systems of the vast majority of industrialised countries make available to achieve these objectives.[163] Let us together try to understand why and how.

We have been often told that the primary, if not exclusive, purpose of employment regulation is to protect workers. Certainly, strengthening the bargaining position of workers both in the market and during the relationship with their employers is a crucial objective of modern social protection. But this is a half-truth. Employment regulations have also been designed to give employers broad powers to manage labour. In legal terms, some systems label these rights 'employer powers'; in Anglo-Saxon countries they are more often indicated as 'managerial prerogatives'.[164] Painting a faithful representation of managerial authority in the lifecycle of working relationships represents a starting point when it comes to enforcing and reinforcing limits in both innovative and conventional sectors of the labour market.

Employer powers and managerial prerogatives are often taken for granted, as if they were a natural and irreversible accident. Yet they are not only the result of socio-economic factors such as the low bargaining power of workers or the ownership of the business organisation by the employer. On closer inspection, the employer's powers are legally grounded in labour regulations that incorporate positions of authority into the employment contract, in a way that is quite unique compared to other contracts.[165] These prerogatives are mainly threefold: the power to assign tasks and specify 'what needs to be performed in what order and time period' (direction);[166] the power to evaluate both the performance of such tasks and compliance with orders (supervision); and the power to sanction woefully inadequate or negligent performance of assigned tasks or even disobedience of legitimately given instructions 'so as to elicit cooperation and enforce compliance' (discipline).[167]

Commenting on the particularities of the employment contract at common law, in an illuminating piece of writing Hugh Collins concluded that there is an 'inherent tension between the contract of employment and both respect for civil liberties and respect for equality before the law'.[168] Some of these tensions, he argued, are 'misconceived as inherent in the legal institution when they are merely contingent'.[169] Nonetheless, he found, the institution of the contract of employment is 'in some respects both illiberal and inegalitarian'.[170] Drawing on Otto Kahn-Freund, Collins distinguished between employees' submission and subordination. The first occurs when they enter into a contract of employment whose terms are dictated or almost entirely dictated by the employer and 'where there may be no reasonable alternatives to earn an income but to take this job'. Subordination, instead, corresponds to an employee's 'being subject to the hierarchical control of the employer or manager'. This is, in his words, 'a power relationship constructed by the contract of employment and supported by the law',[171] or, even better, its reason for being.

The concept of subordination is, of course, well-known in the civil law tradition as the quintessential element of the contract of employment. What renders a work arrangement a contract of employment, according to the French Court of Cassation is the 'link of subordination' between the employer and the employee.[172] The French Labour Code provides that 'working time is the time during which the employee is at the employer's disposal and complies with her directives [...]'.[173] Subordination is what makes a worker an 'employee' according to the Italian Civil Code, as the Italian legal term for 'employee' is, in fact, *'lavoratore subordinato'*. The Civil Code also explicitly sanctions a hierarchical link existing between employers and their workers. Article 2086 provides that entrepreneurs are 'the heads [*capi*] of the firm and [their] collaborators hierarchically depend on [them]'. This article significantly reflects the cultural and political ideology of the fascist lawmakers who drafted the Civil Code in 1942. Although the legislation enacted during the democratic era materially 'tamed' its original intent, unlike other provisions governing the enterprise and labour relations, which were implicitly or explicitly abrogated as from the end of the fascist regime, Article 2086 is still considered to be in force. It perfectly conveys the idea of 'private government' as outlined by Elisabeth Anderson in her writings, namely the notion that authority and hierarchy sanctioned by the law can extend far beyond the State and public powers and manifest itself aggressively in the modern employment relationship.[174] Albeit Anderson primarily focuses on common law systems and particularly that of the US, the underlying power structure of the employment relationship is analogous to the one in civil law countries. In short, it is no coincidence that many legal systems refer to 'subordination' when talking about employees!

The presence of wide latitude in exercising powers at work is what traditionally distinguishes subordinate employment from self-employment in legal terms.[175]

As a reaction to the existence of these powers and as compensation for the obligations and duties that employees derive from them, in many legal systems employment regulation has gradually provided a series of safeguards and protections in favour of employees. Although this rule has slowly changed in several countries such as Spain, the UK, Canada, Austria and Italy, self-employed workers, who are not subject to the employers' powers, have not commonly received any specific legal protection.

The legally sanctioned powers of employers respond to precise economic and organisational needs of firms that were detailed by Nobel laureates in economics, Ronald Coase and Oliver Williamson. As argued above, Coase was the first to illustrate that their essential function is to enable firms to limit their costs.[176] Think of the expense, in terms of time and resources, of searching for and selecting other contractors in the market, and then finding information, negotiating terms of engagement, drafting contracts and executing them (as well as verifying the outcome). Imagine that you run a business, need workers and have to sit down and negotiate with each of them, come to an agreement and enforce it every time new work is needed, or you have to change previously established processes. It would be a permanent production paralysis, with unsustainable transaction costs. Gaja would have spent all his days discussing with the sharecroppers whether it was worth picking that unripe bunch. Firms exist (and decide to integrate vertically) in order to replace countless costly contractual transactions with hierarchical relationships that do not require them to agree, day by day, minute by minute, with their employees. There is an initial negotiation, and perhaps this is repeated periodically, but once an agreement has been reached, the parties accept that one will be able to direct the other without requiring their consent each time – an exception to general legal principle which postulates that any alterations made to a contract are invalid unless agreed upon by both parties.

Within advanced countries, the keystone on which the hierarchy that makes firms function rests, is precisely the employment relationship, an arrangement that is in itself incomplete and updatable,[177] capable of effectively synthesising a bundle of managerial powers that constitute the authority of the employer, in exchange for a promise of economic and contractual security. In a vertically integrated firm, these powers are often delegated to managers, the 'visible hand' of the entrepreneur, as economic historian Alfred Chandler called it.[178]

Giovanni Gaja decided to employ former sharecroppers as wage employees in order to pursue his own vision, but also, and above all, to be able to give detailed and binding orders on how to manage the harvest. He was looking for a contractual template that would allow for the fully-fledged exercise of managerial prerogatives. The employment contract was the perfect solution. Managerial powers allow employers to run their business and respond quickly to circumstances that could not be precisely foreseen when the contract was negotiated. In other words, they allow entrepreneurs not to have to continually obtain the consent of employees and make them vested with the authority to issue unilateral commands, within the limits of what is reasonable and legal, to monitor workers' performances and to sanction employees who do not comply with the rules.

Subordination and the managerial prerogatives that make the employment contract a crucial element of capitalist production did not come about by chance. Rather, they stem from precise legislative interventions introduced in pre-industrial times and at the dawn of industrialisation. Simon Deakin and Gillian Morris,[179] for instance, refer in their landmark textbook to the Master and Servant Acts enacted in Britain in the nineteenth century and to legislation passed in earlier times that provided for the abatement of wages and the imprisonment of servants and labourers for 'misdemeanour, miscarriage or ill behavior'.

Absconding from and refusing to work was also criminally sanctioned and the courts issued prison sentences for breach of servants' contractual obligations, a practice enshrined in legislation, together with sanctions for embezzlement of the goods and raw materials of their masters. Master and Servant legislation was also enacted in the British colonies, becoming a consistent feature of common law jurisdictions.[180] In the US, the so-called 'Black Codes' adopted in the Southern states after the end of the Civil War disciplined African-Americans by forcing them to enter into annual labour contracts, by making vagrancy a criminal offence punishable with penal labour and perpetuating slavery-like forms of domination.[181] In civil law countries, public and criminal regulation to police the workforce were introduced since the Ancien Régime. The legislation imposing the *livret du travail*, for instance, ensured that workers could not leave their workplace in search of another occupation without the consent of their employers or before having fully repaid any wage advance or outstanding debt towards them.[182] In France, workplace regulations issued unilaterally by masters were also a crucial way of establishing private forms of disciplinary powers. In the early decades of the nineteenth century, the *conseils de prud'hommes* and the *justices de paix* – also in accordance with the Revolutionary ideals of equality among citizens – refused to enforce these regulations unless it was proved that workers had genuinely agreed with their introduction. In the second half of the century, however, the higher courts, and particularly the *Cour de Cassation*, upheld their unilateral introduction by employers, and therefore, materially sanctioned the authority of the latter over the workforce.[183]

With time, custom, and practice, this authoritarian model of enforcing contractual obligations and labour discipline of servants and labourers seeped into the common law construction of the contract of employment and the civil law notion of subordination. Deakin and Morris observed that managerial prerogatives 'do not simply result from the employer's superior bargaining power prior to the agreement'.[184] They are 'underpinned by certain legal norms that today take the form of the common law implied terms of the contract of employment', such as the employees' obligation of fidelity and obedience, 'which can be traced back in many cases to the master and servant legislation of the nineteenth century and before'.[185]

These models have long constituted the legal framework of subordinate employment and have become an integral part of regulation in every country in the world. This regulation, therefore, does much more than protect workers. First, it assigns to management the unilateral power to direct, control and regulate human labour, and thus, ultimately the body and mind activities of other human beings; at the same time, it must reconcile these almost 'seignorial' prerogatives with respect for human dignity, which is essential for safeguarding the principle of equality in a democratic society. One of the fundamental tasks of modern employment and labour law is to rationalise and limit, one might say constitutionalise, the employers' powers.[186]

Algorithmic management threatens to disempower this model, as it allows bosses to dodge legal rules limiting the extent of managerial prerogatives. This dimension of employment regulation is far too often neglected in mainstream accounts of the employment relationship, particularly in economic debates and policymaking. It is high time for a much more attentive and critical analysis of these elements to be spread beyond labour law scholarship. This was the purpose of Elizabeth Anderson's writings on private government in the US. Commenting on these writings, the historian David Bromwich summarised her arguments as a claim that 'political theory should not stop at the door of the workplace'.[187]

To two Italian lawyers, this expression inevitably suggests the notion of 'bringing the Constitution into the factories'. This was a long-held demand of the Italian labour movement since the new democratic Constitution came into force in 1948. This Constitution, a remarkably progressive one at the time of its approval, protects crucial labour and employment rights, including freedom of association and the right to strike, the right to paid holidays and a fair and just remuneration, among others. The first two decades of the new constitutional era, however, were marked by intense political and labour conflicts whose effects reverberated within workplaces. Trade union representatives and members were commonly dismissed, demoted and 'confined' in 'punitive work units'. Although these conducts violated the spirit of the Constitution, there were no adequate legal tools to react to them. The legal framework for employment was still the one devised by the fascist regime that had introduced the Civil Code, with its strong deference to entrepreneurial powers and hierarchy. Only with the coming into force in 1970 of the *Statuto dei lavoratori*, could commentators acknowledge that the 'Constitution had entered the factory'.[188]

The *Statuto* had a strong collective rights component, inspired, among others, by the US' Wagner Act. It promoted trade union activity within the workplace, it established the right to appoint workers' representatives within work units, and prohibited anti-union discrimination and other unfair labour practices, including those conflicting with the constitutional right to strike. The most ground-breaking component of the *Statuto*, however, was the protection of individual workers' rights as a means to reinforce collective rights.[189] The new legislation provided a right to be reinstated in the workplace in the case of unfair dismissal in larger workplaces (and not only in the case of discrimination, as in other countries), a ban on arbitrary transfers to other work units, and, in the case of a demotion, a right to be reinstated to the previous post or a comparable one. A series of forms of protection of civil liberties at the workplace accompanied these provisions, including the right to freedom of speech at work, safeguards against arbitrary searches and a ban on employing armed guards to monitor workers.

Protections analogous to those of the *Statuto* have been enacted in many countries during the twentieth century and constitute an essential part of employment regulation in these systems.[190] In the last decades, however, employment and labour protection have often been criticised for being inefficient and obsolete.

Those who want to scrap employment protection should be asked how the suppression of those rights can be reconciled with a genuinely democratic society, but this would be an exercise in futility. Usually, they either do not know what employment regulation is about or do not think that the rule of law also applies at work. The pandemic offered a perfect demonstration of how business powers can be exerted cynically, without the necessary counterbalances. In dealing with the emergency, many governments first left it to the discretion of companies to decide whether to resort to remote working, presenting it in principle as a simple option and not as a compulsory practice whenever it was technically feasible. It was also left to the unilateral decision of companies to put their staff on furlough or force them to take leave and to decide whether to discontinue precarious and non-standard workers. Even when it came to identifying essential activities, the margin of choice left to businesses was very wide. In some cases, it took threats of trade union mobilisation to suspend work in many companies whose services were anything but essential. In small and medium-sized enterprises, where trade unions are often non-existent, the crisis marked an unprecedented expansion of de facto managerial powers, even when there was a risk of negative impacts on the health and safety of the workers involved and on society at large.

To conclude this section, we must refute some other clichés about the alleged inadequacy of existing legal and social institutions to respond to the changing needs of our economies. Employment regulation is often portrayed as a relic of the past. Considering how this regulation is pivotal to facilitate industrial and post-industrial forms of business production, on the one hand, and to protect democratic societies from the abuses of managerial dominance, on the other, mainstream theories must be rejected. It is an ideological hypothesis to justify any circumvention of existing protections on the pretext of their alleged inability to cope with present and future social challenges. This rhetoric is more aimed at reinstating the harshest experiences of the industrial and proto-industrial eras, providing command, control and discipline without any labour protection surrounding them.[191]

The casual and precarious nature of work arrangements is too often presented as the price to be paid for innovation, without distinguishing between those who renew their organisational models and introduce new tools to genuinely increase their productivity and those who argue that employment protection should be dismantled to allow us to order pizza via smartphone. The unilateral flexibility of platforms to decide minute by minute whom to hire and remunerate without any guarantees is thus marketed as an indispensable tool for the corporation of the future. What's more, it is often claimed that this flexibility is matched by the workers' ability to connect and work whenever they like. As we have heard in relation to the riders of the food delivery apps or the drivers of ride-hailing platforms, the intrusive and pervasive nature of certain organisational and control practices and the low pay makes this alleged flexibility a mirage,[192] mainly aimed at avoiding the perceived burdens of labour and employment regulations.[193]

Finally, there is another 'weapon of mass distraction' that is always armed when dealing with these issues – by offering employment protections, workers will lose the ability to work whenever they want; they will have to work fixed and rigid hours. In a world where flexible forms of work, free from fixed hours and places of work, without giving up any of the protections at work exist, and where technology makes it possible to calculate to the second who will be available to do what at any given time, these statements ring out as being deeply hypocritical. There is no basis for the argument that the flexibility to decide when and if to work is radically incompatible with the employment relationship, when periods of work are characterised by exposure to the control and discipline typical of subordination. It is important to note that flexible organisational modules can comfortably coexist with the employment contract, as decades of business innovations and case law have shown.

Unfortunately, some policymakers and courts still tend to regard rigid schedules as quintessential to employment. In the US, this is how some courts established that Uber drivers were self-employed and this is what the US Department of Labour under Trump's administration claimed. In Italy, when deciding on the employment status of food-delivery riders, some courts still applied 30-year-old judicial precedents on delivery work dating back to a time when there were no GPS to monitor the exact location and speed of delivery drivers, no algorithms to assign work and no consumer ratings to assess it (and smartphones were also a long way off). This kind of attitude has started to evolve.

Judges in many European countries have changed their approach on this point: there can be subordination even without time constraints. When managerial prerogatives are exercised by means of less visible digital tools, a worker's limited flexibility in deciding whether, when and where to provide their service should not exclude the possibility of them having access to the protective regime of labour law. To give an example, the Spanish Supreme Court[194] explained that, in a digitised labour market where workplaces are decentralised, workforces fragmented and organisations networked, the notion of dependence has become flexible. It can apply when a worker's contribution is functionally integrated into the company's core business.[195]

Workers could have a considerable amount of autonomy in the deployment of the allocated task – granted by programmatic orders or by a particular mode of organisation – yet they could still be subject to 'upstream' managerial power,[196] as the experience of large amounts of people working from home has also shown.

Instead, over-reliance on arrangements that are excluded from meaningful protection can result in lower productivity growth because this model erodes firm-specific skills and decouples managerial power from protective obligations.[197]

B. Moving Towards a Universal Model of Protection for Modern Times?

It is certainly true that the standard employment relationship was assumed to be doomed too early in the academic and public debate. Years ago, labour law scholar Guy Davidov put together some excellent arguments to refute this recurrent misconception.[198] Taking up a misquote attributed to Mark Twain, the paper was entitled: 'the reports of my death are greatly exaggerated'. One can certainly reflect on the capacity of the standard employment relationship model to offer answers to the changing contingencies of today's world of work, where discontinuity and instability prevail. But the eulogy for subordinate employment has often been wrongly delivered.

Nonetheless, it is undeniable that, for several decades now, in industrialised countries all over the world, the number of 'dependent' self-employed workers has grown considerably. This phenomenon has not had one single cause. Profound changes in business models since the 1970s, as well as the mentioned tendency to 'fissurise' companies by outsourcing ever larger parts of production processes to external suppliers, while exploiting the growing technological interconnection to maintain a strong coordination of these outsourced 'fragments' of the business, have played an essential role. The growth of the service sector to the detriment of manufacturing has been equally important, accompanied by a continuous erosion – both in terms of membership and influence – of those trade union and political movements that had the most represented workers in the twentieth century industry.

The law, especially in Anglo-Saxon countries, has favoured this disintegration by creating increasing hurdles to trade union organising and action and defanging the labour movement just when it was facing new business strategies. In many industrialised countries, the years between the 1970s and 1980s represented a moment of 'escape' from subordination and labour law. It was precisely at that time that companies began to resort to self-employment arrangements that often did not correspond to genuine managerial autonomy or economic independence of the worker. The savings in direct costs, in terms of wages and social contributions, and indirect costs, in terms of regulatory protection, were enormous. Sometimes, part of the tax and social security savings was paid to workers in the form of a higher net income than would have been paid in the case of employment. Obviously, it was not only about flagrant cases of evasion, but it is undeniable that there were abuses and that administrative and judicial controls failed to contain them.

All this has greatly broadened the boundaries of the grey area between employment and self-employment,[199] without any particular protection or sufficient strength on the side of contractors to compete and protect themselves 'with their bare hands' on the market. Not even when these workers were given more autonomy in managing their own work and schedules, and perhaps even the possibility of working for other clients, did they achieve the economic and organisational independence typical of a traditional self-employed person.

In the US, in the wake of gig economy, some commentators have proposed adopting an intermediate category of workers between employment and self-employment in order to partially shield platform workers without forcing platforms to comply with the bulk of labour law.[200] For the time being, however, nothing has been done about this,[201] except in California, where the platforms managed to get a huge 'free out of jail' card by means of a referendum.

After a landmark ruling of California Supreme Court in its *Dynamex* judgment, lawmakers passed a Bill, AB5, setting a three-pronged test to determine a worker's employment status. Businesses that seek to treat workers as independent contractors must show that: '(A) the person is free from the control and direction of the hiring entity in connection with the performance of the work, both under the contract for the performance of the work and in fact. (B) The person performs work that is outside the usual course of the hiring entity's business. (C) The person is customarily engaged in an independently established trade, occupation, or business of the same nature as that involved in the work performed'.[202] This test should, in principle, be used by courts for the purposes of applying the Californian Labor Code, the Unemployment Code and the Industrial Welfare Commission Wage Orders.[203]

After the Bill entered into force, platforms tried their best to litigate against the test, alleging that their contractors did not fall into it. They failed. In the meantime, they decided to engage in a political campaign to neutralise the impact of the new legislation. A referendum proposition – Prop 22 – was thus introduced to carve out an exemption for platforms workers from the law. During the November 2020 election, Californian voters were thus also asked to decide on adopting a 'Protect App-Based Drivers and Services Act'. The Act, aimed at excluding most platform workers from the application of the ABC test, was supported by many labour platforms, including by creating the appearance of grassroots endorsement by their workers. They invested an astounding reported $200 million on the campaign, placing ads everywhere and bombarding their users and workers with messages supporting the Proposition. They also portrayed the AB5 legislation as a lethal threat to the flexibility afforded by their business model. Californian voters approved the proposal. The investment immediately repaid itself abundantly. Uber's market value rose by 14 per cent, circa $9 billion (with a 'b') after the vote. As a result, the platform workers at issue are now classified as self-employed, with certain limited protections applying to them, including non-discrimination safeguards, a healthcare subsidy, reimbursement of some car expenses, occupational accident insurance and minimum earnings for effective working time.[204]

Unsurprisingly, the Uber CEO Dara Khosrowshahi declared: 'Going forward, you will see us more loudly advocate for new laws like Prop 22, which we believe strike the balance between preserving the flexibility that drivers value so much, while adding protections that all gig workers deserve [...] It's a priority for us to work with governments across the U.S. and the world to make this a reality'.[205] Launching a flagship white paper contributing to the European consultation on potential measures addressing platform work, the CEO said any EU regulation on platform work needed to be 'grounded in the principles drivers and couriers say are most important to them: flexibility and control over when and where they want to work'.[206] The 'independent plus' model sanctioned by Proposition 22, however, is mostly a cover up (recently, the Alameda County Superior Court ruled that it is unconstitutional, but appeals are expected). In Europe, a Prop 22-like model would only graciously concede rights that already apply to workers, including health insurance and non-discrimination, and strip them of most of the protection fought and won in court.

It ultimately boils down to an old 'third category' approach that had been advocated in the past to protect gig workers. It corresponds to a hybrid status between employment and self-employment, offering a fraction of the protection that workers would receive if they were classified as employees. This proposal is not unprecedented. Third categories, of course, vary extensively among countries, with some legal systems offering meaningful protection, as in the case of the UK, where 'workers' enjoy the right to the national minimum wage, collective labour rights, working time and non-discrimination protection. Yet, this is certainly not the case of the new Californian status. Pursuant to the new Californian model, platform workers there will still be entitled to more than ordinary independent contractors receive, it can be argued. But this is not a glass half-empty or half-full scenario.[207]

Proposals for a third category reflexively appear to be an easy solution, tailor-made for the manifold problems surfacing in the platform economy. That initial reaction, however, is tempered upon further study of the content and history of the implementation of the third category in other nations. In a paper co-authored with labour law professor Miriam A Cherry,[208] one of the authors of this book examined the experiences of other countries to learn winning strategies and regulatory fiascos. Indeed, the implementation of intermediate categories in various nations highlights both successes and problems. For instance, Canada's passage of legislation in the 1970s created a new category of 'dependent contractors' through revising the definition of 'employee' in various statutes. The practical result was to bring more workers within the scope of protection. A 'safe harbour' for workers, based on economic dependency, was introduced. The measure seems to have worked well in terms of expanding the coverage of the laws to a larger number of workers.

Contrarily, in Italy's experimentation with the in-between category, businesses were reported to be trying to take advantage of a discounted status of *quasi-subordination* to evade regulations applicable to employees. The quasi-subordinate category, in practice, created a loophole that resulted in less protection. Its adoption led to widespread arbitrage of the categories, with businesses moving employees into a 'bogus' status in the quasi-subordinate category. Through the years, the lawmakers attempted to make the requirement for a genuine recourse to quasi-subordinate arrangements more stringent, also reducing incentives and room for arbitrage. The result, however, was increased litigation and huge legal uncertainty, so that, since 2015, the lawmakers have started to significantly roll back quasi-subordination. In particular, the new law provided that all workers whose work is organised by the other party (basically all the quasi-subordinate) should be covered by labour and employment protection, unless a collective agreement signed by the most representative unions provides otherwise. After some initial discussion in lower courts, and some legislative adjustments, most Italian judges, including the Supreme Court, now deem that food-delivery riders fall under this legislation,[209] however the platforms' attempts to dodge its application are not over.[210]

Spain provides another notable example of a legal system that adopted a third category, but only for a very few workers. The law assumes that workers predominantly working for one business are economically dependent self-employed. Looking at the reasons for the limited use of this category, it comes down to a heavy burden of requirements to be met, including the use of a rigorous economic threshold. Germany's category of employee-like persons requires that workers rely predominantly on another entity for their total income, the need for social protection comparable to an employee and the personal nature of work performed on the basis of a contract for services (without staff). Both the Spanish and German cases arguably leave a great deal to be desired. Recent comparative studies have shown that the introduction of these intermediate categories has not sufficiently protected all workers in need of this protection.[211]

Adding a new category, among other things, expands the possibility for 'legal status shopping', thus shifting the grey zone between employment and self-employment somewhere else, without erasing it. This could also lead to an increase in the complexity of litigation, since there are disputes over the boundaries between three categories instead of two. In the UK it took going to the Supreme Court to have a final judgment ruling that Uber drivers fit the 'worker' intermediate category.[212] A few critical points also remain unresolved. Self-employed workers, including those who are in intermediate categories, often remain excluded from fundamental rights such as the prohibition of discrimination and trade union rights, which – also at European level – are de facto significantly restricted for those who are not subordinate.[213] In various countries, including Italy, France and the UK, different proposals have been proposed to make some fundamental labour protections universal, by trade unions and scholars close to the labour movement.[214]

A particularly important proposal was presented, at the international level, by the Global Commission on the Future of Work of the International Labour Organisation. The ILO is a specialised United Nations agency dealing with labour and is managed, uniquely among large international organisations, by 'tripartite' bodies made up of representatives of national governments, trade unions and employers' associations from around the world. In 2019, the ILO celebrated its centenary, having been established in 1919 by the Treaty of Versailles that ended World War I, on the consideration that 'universal and lasting peace can be established only if it is based upon social justice'. On the occasion of the centenary, the ILO decided to convene a Global Commission of 27 independent experts from academia, business and labour and from different geographical backgrounds.[215] The commission was mandated to formulate proposals to guide the work of the ILO during its second century. Among these, the Commission suggested the adoption of a Universal Labour Guarantee (ULG).

The ULG would encompass, first and foremost, the Fundamental Principles and Rights at Work that the ILO already considers universal and valid for all workers without distinction between the employees and the self-employed: freedom of association and the right to collective bargaining, elimination of forced labour, abolition of child labour and elimination of discrimination at work. The pursuit of these goals is already mandatory for all ILO Member States. The ULG would add to these universal rights the protection of occupational health and safety and the guarantee of 'limits on hours of work' and 'an adequate living wage'. For the Commission, these rights should be guaranteed regardless of employment status and would therefore also cover the self-employed. For the time being, the ILO has very loosely accepted the recommendation made by its independent experts. The Future of Work Initiative culminated in the adoption of the ILO Declaration for the Future of Work in 2019. The Declaration largely followed the path set out by the Global Commission, although it did not expressly endorse some of its most forward-looking proposals, including the Universal Labour Guarantee.[216] The very fact that it is being discussed, however, is a significant step forward in the debate on the future of work.

It is increasingly clear that international labour law can no longer protect only employees. In 2019, in adopting a landmark Convention against violence and harassment in the world of work, delegates of Member States, trade unions and employers at the ILO agreed that all workers, including the self-employed but also volunteers, those who have lost their jobs and those seeking them, should be protected against violent and harassing conducts. The universalism of certain protections is therefore progressively more central to labour discussions.

In this regard, a few years ago labour lawyers Mark Freedland and Nicola Countouris proposed a sort of 'Copernican revolution' in labour law. Instead of chiselling away at the boundaries between employment, self-employment and intermediate categories, labour law should protect everyone who predominantly 'works personally'.[217] All workers, regardless of employment status, should be protected unless they themselves employ other people or have the means, capital and customers to make them de facto small businesses. This proposal, recently supported by one of the authors of this book, acknowledges once and for all that the need for protection does not only concern workers in an employment relationship. And it acknowledges the fact that new technologies are blurring the line between employment and self-employment, allowing companies to expand their managerial prerogatives, including through software and algorithms, far beyond the notion of formal employment.

This is, of course, a sweeping and far-reaching idea that would require time and adjustment, including through collective bargaining. However, it would have the merit of overturning the current protective paradigm based on the burden to prove, often with insurmountable practical difficulties, that one is an employee rather than a self-employed person, with all the uncertainties that this entails. Moving in this direction would certainly mean a revision of the traditional legal categories. But, on closer inspection, the practical results might not be so distant from covering all limb (b) workers under employment and labour law from day one in the UK, a proposal endorsed by the Labour Party,[218] or from genuinely and evenly applying the 2015 reform on quasi-subordination in Italy that extends labour protection to all self-employed persons whose performance is organised by the principal. It would, however, be a more transparent and clearer way of extending labour and employment rights making amends for the fact too many self-employed workers have, until now, almost always been deliberately left without effective protection. It could also contribute to going beyond hierarchical relationships, introducing new models to empower organisations and involving workers in decision-making. A much needed overcoming of strict hierarchy schemes in the world of work, though, is totally unrealistic if the key criterion for the attribution of rights remains the concept of subordination.

The fact that an increasingly large segment of the non-waged workforce is deserving and in need of protection has emerged dramatically during the pandemic. Both in the US and in many European countries, lawmakers have adopted partial support measures for the self-employed. Measures have included cash payments to the self-employed such as the Self-Employment Income Support Scheme (SEISS) in the UK, extension of unemployment benefits, income subsidies and tax and mortgage breaks.[219] Sometimes these measures included casual and platform workers, with income-replacement schemes no longer dependent upon the existence of a standard employment relationship. Too often, however, despite the attempt to extend the social safety net beyond the boundaries of employment, these workers fell through the cracks of protection.[220] Hopefully, this partial inclusion of the self-employed in protective schemes will not vanish at the end of the current crisis, but instead be extended and become part of the structure, correcting the distortions and limitations that marked the emergency measures. The need to protect these workers is anything but contingent. It is therefore a positive thing that action was taken in their favour during the health emergency, but it must be understood once and for all that a new fundamental equilibrium is sorely needed in the direction of greater protection for all workers.

C. The Big Family of Non-Standard Forms of Employment

One of the most stubborn clichés circulating about platform work is the idea that it can be considered an entirely novel phenomenon, to be addressed with radical regulatory paradigm shifts. Without mincing words, this is not the case, much to the chagrin of pundits. Platform-mediated work is not significantly different from other forms of non-standard work that have gained prominence over the past 40 years.[221]

The term 'non-standard work' refers to the large family of jobs that depart from the standard employment relationship (SER). The SER is the form of work that is still the most common in the industrialised world, defined as full-time, permanent employment with a formal, direct relationship between the worker and the employer.[222] Non-standard work 'deviates' along several axes (temporal, spatial, degree of protection) from this form of work around which most employment rights and labour protection have been built.[223] Almost everywhere, the core of labour and employment protection as well as social security have been primarily designed around a prototype of worker and from a very gendered perspective.[224] Historically, the model of full-time work was mainly linked to a 'male breadwinner' model. This breadwinner was responsible for bringing home the wages, while women's work was often relegated to a secondary protective model (eg, homework) or was excluded from protection altogether (eg, unpaid care work).

Back to the future? It has been questioned whether 'organizing work in standard, hierarchical employment relations and internal labor markets in the post–World War II period may have been more of an historical irregularity than is the use of nonstandard employment relations'.[225] Turning to statistics, half of all new jobs created in the last decade have been non-standard, while over 25 per cent of the EU-28 workforce is engaged in casual and atypical forms of work.[226] In recent decades, non-standard work in industrialised countries has grown significantly not only in numbers but also in public perception. In the US the percentage of workers engaged in alternative arrangements – such as contractors, temporary agency workers, and on-call and gig workers – rose from 10.1 per cent in 2005 to 15.8 per cent in 2015.[227] Non-standard work now makes up around one in three jobs in OECD countries and 40 per cent in the European Union.[228]

The issue of 'precariousness' of non-standard workers has been at the heart of the debate about employment and labour issues for years. It is precisely for this reason that those most familiar with the evolution of the world of work in recent decades can barely keep their cool when non-standard work arrangements are presented as 'new' forms of work. Incidentally, we prefer the term 'non-standard work' to 'precarious work'.[229] First, not all non-standard forms of work are precarious. Workers who want to devote part of their time to other activities may, for example, prefer a part-time contract, as long as it has stable hours and decent remuneration (unfortunately, in most industrialised countries, this form is increasingly rare: much more frequent is an involuntary part-time model, where people work part-time not by choice, but due to lack of full-time opportunities, sometimes even working two or more part-time jobs). More importantly, precarious work extends a long way beyond non-standard work. Even permanent and full-time employment can be unstable and insecure, afflicted by low wages, unhealthy working environments, working hours not reconcilable with private life, lack of trade union protection and limited access to credit.

In this respect, yet another false myth should be dispelled. That is, the one that pits so-called 'insiders' (presumed to be 'protected', usually identified with anyone with a standard employment contract) against 'outsiders' (those excluded from the world of permanent, full-time work).[230] It is not as simple as it seems: precarious employment involves large amounts of standard employment. The insider-outsider distinction is, simply, a hallucination. On top of this, and somehow contradictorily, literature has supported the idea that non-standard forms of employment might result in a 'win-win' situation for workers and businesses. Conversely, research shows that the disadvantages seem to dominate for the workers, and particularly for already vulnerable groups, such as young workers, women with childcare responsibilities or migrants.[231] These arrangements transfer the costs of training, skill acquisition and capital investment, and the risks of variations in demand from employer to employee and welfare systems.[232]

What exactly is non-standard work? There are many possible classifications. We rely on the one adopted by the International Labour Office – the secretariat of the ILO, in a 2016 report – as a result of an in-depth discussion with experts selected by trade union movements, business associations and governments from all around the world.[233] The Office identified four macro-forms of non-standard work. First, temporary work, which includes all fixed-term work, including jobs for a given period of time, contracts for the completion of a particular project, and seasonal work (especially in the tourism, agriculture and food sectors). These jobs can be either long or short term, in the latter case they take the form of casual work or daily work, still prevalent in the economies of the global South, but certainly not unknown in other latitudes, especially in the countryside, in retail and in the hospitality sector.[234]

The ILO report also included part-time work in the list of non-standard arrangements; here people work less hours than average. This is the most stable form of part-time work and the one that is most compatible with other work and non-work activities. Part-time is said to be voluntary if it is the worker who chooses a reduced schedule, involuntary when it is due to the absence of full-time job offers. Among those workers in the EU employed part-time in 2017, over a quarter (26.4 per cent) did not voluntarily choose this working pattern. The highest shares of involuntary part-time work across the EU were recorded in Greece (70.2 per cent of part-time workers) and Cyprus (67.4 per cent), followed by Italy (62.5 per cent), Spain (61.1 per cent), Bulgaria (58.7 per cent), Romania (55.8 per cent), Portugal (47.5 per cent) and France (43.1 per cent).[235] Involuntary part-time work can lead to a permanent condition of underemployment, where workers spend as much time looking for jobs as they do working for pay.

The ILO also considers so-called marginal part-time as part-time work. In marginal part-time work, one does not know in advance if and when they will work because the employer reserves the right to call (and pay) the worker only if and when they are sure to use them (in Ireland, these types of arrangements were called 'if and when' contracts for a reason). These forms of work, somewhere between part-time and the most casual forms of temporary work, are increasingly widespread in industrialised countries and often have evocative names such as zero-hours contracts in the UK (meaning that the employer gives no guarantee of calling the worker), on-demand work in the Netherlands or on-call work in Germany (where they are often a specific form of the better known 'mini-jobs', a primary source of income for many households).[236] In Italy the terms 'on-call' or 'intermittent' work have been in use (but there have been many forms of work designed to offer the employer maximum flexibility in calling and paying the worker on an 'if and when' basis, such as voucher-based work). In the UK, an overview of statistics reveals that 30 per cent of the people who are on temporary contracts would rather have a permanent arrangement and regular work; a percentage close to 50 per cent among those on zero-hour contracts.[237]

Then there is 'multi-party' employment. This is how the ILO identifies those forms of work in which the worker's activity is directed or used wholly or partly by someone other than their employer, breaking the standard 'bilaterality' of employment contracts. It includes first and foremost agency work, a scheme in which an agency hires a worker and sends them 'on mission' to a user firm, which pays the cost of the work and a fee to the agency. But the category also includes subcontracting, franchising or other forms of supply-chains arrangements whereby increasingly larger parts of the business cycle are outsourced to other entities. Very often, however, principals are able to impose meticulous compliance with their own production standards and lowest-cost contractual conditions. In these cases, the workers of the subcontractor can end up paying the price of lower wages and unsatisfactory working conditions without being able to bargain directly with the 'lead' firm. In industrialised countries, the most unfavourable consequences of these labour-brokering practices are often found in the logistics and hospitality sectors and in the agri-food industry.

In addition, the grey area between employment and self-employment is becoming increasingly wide. Freelancers used to be knights without a fixed master who were free to offer their services to the highest bidder (their 'lance', therefore, was 'free').[238] Similarly, self-employment can be a liberating choice for those who want to avoid the constraints of subordination and are able to compete on the relevant market independently. For many self-employed workers, however, this is not the case. Principals impose the nominally 'self-employed' format in order to save on labour costs – which are much lower in terms of protection and expenses than in the case of employment – in the face of time or hierarchical constraints that are completely incompatible with the independence of true self-employment.[239] This is what is referred to as 'bogus' self-employment. Think of the many 'independent contractors' who do exactly the same job as people engaged as employees in comparable situations, and costing so much less in social security and taxation terms as well as in labour protection (no minimum wages, overtime, paid holidays etc).[240] The last form of non-standard work is 'dependent self-employment'. In this format, although some of the typical features of subordination, such as a strong power of direction on the part of the employer or a fixed compensation and hours, can be lacking, freelancers here are dependent on one or very few clients and have no independent access to the market. Thus, they are much more dependent on clients than traditional self-employed workers.[241] Many of the workers in the intermediate categories discussed in the previous section fall under this definition.

Why are we discussing these classifications? To explain how much platform work has in common with all these arrangements. The resemblance to temporary and casual work, as well as to some forms of 'marginal' part-time and on-demand work, is obvious; platform work is often carried out for short or very short periods (even a few minutes) with no guarantee of being offered new work at the end of each task.[242] The similarities with 'multi-party' employment should also not be overlooked. In fact, platforms play a very similar role to employment agencies.[243] Intermediaries operate within both remote and location-based work platforms. They may organise the supply and demand for specific jobs and even the execution of these jobs on behalf of other clients, who may be inexperienced in crowdwork operations, or they may provide workers with the means for the execution of the service, typically cars in transport services, in exchange for a percentage of the fees. In fact, the Parliamentary Resolution on a European Agenda for the collaborative economy stated that 'many intermediating online platforms' are 'structurally similar to temporary work agencies'.[244] All this obviously complicates the legal framework as well as the prospects for transparency and protection of workers and, in the event of a dispute, makes it even more difficult to correctly ascribe obligations and responsibilities. It can also pave the way to material abuses, as happened with some platforms in Italy and Spain.[245]

It is important to reflect on how platform work often falls into the grey area between employment and self-employment. Almost all platform workers are classified as self-employed by the platforms, who also exploit the fallacy under which these forms of work are perceived as 'amateurish' in nature. The reality, however, is much more intricate, given the inherent diversity of platform work, which can be regarded as anything but a homogeneous legal category. This is also due to the presence, alongside genuinely autonomous forms of work, of cases in which work autonomy is, quite simply, imaginary.

It is clear, therefore, that platform work is not a new phenomenon, nor is it unrelated to other consolidated trends. These include the erosion of standard employment, the reduction in the duration of jobs, but also the rise of intricate subcontracting and 'fissuring' schemes, or the increasing casualisation of work arrangements and the broadening of the grey area between self-employment and employment.

The analysis of platform work must therefore take into account what we already know about other non-standard forms of work. The ILO reports that although these can sometimes be 'stepping stones' to more stable contracts and better working conditions, this is by no means automatic. Adequate regulation is essential to prevent non-standard work from 'trapping' particularly the most vulnerable groups of workers – women, young people, migrants and the elderly – in a 'dead end' of short-term jobs and poor opportunities.[246] All too often, people tend to approach work and frame reforms with an eye only on the number of employed people (a figure often 'adulterated' by arbitrary classifications), forgetting that a functioning labour market is not only one that employs more people but also one that employs them meaningfully. Alarmed by the numbers of the unemployed and of the persons outside the labour force (those not even looking for a job), national governments, often pushed by international institutions such as the World Bank and the International Monetary Fund, have manifestly favoured quantity over quality of work, facilitating recourse to some non-standard forms of work, without worrying too much about what this entails in terms of the quality of work and its conditions.

Of course, the picture of non-standard work is not entirely grim: it can respond to genuine flexibility needs of workers and firms.[247] But it cannot be ignored that non-standard workers suffer from a substantial gap in protections and rights compared to others: lower wages for the same tasks, despite all prohibitions and non-discrimination principles, a dearth of opportunities for training and career development and poorer occupational health and safety standards. In addition, they have limited access to the protection of their rights through collective bargaining, which is sometimes also linked to the mistrust of the standard workforce towards temporary and contingent workers and the traditional difficulty of trade unions in dealing with them. Nevertheless, the obstacles to unionisation are also of a regulatory nature (in certain countries, anti-trust regulation does not allow the self-employed to unionise; the European Union institutions themselves, as we shall see, have a contradictory view on the matter). Many obstacles stem from the fear of those who have a temporary contract (be it short or long) joining a union or striking for fear of not having their contract renewed when it expires. These critical issues also affect platform work. The threat of unrest is stifled by companies using anti-union shutdowns or antitrust lawsuits.

In many continental European countries, over the last two decades lawmakers have progressively removed certain restrictions on the use of fixed-term and agency work. In particular, the obligation to provide objective reasons justifying why these contracts are entered into instead of resorting to standard employment has been, in alternating phases, severely limited or eliminated. It has not been considered, however, that removing these constraints would have encouraged firms to meet their needs, even permanent ones, by increasingly resorting to temporary work. This is why we cannot pretend to ignore the fact that reliable regulation has a strong impact in shaping the behaviour of companies.

Nor can it be ignored that once the regulation of non-standard arrangements is loosened, it is extremely difficulty to re-regulate them, by increasing the protection for workers, as firms adjust their business models to the new deregulated reality and, as a consequence, this reality becomes irreversible. To give an example, in 2018 the Italian government introduced a mild measure to re-regulate temporary work, which brought the regulation of these arrangements back to the level of protection of comparable countries such as France and, more recently, Spain thanks to the labour-market reform agreed among government, the trade unions and employers.[248] The new rules were felt as an unacceptable imposition by a very vocal part of the Italian business world. Many commentators focused only on how many workers would hypothetically be left out in the cold because of the new legislation. The same charade was performed some years earlier when voucher-based work schemes were restricted, after previous reforms had blown their use out of proportion to their original purpose and to international best practices, whereby vouchers are only used for domestic work and odd jobs. Despite non-standard work routinely making headlines, few ever question the quality of these jobs in terms of wages, protection and opportunities.

All eyes are focused on the number of people employed, while the analysis of working conditions is constantly postponed. The same, unfortunately, happens with platform work. Opinion leaders present every regulatory intervention as an aggravation that will only lead to the reduction of jobs or, to 'undeclared work', as if undeclared work were a legitimate option and not a practice to be addressed with more resources to support the activities of labour inspectorates, which are often underfunded and understaffed. We believe, instead, that this entrenched downward spiral of working conditions and protection should be reversed, rather than resigning ourselves to sacrificing every regulatory possibility on the altar of the number of people employed. In the final chapter this book proposes a new map for the era of radical digital advancements.

---

[1] O Solon, 'The rise of "pseudo-AI": how tech firms quietly use humans to do bots' work' *The Guardian* (6 July 2018) www.theguardian.com/technology/2018/jul/06/artificial-intelligence-ai-humans-bots-tech-companies.

[2] The ecosystem of platforms is very diverse, including payment systems (Paypal or Revolut), social networks (Facebook and TikTok), entertainment businesses (Spotify or Netflix) or information providers (Google News and Reddit), and services related to mobility and hospitality (ShareNow and AirBnB). Where the element of renting or purchasing a good prevails, the personal services associated with the exchange are ancillary to the main activity. See generally J Van Dijck, T Poell and M De Waal, *The Platform Society. Public Values in a Connective World* (Oxford, Oxford University Press, 2018). Apart from a few quick strolls into neighbouring areas, this chapter exclusively deals with platforms that exchange work.

[3] V Dubal, 'Digital Piecework' (*Dissent*, Autumn 2020) www.dissentmagazine.org/article/digital-piecework.

[4] A Aloisi, 'Commoditized workers: case study research on labor law issues arising from a set of "on-demand/gig economy" platforms' (2016) 37(3) *Comparative Labor Law & Policy Journal* 653–90.

[5] B Rogers, 'Employment rights in the platform economy: getting back to basics' (2016) 10 *Harvard Law Policy Rev* 479–520; see also O Lobel, 'The gig economy & the future of employment and labor law' (2017) 1 *University of San Francisco Law Review* 51–73.

[6] N Lomas, 'Uber lobbies for "Prop 22"-style gig work standards in the EU' (*TechCrunch*, 15 February 2021) https://techcrunch.com/2021/02/15/uber-lobbies-for-prop-22-style-gig-work-standards-in-the-eu/.

[7] V De Stefano, 'The rise of the "just-in-time workforce": On-demand work, crowdwork and labour protection in the "gig-economy"' (2016) 37(3) *Comparative Labor Law & Policy Journal* 471–504.

[8] As *The Guardian* put it: you can summon 'chips and vodka on New Year's Eve, say, and then aspirin on New Year's Day'. S Subramanian, 'How our home delivery habit reshaped the world' *The Guardian* (21 November 2019) www.theguardian.com/technology/2019/nov/21/how-our-home-delivery-habit-reshaped-the-world.

[9] *O'Connor et al. v Uber Technologies, Inc.*, No. 13-03826-EMC (N.D. Cal. 2015). *Cotter et al. v Lyft Inc.*, Order Denying Cross-Motion for Summary Judgement, No. 13-cv-04065-VC (N.D. Cal. 2015).

[10] CEPS, EFTHEIA and HIVA-KU Leuven, 'Study to Gather Evidence on the Working Conditions of Platform Workers. VT/2018/032 Final Report' (2020).

[11] OECD, 'Gig Economy Platforms: Boon or Bane?' in *Economics Department Working Paper 1150* (OECD, 2019); S Riso, *Mapping the Contours of the Platform Economy* (Working Paper, Eurofound, 2019). A Pesole, C Urzi Brancati, E Fernández Macías, F Biagi and I González Vázquez, *Platform Workers in Europe* (Luxemburg, Publications Office of the European Union, 2018).

[12] C Urzì Brancati et al, *Digital Labour Platforms in Europe: Numbers, Profiles, and Employment Status of Platform Workers* (Luxemburg, Publications Office of the European Union, 2019).

[13] J Berg, 'Income security in the on-demand economy: findings and policy lessons from a survey of crowdworkers' (2016) 37(3) *Comparative Labor Law & Policy Journal* 543–76.

[14] Consultation Document Second-phase consultation of social partners under Article 154 TFEU on possible action addressing the challenges related to working conditions in platform work (SWD(2021) 143 final).

[15] ILO, World *Employment and Social Outlook 2021: The role of digital labour platforms in transforming the world of work* (International Labour Office, Geneva, ILO, 2021).

[16] J Berg and H Johnston, 'Too good to be true? A comment on Hall and Krueger's analysis of the labor market for Uber's driver-partner' (2019) 72(1) *ILR Review* 39–68. Together with other researchers and academics who have been working on the gig economy for years, we promoted an 'Open Letter on Principles for Ethically Sustainable Research on the Gig Economy'. The text is available on Medium at https://medium.com/@gigeconomyresearchersunited/open-letter-and-principles-for-ethical-research-on-the-gig-economy-3cd27924cc08.

[17] L Zingales, 'Uber and the Sherlock Holmes principle: How control of data can lead to biased academic research' (*ProMarket–Stigler Center*, 9 October 2019) https://promarket.org/2019/10/09/uber-and-the-sherlock-holmes-principle-how-control-of-data-can-lead-to-biased-academic-research/.

[18] A Piasna, 'Counting Gigs: How Can We Measure the Scale of Online Platform Work?' (ETUI Research Paper, 2020).

[19] K Frenken and J Schor, 'Putting the sharing economy into perspective' (2017) 23 *Environmental Innovation and Societal Transitions* 3–10.

[20] A Malhotra and M Van Alstyne 'The dark side of the sharing economy ... and how to lighten it' (2014) 57(11) *Communications of the ACM* 24–27; JB Schor, W Attwood-Charles, M Cansoy, I Ladegaard and R Wengronowitz, 'Dependence and precarity in the platform economy' (2020) 49(5) *Theory and Society* 833–61.

[21] See also Communication of 2 June 2016, A European agenda for the collaborative economy (https://ec.europa.eu/transparency/documents-register/detail?ref=COM(2016)356&lang=en) (a central section is devoted to 'labour law and worker classification').

[22] Eurofound, *New forms of employment* (Luxembourg, Publications Office of the European Union, 2015).

[23] Focusing on three specific types of platform work 'on-location platform-determined work: low-skilled work allocated by the platform and delivered in person; on-location worker-initiated work: low to moderately skilled work where tasks are selected and delivered in person; online contest work: high-skilled online work, where the worker is selected by the client by means of a contest'. The study analyses the complexity of the many profiles by taking into account the composition of the workforce, the regulatory environment, the degree of autonomy and intensity of control, access to social protection, issues related to skills, training and career prospects, as well as income and related tax and social security. Eurofound, *Employment and working conditions of selected types of platform work* (Luxembourg, Publications Office of the European Union, 2018).

[24] The term 'crowdsourcing' was coined in 2006. See J Hove, 'The Rise of Crowdsourcing' (*Wired*, 1 June 2006) www.wired.com/2006/06/crowds/.

[25] ILO, 'Work for a Brighter Future, Report of the Global Commission on the Future of Work, 2019', available at www.ilo.org/global/publications/books/WCMS_662410/lang--en/index.htm; Pesole et al (n 11). J Berg et al, *Digital labour platforms and the future of work, Towards Decent Work in the Online World* (Geneva, International Labour Organisation, 2018).

[26] A Sundararajan, *The Sharing Economy: The End of Employment and the Rise of Crowd-Based Capitalism* (Cambridge, MIT Press, 2016). But see R Calo and A Rosenblat, 'The Taking Economy: Uber, Information, and Power' (2017) 117 *Columbia Law Review* 1623–90.

[27] R Botsman and R Rogers, *What's Mine is Yours. The rise of collaborative consumption* (New York, HarperBusiness, 2011). For a critical perspective, see T Slee, *What's Yours is Mine: Against the Sharing Economy* (New York, O/R Books, 2015).

[28] U Huws, *Reinventing the Welfare State: Digital Platforms and Public Policies* (London, Pluto Press, 2020).

[29] AJ Ravenelle, *Hustle and Gig: Struggling and Surviving in the Sharing Economy* (Oakland, University of California Press, 2019).

[30] S Cagle, 'The sharing economy was always a scam' (*OneZero*, 3 March 2019) https://onezero.medium.com/the-sharing-economy-was-always-a-scam-68a9b36f3e4b.

[31] M Jeffery, 'Not Really Going to Work? Of the Directive on Part-Time Work, "Atypical Work" and Attempts to Regulate It' (1998) 17(3) *Industrial Law Journal* 193–213. See also J Murray, 'Social justice for women? The ILO's Convention on part-time work' (1999) 15(1) *International Journal of Comparative Labour Law and Industrial Relations* 3–19. D McCann, 'Equality through Precarious Work Regulation: Lessons from the Domestic Work Debates in Defence of the Standard Employment Relationship' (2014) 10(4) *International Journal of Law in Context* 507–21.

[32] J Prassl, *Humans as a Service: The Promise and Perils of Work in the Gig Economy* (Oxford, Oxford University Press, 2018).

[33] C Codagnone, F Biagi and F Abadie, *The Passions and the Interests: Unpacking the 'Sharing Economy'* (Luxemburg, JRC Science for Policy Report, 2016).

[34] S Butler, 'Deliveroo accused of "creating vocabulary" to avoid calling couriers employees' *The Guardian* (5 April 2017) www.theguardian.com/business/2017/apr/05/deliveroo-couriers-employees-managers?CMP=gu_com.

[35] *The Economist*, 'Workers on tap' (*The Economist*, 30 December 2014) www.economist.com/leaders/2014/12/30/workers-on-tap. The expression is coupled with Uber's promise to make 'transportation that is as reliable as running water'. See Uber, 'Transportation That Is As Reliable As Running Water' (*Uber Blog*, 4 September 2015) www.uber.com/en-au/blog/melbourne/transportation-that-is-as-reliable-as-running-water/. See also J Ticona, *Left to our own devices: Coping with insecure work in a digital age* (Oxford, Oxford University Press, 2022).

[36] E Pollman and JM Barry, 'Regulatory entrepreneurship' (2016) 90(3) *Southern California Law Review* 383–448.

[37] P Coccorese, 'Protestano i lavoratori di Foodora: "Siamo sottopagati, non fate più ordinazioni"' (*La Stampa*, 9 October 2016) www.lastampa.it/torino/2016/10/09/news/protestano-i-lavoratori-di-foodora-siamo-sottopagati-non-fate-piu-ordinazioni-1.34784341/.

[38] IZA, 'Social Protection Rights of Economically Dependent Self-Employed Workers' 2013 IZA Research Report No. 54, 19.

[39] S Greenhouse, 'False Freedom: Sharing the Scraps from the Perilous Gig Economy' (*Literary Hub*, 7 August 2019) https://lithub.com/false-freedom-sharing-the-scraps-from-the-perilous-gig-economy/; S Steward, 'Five myths about the gig economy. No, Uber drivers don't have much flexibility' *The Washington Post* (24 April 2020) www.washingtonpost.com/outlook/five-myths/five-myths-about-the-gig-economy/2020/04/24/852023e4-8577-11ea-ae26-989cfce1c7c7_story.html.

[40] D Georgiou, '"Business Risk-Assumption" as a Criterion for the Determination of EU Employment Status: A Critical Evaluation' (2021) *Industrial Law Journal*.

[41] In *Sorry We Missed You* (2019), Ken Loach depicts the inhumane situation of a worker 'onboarded' with a parcel delivery company on a zero-hour contract, still under the thumb of the manager, who dictates routes, shifts and targets.

[42] J Tolentino, 'The gig economy celebrates working yourself to death' (*The New Yorker*, 22 March 2017) www.newyorker.com/culture/jia-tolentino/the-gig-economy-celebrates-working-yourself-to-death.

[43] Case C-217/05 *Confederación Española de Empresarios de Estaciones de Servicio v Compañía Española de Petróleos SA* [2006] ECR I-11987; Case C-97/08 *Akzo Nobel NV and Others v Commission of the European Communities* [2009] ECR I-8237.

[44] Employment Tribunal, *Mr Y Aslam, Mr J Farrar and Others v Uber*, Case Numbers: 2202551/2015 & Others.

[45] J Woodcock and M Graham, *The Gig Economy: A Critical Introduction* (Cambridge, Polity, 2019).

[46] ILO, *World Employment and Social Outlook 2021: The role of digital labour platforms in transforming the world of work* (Geneva, International Labour Office, 2021).

[47] N van Doorn, E Mos and J Bosma, 'Disrupting "Business as Usual": How COVID-19 is impacting platform-mediated labor and social reproduction' (*Platform Labor*, 11 May 2020) https://platformlabor.net/blog/disrupting-business-as-usual; S Emerson, 'The coronavirus puts

restaurants at the mercy of the tech industry' (*OneZero*, 4 May 2020) https://onezero.medium.com/the-coronavirus-puts-restaurants-at-the-mercy-of-the-tech-industry-e104f6e670f4.

[48] R Roy, 'Doordash and Pizza Arbitrage. There is such a thing as a free lunch' (*Margins*, 17 May 2020) www.readmargins.com/p/doordash-and-pizza-arbitrage.

[49] See also D Evans, 'Uber and Lyft rides are more expensive than ever because of a driver shortage' (*CNBC*, 1 September 2021) www.cnbc.com/2021/08/31/why-uber-and-lyft-rides-are-more-expensive-than-ever.html.

[50] R Roroohar, *Don't Be Evil: How Big Tech Betrayed its Founding Principles – and All of Us* (New York, Currency, 2019). T Scholz, *Uberworked and Underpaid: How Workers are Disrupting the Digital Economy* (Cambridge, UK and Malden, USA, Polity Press, 2017).

[51] D Khosrowshahi, 'An Operating System for Everyday Life' (*Uber Blog*, 26 September 2019) www.uber.com/newsroom/everyday-life-os/.

[52] This also applies to rule-makers. In 2019, the French Parliament adopted a new law on social mobility orientation. As long as a social responsibility charter was approved between the platform and administrative authorities, the provisions of the agreement could not have been used in court to bring a reclassification lawsuit. This would have egregiously undermined the possibility for drivers and couriers to challenge an inappropriate contractual label, thus preventing the courts from carrying out their own assessment when ruling on a reclassification lawsuit. This section of the law was deemed unconstitutional by the French Constitutional Court. Law 2019-1428 (24/12/2019) on mobility orientation (LOM). See Conseil Constitutionnel, Décision n° 2019-794 DC 20/12/2019.

[53] Paragraph 11, R198 – Employment Relationship Recommendation, 2006 (No. 198). See International Labour Office, *Regulating the employment relationship in Europe: A guide to Recommendation No. 198* (Geneva, International Labour Office, 2013). The Court of Justice of the European Union has repeatedly held that 'the essential feature of an employment relationship is that, for a certain period of time, a person performs services for and *under the direction* of another person, in return for which he receives remuneration'. Case C-216/15 *Betriebsrat der Ruhrlandklinik v Ruhrlandklinik* [2016] EU:C:2016:518. N Countouris, 'The Concept of "Worker" in European Labour Law: Fragmentation, Autonomy and Scope' (2018) 47(2) *Industrial Law Journal* 192–225. E Menegatti, 'Taking EU Labor Law Beyond the Employment Contract: The Role Played by the European Court of Justice' (2020) 11(1) *European Labour Law Journal* 26–47. S Deakin, 'The Comparative Evolution of the Employment Relationship' in G Davidov and B Langille (eds), *Boundaries and Frontiers of Labour Law* (Oxford, Hart, 2006).

[54] Article 3(2) Proposal for a Directive of the European Parliament and of the Council on improving working conditions in platform work COM(2021) 762 final 2021/0414 (COD).

[55] V De Stefano et al, *Platform Work and the Employment Relationship* (Geneva, International Labour Organization, 2021). See also S Garben, *Tackling social disruption in the online platform economy* (Brussels, FEPS Policy Paper, 2019).

[56] The unilateral wording of the clauses regulating the relationship leaves no room for the possibility of negotiating better or even different treatment than that envisaged and drawn up by the company. In the Anglo-Saxon world, such agreements are called clickwrap or clickthrough. J Tomassetti 'Algorithmic Management, Employment, and the Self in Gig Work' in D Das Acevedo (ed), *Beyond the Algorithm: Qualitative Insights for Gig Work Regulation* (Cambridge, Cambridge University Press, 2020); NJ Davis, 'Presumed assent: The judicial acceptance of clickwrap' (2007) 22(1) *Berkeley Technology Law Journal* 577–98; MJ Radin, *Boilerplate: The Fine Print. Vanishing Rights, and the Rule of Law* (Princeton, Princeton University Press, 2014).

[57] C Cant, *Riding for Deliveroo. Resistance in the New Economy* (Cambridge, Polity Press, 2020). See also Focus on Labour Exploitation, 'The gig is up: Participatory research with couriers in the UK app-based delivery sector' (Participatory Research Working Paper 3, 2021).

[58] A Rosenblat, *Uberland: How algorithms are rewriting the rules of work* (Oakland CA, University of California Press, 2018). See also A Shapiro, 'Between autonomy and control: Strategies of arbitrage in the "on-demand" economy' (2018) 20(8) *New Media & Society* 2954–71.

[59] MA Cherry, 'Employment Status for "Essential Workers": The Case for Gig Worker Parity' (2021) 55(2) *Loyola of Los Angeles Law Review*.

[60] K Howson, F Ustek Spilda, A Bertolini, R Heeks, F Ferrari, S Katta and M Cole, 'Stripping back the mask: Working conditions on digital labour platforms during the COVID-19 pandemic' (2022) *International Labour Review*.

[61] A Cefaliello, 'Beyond status: the long road towards effective health and safety rights for on-demand workers' (*UK Labour Law Blog*, 16 June 2021) https://uklabourlawblog.com/2021/06/16/beyond-status-the-long-road-towards-effective-health-and-safety-rights-for-on-demand-workers-by-aude-cefaliello/.

[62] B Merchant, 'Coronavirus is speeding up the amazonification of the planet' (*OneZero*, 19 March 2020). https://onezero.medium.com/coronavirus-is-speeding-up-the-amazonification-of-the-planet-21cb20d16372. L Smiley, 'The Shut-in Economy' (*Matter*, 25 March 2015) https://medium.com/matter/the-shut-in-economy-ec3ec1294816.

[63] N Van Doorn and A Badger, 'Platform capitalism's hidden abode: producing data assets in the gig economy' (2020) 52(5) *Antipode* 1475–95.

[64] J Woodcock, 'The algorithmic panopticon at Deliveroo: Measurement, precarity, and the illusion of control' (2020) 20(3) *Ephemera* 67–95. J Dzieza, 'Revolt of the Delivery Workers' (*Curbed*, 13 September 2021) www.curbed.com/article/nyc-delivery-workers.html.

[65] Tribunal of Bologna, Order no. 2949/2019, 31 December 2020, 19. C Safak and J Farrar, 'Managed by Bots. Data-Driven Exploitation in the Gig Economy' (London, Worker Info Exchanges, 2021) www.workerinfoexchange.org/wie-report-managed-by-bots.

[66] Tribunal Supremo, 'Sala de lo Social' Case 4746/2019 (2020); Cour de Cassation, Chambre Sociale, Arrêt 374 (19-13.316, 2020).

[67] A Marshall, 'Uber changes its rules, and drivers adjust their strategies' (*Wired*, 2 October 2020) www.wired.com/story/uber-changes-rules-drivers-adjust-strategies/.

[68] Woodcock (n 64).

[69] S Silberman and L Irani, 'Operating an employer reputation system: Lessons from Turkopticon. 2008-2015' (2016) 37(3) *Comparative Labor Law & Policy Journal* 505–42.

[70] W Däubler, 'Challenges to labour law' in A Perulli (ed), *L'idea di diritto del lavoro, oggi. In ricordo di Giorgio Ghezzi* (Padova, Cedam, 2017).

[71] M Finkin, 'Beclouded work in historical perspective' (2016) 37(3) *Comparative Labor Law & Policy Journal* 603–18. See also VD Dubal, 'The Time Politics of Home-Based Digital Piecework' (2020) *The Future of Work in the Age of Automation and AI c4ejournal*; S Moore and K Newsome, 'Paying for free delivery: dependent self-employment as a measure of precarity in parcel delivery' (2018) 32(3) *Work, Employment and Society* 475–92.

[72] K Gregory, '"My Life Is More Valuable Than This": Understanding Risk among On-Demand Food Couriers in Edinburgh' (2020) 235(2) *Work, Employment and Society* 316–31. See also P Bérastégui, *Exposure to psychosocial risk factors in the gig economy: a systematic review* (Brussels, European Trade Union Institute, 2021).

[73] A Booth, 'Buenos Aires judge bans delivery apps after road accidents spike' *The Guardian* (16 August 2019) www.theguardian.com/cities/2019/aug/16/buenos-aires-judge-bans-delivery-apps-after-road-accidents-spike.

[74] O De Simone, 'Napoli, rider aggredito di notte dal branco: denunciati un 15enne e un 17enne' (*Il Mattino*, 5 September 2021) www.ilmattino.it/napoli/cronaca/napoli_rider_aggredito_branco_denunciati_minorenni-6177214.html.

[75] A Newman, 'DoorDash Changes Tipping Model After Uproar From Customers' *The New York Times* (24 July 2019) www.nytimes.com/2019/07/24/nyregion/doordash-tip-policy.html?smid=url-share.

[76] J Stanford, 'Bring your own equipment and wait for work: Working for Uber is a lot like being a dock worker a century ago' *The Star* (17 November 2019) www.thestar.com/business/opinion/2019/11/17/bring-your-own-equipment-and-wait-for-work-working-for-uber-is-a-lot-like-being-a-dock-worker-a-century-ago.html.

[77] J Meijerink, A Keegan and T Bondarouk, 'Having their cake and eating it too? Online labor platforms and human resource management as a case of institutional complexity' (2020) *The International Journal of Human Resource Management* 1–37; J Rubery and F Wilkinson, 'Outwork and segmented labour markets' in F Wilkinson (ed), *The Dynamics of Labour Market Segmentation* (London, Academic Press, 1981).

[78] T O'Reilly, *WTF?: What's the future and why it's up to us* (New York, Harper Collins, 2017); GF Davis, 'What might replace the modern corporation? Uberization and the web page enterprise' (2016) 39(2) *Seattle University Law Review* 501–16.

[79] M Piore and C Sabel, *The Second Industrial Divide: Possibilities for Prosperity* (New York, NY, Basic Books, 1984).

[80] In many judicial systems the 'Uber Pop' version (the service for non-professional drivers) was banned for unfair competition or non-compliance with transport regulation. J Posaner and M Heikkilä, 'Uber loses London operating license' (*Politico Europe*, 25 November 2019) www.politico.eu/article/uber-loses-london-operating-license-over-pattern-of-failure/.

[81] When asset specificity, uncertainty and frequency are high, firms may find it more convenient to grow in a vertically integrated fashion, establishing a non-market governance system. HA Simon, 'A formal theory of the employment relationship' (1951) 19(3) *Econometrica* 293–305; OD Hart and

J Moore, 'On the design of hierarchies: Coordination versus specialization' (2005) 113(4) *Journal of Political Economy* 675–702.

[82] T Goodwin, 'The battle is for the customer interface' (*TechCrunch*, 4 March 2015) https://tech crunch.com/2015/03/03/in-the-age-of-disintermediation-the-battle-is-all-for-the-customer-interface/. MC Munger, *Tomorrow 3.0: Transaction costs and the sharing economy* (Cambridge, Cambridge University Press, 2018).

[83] B Holmström, and J Roberts, 'The boundaries of the firm revisited' (1998) 12(2) *Journal of Economic Perspectives* 73–94.

[84] WW Powell, 'Neither market nor hierarchy: Network form of organization' in BM Staw and LL Cummings (eds), *Research in Organizational Behavior* (Greenwich, Conn.: JAI Press, 1990).

[85] RJ Gilson, CF Sabel and RE Scott, 'Contracting for innovation: Vertical disintegration and inter-firm collaboration' (2009) 109(3) *Columbia Law Review* 431–502. See also L Corazza and O Razzolini, 'Who is an employer?' in MW Finkin and G Mundlak (eds), *Research Handbook in Comparative Labor Law* (Cheltenham, Edward Elgar Publishing, 2015).

[86] TW Malone, J Yates and RI Benjamin, 'Electronic markets and electronic hierarchies' (1987) 30(6) *Communications of the ACM* 484–97. See also M Castells, *The Rise of the Network Society* (New York, Wiley, 2010).

[87] DS Evans and R Schmalensee, *Matchmakers: The New Economics of Multisided Platforms* (Boston, MA, Harvard Business School Press, 2016).

[88] GG Parker, MW Van Alstyne and S Paul Choudary, *Platform Revolution: How Networked Markets are Transforming the Economy and How to Make Them Work for You* (New York, WW Norton & Company, 2016).

[89] A Aloisi, 'Hierarchies Without Firms? Vertical Disintegration, Outsourcing and the Nature of the Platform' (2020) 8 *Quaderni del Premio Giorgio Rota* 11–32. See also E Tucker, 'Towards a political economy of platform-mediated work' (2020) 101(3) *Studies in Political Economy* 185–207.

[90] J Tomassetti, 'Does Uber redefine the firm? The postindustrial corporation and advanced information technology' (2016) 34(1) *The Hofstra Labor & Employment Law Journal* 1–78. See also F Zhu and M Iansiti, 'Why some platforms thrive and others don't' (*Harvard Business Review*, January–February 2019) https://hbr.org/2019/01/why-some-platforms-thrive-and-others-dont.

[91] JR Deckop, R Mangel and CC Cirka, 'Getting more than you pay for: Organizational citizenship behavior and pay-for-performance plans' (1999) 42(4) *Academy of Management Journal* 420–28. See also N Foss and Klein, 'No boss? No thanks' (*AEON*, 14 January 2019) https://aeon.co/essays/no-boss-no-thanks-why-managers-are-more-important-than-ever; R Sennett, *The Corrosion of Character: The Personal Consequences of Work in the New Capitalism* (New York and London, 1998).

[92] Tomassetti (n 90).

[93] U Muehlberger, *Hierarchies, relational contracts and new forms of outsourcing* (ICER Working Paper, 2005, No. 22).

[94] KVW Stone, *From Widgets to Digits: Employment Regulation for the Changing Workplace* (New York, Cambridge University Press, 2004).

[95] A De Franceschi, 'Uber Spain and the "Identity Crisis" of Online Platforms' (2018) 1 *Journal of European Consumer and Market Law* 1–4.

[96] United States District Court, Northern District of California, *O'Connor et al. v Uber Technologies, Inc., et al.*, Order Denying Cross-Motion for Summary Judgement, 11 March 2015, Document 251.

[97] Opinion of Advocate General Szpunar delivered on 11 May 2017, *Asociación Profesional Elite Taxi v Uber Systems Spain*, para 52.

[98] A Spicer, 'No bosses, no managers: The truth behind the "flat hierarchy" façade' *The Guardian* (30 July 2018) www.theguardian.com/commentisfree/2018/jul/30/no-bosses-managers-flat-hierachy-workplace-tech-hollywood.

[99] H Collins, 'A Review of The Concept of The Employer by Dr Jeremias Prassl' (University of Oxford, Faculty of Law, 10 November 2015) www.law.ox.ac.uk/content/labour-law-0/blog/2015/11/review-concept-employer-dr-jeremias-prassl.

[100] A Wiener, 'Our ghost-kitchen future' *The New Yorker* (20 June 2020) www.newyorker.com/news/letter-from-silicon-valley/our-ghost-kitchen-future. See also P Haek, 'Cities' next headache: Ultrafast grocery delivery' (*Politico*, 26 January 2022) www.politico.eu/article/ultrafast-grocery-delivery-city-europe-eu/.

[101] B Rogers, *Data and Democracy* (Cambridge MA, MIT Press, 2022).

[102] D Weil, *The Fissured Workplace* (Cambridge, MA, Harvard University Press, 2014).

[103] D Weil, 'Call Uber and Lyft drivers what they are: employees' *Los Angeles Times* (5 July 2019) www.latimes.com/opinion/op-ed/la-oe-weil-uber-lyft-employees-contractors-20190705-story.html.

[104] N Srnicek, *Platform Capitalism* (Cambridge, Polity, 2016).

[105] D Méda, *The Future of work: The meaning and value of work in Europe* (Geneva, ILO Research Paper, No. 18, 2016).

[106] Commission Recommendation of 26 April 2017 on the European Pillar of Social Rights, C(2017)2600 final; Interinstitutional Proclamation on the European Pillar of Social Rights (2017/ C 428/09); European Commission, 'Statement of President Juncker on the Proclamation of the European Pillar of Social Rights' (2017), available at https://ec.europa.eu/commission/presscorner/ detail/en/STATEMENT_17_4706. For a development, see European Commission, 'The European Pillar of Social Rights Action Plan', COM(2021)102 final, Communication from the Commission (4 March 2021). See S Garben, 'The European Pillar of Social Rights: An Assessment of its Meaning and Significance' (2019) 21 *Cambridge Yearbook of European Legal Studies* 101–27.

[107] V Hatzopoulos, *The Collaborative Economy and EU Law* (Oxford, Hart Publishing, 2018).

[108] Ursula von der Leyen, Mission letter to Nicolas Schmit, Commissioner-designate for Jobs (2019).

[109] V Schmidt, *Europe's Crisis of Legitimacy: Governing by Rules and Ruling by Numbers in the Eurozone* (Oxford, Oxford University Press, 2020). See also M Sandbu, 'Europe has rediscovered the social market economy' (*Financial Times*, 19 December 2021) www.ft.com/content/c6760232-80cc-4a2 5-a1a1-7315f620b63c.

[110] Directive 97/81 of 15 December 1997 concerning the Framework Agreement on part-time work, Directive 1999/70 of 28 June 1999 concerning the Framework Agreement on fixed-term work, and Directive 2008/104 of 19 November 2008 on temporary agency work.

[111] N Countouris, 'EU Law and the Regulation of "Atypical" Work' in A Bogg, C Costello and ACL Davies (eds), *Research Handbook on EU Labour Law* (Northampton, MA, Edward Elgar, 2016) 253.

[112] M Bell, 'Between Flexicurity and Fundamental Social Rights: The EU Directives on Atypical Work' (2012) 1 *European Law Rev* 31–48. See also A Broughton et al, 'Flexible Forms of Work: "Very Atypical" Contractual Arrangements' (EurWork Observatory, 2010); A Aloisi, 'Platform Work in the European Union: Lessons Learned, Legal Developments and Challenges Ahead' (2022) 13(1) *European Labour Law Journal* 4–29.

[113] S Deakin, 'New forms of employment: Implications for EU-law – The law as it stands' (European Labour Law Network – 7th Annual Legal Seminar, The Hague, 2014).

[114] S Deakin and A Koukiadaki, 'The sovereign debt crisis and the evolution of labour law in Europe' in N Countouris and M Freedland (eds), *Social Europe and the Crisis of Idea(l)s* (Cambridge, Cambridge University Press, 2013); S Garben, C Kilpatrick and E Muir, 'From Austerity Back to Legitimacy? The European Pillar of Social Rights: A Policy Brief' *EU Law analysis* (2017).

[115] J López, A de le Court and S Canalda, 'Breaking The Equilibrium Between Flexibility And Security – Flexiprecarity as the Spanish Version of the Model' (2004) 5(1) *European Labour Law Journal* 22–42.

[116] For a USA perspective, see P Akman, 'Online Platforms, Agency, and Competition Law: Mind the Gap' (2019) 43(2) *Fordham International Law Journal* 209–319.

[117] European Commission, Communication from the Commission to the European Parliament, the Council, the European Economic and Social Committee and the Committee of the Regions, A European agenda for the collaborative economy COM/2016/0356 final 02/06/2016.

[118] ibid.

[119] European Parliament, Resolution on an 'European agenda for the collaborative economy' 2017/2003(INI) – 15/06/2017.

[120] ibid.

[121] Directive (EU) 2019/1152 of the European Parliament and of the Council of 20 June 2019 on transparent and predictable working conditions in the European Union. See B Bednarowicz, 'Delivering on the European Pillar of Social Rights: The New Directive on Transparent and Predictable Working Conditions in the European Union' (2019) 48(4) *Industrial Law Journal* 604–23.

[122] Recital 5.

[123] The CJEU has repeatedly held that 'the essential feature of an employment relationship is that, for a certain period of time, a person performs services for and under the direction of another person, in return for which he receives remuneration, the legal characterisation under national law and the form of that relationship, as well as the nature of the legal relationship between those two persons, not being decisive in that regard'. Case C-216/15 *Betriebsrat der Ruhrlandklinik v Ruhrlandklinik* [2016] EU:C:2016:518. What is more, according to settled case law, the control test can also be passed in case of tenuous elements of subordination. Case C-232/09 *Dita Danosa v LKB Līzings SIA* [2010] EU:C:2010:674. See also L Nogler, *The Concept of 'Subordination'* (Trento, Università degli Studi di Trento, 2009). Thanks to its institutional legitimacy, the CJEU has progressively adopted a wide-ranging

and relaxed notion of subordination, which 'does not require an employer to be constantly watching over the shoulders of a worker'. ibid at para 96.

[124] CJEU, Case C-692/19 *B v Yodel Delivery Network Ltd* [2020] EU:C:2020:288 (adopting a rather formalistic approach, without going far enough so as to provide useful elements to update the classical analysis of the existence of an employment relationship).

[125] M Risak and T Dullinger, *The Concept of 'Worker' in EU Law: Status Quo and Potential for Change* (Brussels, ETUI Research Paper, 2018).

[126] Communication of 19 October 2020, 'Commission Work Programme 2021' (COM(2020) 690).

[127] See https://ec.europa.eu/commission/presscorner/detail/en/qanda_21_821. S Fernandes and Kerneïs, 'The Porto Social Summit: Turning Principles into Actions' (*Jacques Delors Institute*, 3 May 2021) https://institutdelors.eu/en/publications/sommet-social-de-porto-passer-des-principes-a-laction/.

[128] Proposal for a Regulation of the European Parliament and of the Council laying down harmonised rules on Artificial Intelligence (Artificial Intelligence Act) and amending certain Union legislative acts COM(2021) 206 final.

[129] Recital 36 of the Proposed Regulation. See also Annex III of the Proposed Regulation ('AI systems intended to be used for recruitment or selection of natural persons, notably for advertising vacancies, screening or filtering applications, evaluating candidates in the course of interviews or tests'; and 'AI intended to be used for making decisions on promotion and termination of work-related contractual relationships, for task allocation and for monitoring and evaluating performance and behavior of persons in such relationships').

[130] European Parliament resolution of 16 September 2021 on fair working conditions, rights and social protection for platform workers – new forms of employment linked to digital development (2019/2186(INI)).

[131] Recital 16, ibid.

[132] M Kullmann, '"Platformisation" of Work: An EU Perspective on Introducing a Legal Presumption' (2022) 13(1) *European Labour Law Journal* 66–80.

[133] Jefatura del Estado, 'Real Decreto-ley 9/2021, de 11 de mayo, por el que se modifica el texto refundido de la Ley del Estatuto de los Trabajadores, aprobado por el Real Decreto Legislativo 2/2015, de 23 de octubre, para garantizar los derechos laborales de las personas dedicadas al reparto en el ámbito de plataformas digitales' (2021) 113 BOE 56733.

[134] J Muldoon, 'How Gig Economy Corporations Are Circumventing Spain's Labour Laws' (*Tribune*, 14 August 2021) https://tribunemag.co.uk/2021/08/how-gig-economy-corporations-are-circumventing-spains-labour-laws.

[135] Law No. 128/2019 amending Decree 101/2019 on urgent measures for the protection of work.

[136] Law 2016-1088 (8/8/2016) on labour, the modernisation of social dialogue and securing of professional careers. See new Article L. 7341-1 and Article L. 7342-1 of the French Labour Code. See B Palli, 'Regulation of Platform Work in France: From Voluntary Charters to Sector-Wide Collective agreements?', *Mutual Learning Programme, DG Employment, Social Affairs and Inclusion* (European Commission, 2020).

[137] C Hießl, 'Case Law on the Classification of Platform Workers: Cross-European Comparative Analysis and Tentative Conclusions' (2022) *Comparative Labour Law & Policy Journal*, available at https://papers.ssrn.com/sol3/papers.cfm?abstract_id=3839603; De Stefano et al (n 55).

[138] Case C-256/01 *Debra Allonby v Accrington & Rossendale College* [2004] ICR 1328; Case C 413/13 *FNV Kunsten Informatie en Media v Staat der Nederlanden* [2014] EU:C:2014:2411.

[139] Case C-66/85 *Deborah Lawrie-Blum v Land Baden-Württemberg* [1986] ECR 2121. This trend has resulted in the development of an almost independent meaning of the term 'worker', which was originally established by the CJEU to expansively define the scope of the fundamental freedom of the movement of workers. The purpose is to avoid endangering uniformity at the domestic level by restrictive transpositions excluding certain forms of work from the application of EU labour law. See C-434/15 *Asociación Profesional Elite Taxi v Uber Systems Spain* [2014] EU:C:2017:981. The CJEU stated that '[...] Uber determines at least the maximum fare by means of the eponymous application, [...] the company receives that amount from the client before paying part of it to the non-professional driver of the vehicle, and [...] it exercises a certain control over the quality of the vehicles, the drivers and their conduct, which can, in some circumstances, result in their exclusion' (para 39).

[140] S Sciarra, 'Integration Through Courts: Article 177 as a Pre-Federal Device' in S Sciarra (ed), *Labour law in the Courts* (Oxford, Hart Publishing, 2001).

[141] K Ewing, 'Don't be fooled, Uber is still dodging the minimum wage' (Institute of Employment Rights, 17 March 2021) www.ier.org.uk/comments/dont-be-fooled-uber-is-still-dodging-the-minimum-wage/. See also J Jolly, 'Deliveroo unveils plans to pull out of Spain in wake of "rider law"' *The Guardian*

(30 July 2021) www.theguardian.com/business/2021/jul/30/deliveroo-unveils-plans-to-pull-out-of-spain-in-wake-of-rider-law.

[142] WH Whyte, *The organization man*, (Philadelphia, University of Pennsylvania Press, 2013).

[143] JG Goodale, S Rabinowitz and MA Morgan, 'Effects of top-down departmental and job change upon perceived employee behavior and attitudes: A natural field experiment' (1978) 63(1) *Journal of Applied Psychology* 62–72.

[144] E Tippett, CS Alexander and ZJ Eigen, 'When Timekeeping Software Undermines Compliance' (2017) 19(1) *Yale Journal of Law and Technology* 1–76.

[145] M Stelmaszak Rosa and A Aaltonen, 'As firms collect their data, employees learn to game the system' (*LSE Blog*, 16 January 2020) https://blogs.lse.ac.uk/businessreview/2020/01/16/as-firms-collect-their-data-employees-learn-to-game-the-system/.

[146] RA Jr. Karasek, 'Job Demands, Job Decision Latitude, and Mental Strain: Implications for Job Redesign' (1979) 24(2) *Administrative Science Quarterly* 285–308. A Wrzesniewski and JE Dutton, 'Crafting a Job: Revisioning Employees as Active Crafters of Their Work' (2001) 26(2) *Academy of Management Review* 179–201; BA Groen, MJ Wouters and CP Wilderom, 'Employee Participation, Performance Metrics, and Job Performance: A Survey Study Based on Self-Determination Theory' (2017) 36 *Management Accounting Research* 51–66.

[147] See generally R Bregman, *Humankind: A Hopeful History* (London, Bloomsbury Publishing, 2020); N Raihani, *The Social Instinct: How Cooperation Shaped the World* (London, Jonathan Cape, 2021).

[148] See M Strathern, '"Improving Ratings": Audit in the British University System' (1997) 5(3) *European Review* 305–21.

[149] H Collins, 'Is the Contract of Employment Illiberal?' in H Collins, G Lester and V Mantouvalou (eds), *Philosophical Foundations of Labour Law* (Oxford, Oxford University Press, 2018).

[150] Here the notion of managerial prerogatives can extend far beyond the State and public powers. E Anderson, *Private Government: How Employers Rule Our Lives (and Why We Don't Talk about It)* (Princeton, Princeton University Press, 2017).

[151] G Racabi. 'Abolish the Employer Prerogative, Unleash Work Law' (2022) 43 *Berkeley Journal of Employment and Labor Law* 79–138.

[152] K Rittich, 'Between workers' rights and flexibility: Labor law in an uncertain world' (2010) 54(2) *Saint Louis University Law Journal* 565–83.

[153] R Del Punta, 'Un diritto per il lavoro 4.0' in A Cipriani, A Gramolati and G Mari (eds), *Il lavoro 4.0* (Firenze, Firenze University Press, 2018) 225–50.

[154] H Pruijt, 'Repainting, modifying, smashing Taylorism' (2000) 13(5) *Journal of Organizational Change Management* 439–51.

[155] C Estlund, 'Rethinking Autocracy at Work' (2017) 131(3) *Harvard Law Review* 795–826.

[156] AJ Wood, *Despotism on Demand* (Ithaca, Cornell University Press, 2020).

[157] V Mantouvalou, '"I Lost My Job over a Facebook Post: Was that Fair?" Discipline and Dismissal for Social Media Activity' (2019) 35(1) *International Journal of Comparative Labour Law and Industrial Relations* 101–25.

[158] Del Punta (n 153).

[159] Ep 305: Gaia Gaja on the Past and Future of Barbaresco and Piedmont, Italy. Available at https://winefornormalpeople.libsyn.com/ep-305-gaia-gaja-on-the-past-and-future-of-barbaresco-and-piedmont-italy. This section also draws upon A Aloisi and V De Stefano, 'Regulation and the future of work. The employment relationship as an "innovation facilitator"' (2020) 159(1) *International Labour Review* 47–69.

[160] J Stiglitz, *Incentives and risk sharing in sharecropping* (1974) 41(2) *Review of Economic Studies* 219–55.

[161] W Däubler 'Erleichterung von Innovationen-eine Aufgabe des Arbeitsrechts?' (2004) 59 *Betriebs-Berater*, 2521–25.

[162] HA Simon, 'Organizations and markets' (1991) 5(2) *Journal of Economic Perspectives* 25–44.

[163] L Boltanski and E Chiapello, *The New Spirit of Capitalism* (London, Verso, 2005).

[164] See generally S Young, 'The question of managerial prerogatives' (1963) 16(2) *ILR Review* 240–53.

[165] A Supiot, *Critique du droit du travail* (Paris, Presses Universitaires de France, 1994); see also SA Marglin, 'What do bosses do? The origins and functions of hierarchy in capitalist production' (1974) 6(2) *Review of Radical Political Economics* 60–112; R Edwards, *Contested Terrain: The Transformation of the Workplace in the Twentieth Century* (New York, Basic Books, 1982).

[166] KC Kellogg, MA Valentine and A Christin, 'Algorithms at Work: The New Contested Terrain of Control' (2020) 14(1) *Academy of Management Annals* 366–410.

[167] ibid.

[168] Collins (n 149) 66.

[169] ibid, 66–67.

[170] ibid, 66. Otto Kahn-Freund, for instance, likens the firm to an 'absolute monarchy' where, in principle, all the power is in the hands of the employer. O Kahn-Freund, 'Legal Framework' in AD Flanders and H Armstrong Clegg (eds), *The System of Industrial Relations in Great Britain: Its History, Law and Institutions* (Oxford, Basel Blackwell, 1954).

[171] ibid, 51–53. See also D Cabrelli and R Zahn, 'Theories of Domination and Labour Law: An Alternative Conception for Intervention?' (2017) 33(3) *International Journal of Comparative Labour Law and Industrial Relations* 339–64.

[172] See, for instance, *Cass. soc.*, 13 novembre 1996, in Bull. civ., V, n° 386; pourvoi n° 94-13187.

[173] Article L3121-1, modifié par Loi n° 2016-1088 du 8 août 2016 – art. 8 (V). G Auzero, D Baugard and E Dockès, *Droit du travail* (Paris, Dalloz, 2021).

[174] For a broader discussion, see V De Stefano, '"Master and servers": Collective Labour Rights and Private Government in the Contemporary World of Work' (2020) 36(4) *International Journal of Comparative Labour Law and Industrial Relations* 425–44. See also C Cetty, 'Talking about private government. A review of the argument and its critiques' (*Economic Policy Institute*, 23 September 2021) www.epi.org/unequalpower/publications/talking-about-private-government-a-review-of-the-argument-and-its-critiques/.

[175] J Fudge, 'The future of the standard employment relationship: Labour law, new institutional economics and old power resource theory' (2017) 59(3) *Journal of Industrial Relations* 374–92.

[176] R Coase, 'The nature of the firm' (1937) 16(4) *Economica* 386–405.

[177] CJ Goetz and RE Scott, 'Principles of Relational Contracts' (1981) 67(6) *Virginia Law Review* 1089; Muehlberger (n 93); OE Williamson, *The Economic Institutions of Capitalism: Firms, Markets, Relational Contracting* (New York, Free Press, 1985); P Cappelli and D Neumark 'External churning and internal flexibility: Evidence on the functional flexibility and core-periphery hypotheses' (2004) 43(1) *Industrial Relations: A Journal of Economy and Society* 148–82.

[178] AD Jr Chandler, *The Visible Hand: The Managerial Revolution in American Business* (Cambridge, MA, Harvard University Press, 1977); AD Jr Chandler and H Daem (eds), *Managerial Hierarchies: Comparative Perspectives on the Rise of the Modern Industrial Enterprise* (Cambridge, MA, Harvard University Press, 1989).

[179] S Deakin and G Morris, *Labour Law*, 4th edn (Oxford, Hart Publishing, 2005).

[180] D Hay and P Craven, *Masters, Servants, and Magistrates in Britain and the Empire, 1562–1955* (Chapel Hill, NC, University of North Carolina Press, 2005).

[181] C Anderson, *White Rage. The Unspoken Truth of Our Racial Divide* (New York, Bloomsbury Publishing, 2016). See also EP Thompson, 'Time, Work-Discipline, and Industrial Capitalism' (1967) 38 *Past and Present*, 56–97.

[182] W Steinmetz, *Private Law and Social Inequality in the Industrial Age Comparing Legal Cultures in Britain, France, Germany, and the United States* (Oxford, Oxford University Press, 2000); B Veneziani, 'The Evolution of the Contract of Employment' in B Hepple (ed), *The Making of Labour Law in Europe. A Comparative Study of Nine Countries up to 1945* (London, Mansell Publishing, 1986).

[183] A Cotterau, 'Sens du juste et usages du droit du travail : une évolution contrastée entre la France et la Grande-Bretagne au xixe siècle' (2006) 33(2) *Revue d'histoire du XIXe siècle* 101–20.

[184] Deakin and Morris (n 179), referring to A Fox, *Beyond Contract: Work, Power and Trust Relations* (London, Faber & Faber, 1974); B Caruso, 'The Employment Contract is Dead: Hurrah for the Work Contract! A European Perspective' in KVW Stone and H Arthurs (eds), *Rethinking Workplace Regulation: Beyond the Standard Contract of Employment* (New York, Russell Sage Foundation, 2013) 95–111.

[185] Deakin and Morris (n 179). This section also draws upon V De Stefano, '"Negotiating the Algorithm": Automation, Artificial Intelligence, and Labor Protection' (2019) 41(1) *Comparative Labor Law and Policy Journal* 15–46.

[186] R Dukes, *The Labour Constitution: The Enduring Idea of Labour Law* (Oxford, Oxford University Press, 2014).

[187] D Bromwich, 'Market Rationalization' in Anderson (n 150) 89.

[188] G Giugni, *La memoria di un riformista* (Andrea Ricciardi ed, Bologna, il Mulino, 2007).

[189] F Liso, *La mobilità del lavoratore in azienda: il quadro legale* (Milan, Franco Angeli, 1982).

[190] L Wedderburn L, 'The Italian Workers' Statute – Some British Reflections' (1990) 19(3) *Industrial Law Journal* 154–91.

[191] MA Cherry, 'Beyond misclassification: The digital transformation of work' (2016) 37(3) *Comparative Labor Law & Policy Journal* 544–77; D Landes, *The Unbound Prometheus: Technological*

Change and Industrial Development in Western Europe from 1750 to the Present, 2nd edn (Cambridge, Cambridge University Press, 2014) (arguing that colocation of workers in factories started occurring before the advent of mechanical infrastructure, to exercise organisational power in a more efficient way than in the case of fragmented and less controllable homework).

[192] AJ Wood, M Graham, V Lehdonvirta and I Hjorth, 'Good gig, bad gig: Autonomy and algorithmic control in the global gig economy' (2019) 1(1) *Work, Employment and Society* 56–75. See also See also J Lambert, A Haley-Lock and JR Henly 'Schedule flexibility in hourly jobs: unanticipated consequences and promising directions' (2012) 15(3) *Community, Work & Family* 293–315.

[193] C Perraudin, N Thèvenot and J Valentin, 'Avoiding the employment relationship: Outsourcing and labour substitution among French manufacturing firms, 1984–2003' (2013) 152(3) *International Labour Review* 525–47.

[194] Tribunal Supremo, 'Sala de lo Social' Case 4746/2019 (2020). The UK Supreme Court, *B. V. Uber and others v Aslam and others* [2021] UKSC 5.

[195] A Todolí-Signes, *Notes on the Spanish Supreme Court Ruling That Considers Riders to Be Employees* (2020) *Comparative Labor Law & Policy Journal, Dispatch*. The 'subordination test' can be also passed when subordination is 'tenuous', as the CJEU allowed. Case C-232/09 *Dita Danosa v LKB Līzings SIA* [2010] EU:C:2010:674.

[196] B Sachs, 'Uber: Employee Status and Flexibility' (*On Labor*, 25 September 2015) https://onlabor. org/uber-employee-status-and-flexibility/ ('workers can choose when and how much to work, and can even work without immediate supervision, and still be employees within the meaning of the law'). See also B Sachs, 'Enough with the Flexibility Trope' (*OnLabor*, 15 May 2018) https://onlabor.org/enough-with-the-flexibility-trope/; B Sachs, 'Uber's Flexibility Myth: Reprise' (*OnLabor*, 19 August 2020) https://onlabor.org/ubersflexibility-myth-reprise/. For an overview, see T Katsabian and G Davidov, 'Flexibility, Choice and Labour Law: The Challenge of On-Demand Platforms' (2022) *University of Toronto Law Journal*.

[197] E George and P Chattopadhyay, *Non-standard work and workers: Organizational implications* (Geneva, ILO, 2015); B Walker, 'How does non-standard employment affect workers? A consideration of the evidence' (2011) 36(3) *New Zealand Journal of Employment Relations* 15–30.

[198] G Davidov, 'The reports of my death are greatly exaggerated: "employee" as a viable (though overly-used) legal concept' (2005) https://papers.ssrn.com/sol3/papers.cfm?abstract_id=783484. See also G Davidov, 'Setting Labour Law's Coverage: Between Universalism and Selectivity' (2014) 34 *Oxford Journal of Legal Studies* 543–66.

[199] A Perulli, *Economically dependent/quasi-subordinate (parasubordinate) employment: legal, social and economic aspects* (Brussels, European Commission, 2003); A Supiot, *Beyond Employment. Changes in Work and the Future of Labour Law in Europe* (Oxford, Oxford University Press, 2001).

[200] SD Harris and AB Krueger, *A proposal for modernizing labor laws for twenty-first-century work: The 'independent worker'* (The Hamilton Project, Washington, DC, The Brookings Institution, 2015).

[201] The European Commission has specified that 'there is no intention to create a "third" employment status at EU level, while respecting the choice made by some Member States to introduce it in their national legislation'. Consultation Document, Second-phase consultation of social partners under Article 154 TFEU on possible action addressing the challenges related to working conditions in platform work (SWD(2021) 143 final).

[202] Supreme Court of California 30 April 2018, Case No. S222732, *Dynamex Operations West, Inc. v Superior Court of Los Angeles County*.

[203] K Cunningham-Parmeter, 'Gig-dependence: Finding the real independent contractors of platform work' (2018) 39(3) *The Northern Illinois University Law Review* 379–427.

[204] MA Cherry, 'Dispatch–United States: "Proposition 22: A Vote on Gig Worker Status in California"' (2021) *Comparative Labor Law & Policy Journal, Dispatch*.

[205] JB White, 'Uber CEO sees California ballot initiative as a model for other states' (*Politico*, 11 May 2020).

[206] D Khosrowshahi, 'A Better Deal for European Platform Workers' (*Uber Newsroom*, 15 February 2021) www.uber.com/newsroom/a-better-deal/.

[207] This analysis of Proposition 22 draws upon V De Stefano '"I now pronounce you contractor": Prop22, labour platforms and legislative doublespeak' (*UK Labour Law*, 13 November 2020) https://uklabourlawblog.com/2020/11/13/i-now-pronounce-you-contractor-prop22-labour-platforms-and-legislative-doublespeak-by-valerio-de-stefano/.

[208] MA Cherry and A Aloisi, '"Dependent contractors" in the gig economy: A comparative approach' (2017) 66(3) *American University Law Review* 635–89.

[209] A Aloisi and V De Stefano, 'Delivering employment rights to platform workers' (*il Mulino*, 31 January 2020) https://www.rivistailmulino.it/news/newsitem/index/Item/News:NEWS_ITEM:5018.

[210] P Tamma, 'Italy's labor ministry slams delivery company deal with far-right union' (*Politico*, 17 September 2020) www.politico.eu/article/italys-labor-ministry-slams-delivery-company-deal-with-far-right-union/.

[211] See also the contributions on Austria, Germany, Italy, Spain and the UK published in the special issue of the (2019) 10(3) *European Labour Law Journal*. For an update, see C Schubert, *Economically-dependent Workers as Part of a Decent Economy: International, European and Comparative Perspective* (Munich, C.H. Beck, 2021).

[212] See also A Bogg, 'For Whom the Bell Tolls: "Contract" in the Gig Economy' (Oxford Human Rights Hub, 7 March 2021) https://ohrh.law.ox.ac.uk/for-whom-the-bell-tolls-contract-in-the-gig-economy/.

[213] J Kenner, 'Uber Drivers Are "Workers" – The Expanding Scope of the 'Worker' Concept in the UK's Gig Economy' in J Kenner, I Florczak and M Otto (eds), *Precarious Work. The Challenge for Labour Law in Europe* (Cheltenham, Edward Elgar Publishing, 2019).

[214] In Italy: CGIL, 'Carta dei Diritti Universali del lavoro' (2016). In France: E Dockès (ed), 'Proposition de code du travail' (Paris, Dalloz, 2017). In the UK: K Ewing, Lord J Hendy QC and C Jones, 'A Manifesto for Labour Law: towards a comprehensive revision of workers' rights' (Liverpool, Institute for Employment Rights, 2016).

[215] The paramount objective of providing decent work for all and ensuring a 'human-centred approach' in the digital age has been at the core of the ILO's Future of Work Initiative – a major project launched to mark the centenary of the Organisation (2019). ILO, Report of the Director-General, Report I The Future of Work Centenary Initiative, International Labour Conference, 104th Session, Geneva, 2015, www.ilo.org/wcmsp5/groups/public/---ed_norm/---relconf/documents/meetingdocument/wcms_369026.pdf. ILO Global Commission on the Future of Work, Work for a brighter future (Ginevra, ILO, 2019).

[216] Crucially, the right to occupational health and safety (OSH) at the workplace has not yet been elevated to the rank of fundamental principles and rights at work. The guarantee of an adequate *minimum* wage has been enshrined, instead of the *living* wage suggested by the Commission. Moreover, the Declaration does not broach the idea of expanding working time sovereignty, but instead restates the need to enforce maximum limits on working time. Even if the express formulation 'regardless of their employment status or contractual arrangements' was rejected, opposed among others by the government members of the EU Member States, the Declaration calls to strengthen and expand protection for 'all workers'. Report of the Committee of the Whole: Summary of Proceedings, ILC108-PR6B(Rev.) www.ilo.org/wcmsp5/groups/public/---ed_norm/---relconf/documents/meetingdocument/wcms_711582.pdf, para 1133. See N Potocka-Sionek and A Aloisi, '"Festina Lente": the ILO and EU agendas on the digital transformation of work' (2021) 37(1) *International Journal of Comparative Labour Law and Industrial Relations* 35–64.

[217] M Freedland and N Countouris, *The Legal Construction of Personal Work Relations* (Oxford, Oxford University Press, 2011). One of the authors of this book recently wrote in support of this idea: N Countouris and V De Stefano, *New Trade Union Strategies for New Forms of Employment* (Brussels, ETUC, 2019).

[218] See https://bills.parliament.uk/bills/2876.

[219] D Mangan, E Gramano and M Kullmann, 'An unprecedented social solidarity stress test' (2020) 11(3) *European Labour Law Journal* 247–75.

[220] OECD, *Supporting livelihoods during the COVID-19 crisis: Closing the gaps in safety nets* (Paris, OECD Publishing, 2020).

[221] S Garben, *Protecting Workers in the Online Platform Economy: An overview of regulatory and policy developments in the EU*, European Risk Observatory Discussion paper (2017). See also MJ Walton 'The shifting nature of work and its implications' (2016) 45(2) *Industrial Law Journal* 111–30.

[222] 58% of the workforce in the EU is in indefinite full-time employment.

[223] ACL Davies, *Regulating Atypical Work: Beyond Equality* in N Countouris and M Freedland (eds), *Resocialising Europe in a Time of Crisis* (Cambridge, Cambridge University Press, 2013) 230–49.

[224] J Fudge and R Owens, *Precarious Work, Women, and the New Economy: The Challenge to Legal Norms* (Oxford, Oxford University Press, 2006). See also LF Vosko, *Managing the Margins: Gender, Citizenship, and the International Regulation of Precarious Employment* (Oxford, Oxford University Press, 2009).

[225] AL Kalleberg, 'Nonstandard Employment Relations: Part-Time, Temporary and Contract Work' (2000) 26(1) *Annual Review of Sociology* 341–65. See also T Piketty, *Capital and Ideology* (Cambridge:

Harvard University Press, 2020); Stone and Arthurs (n 184). See also P Doeringer and M Piore, *Internal Labor Markets and Manpower Analysis* (Armonk, ME Sharpe, 1971).

[226] C Barnard and D Georgiou, 'EU Developments in the Labour & Social Field: Jurisprudential and Regulatory Responses to the Digitalisation of Work' in M De Vos (ed), *Technological Disruption in Labour and Employment Law* (Cambridge, Cambridge University Press, 2022).

[227] LF Katz and AB Krueger, *The rise and nature of alternative work arrangements in the United States, 1995-2015* (NBER Working Paper, No. 22667, 2016).

[228] OECD, *In It Together: Why Less Inequality Benefits All* (Paris, OECD Publishing, 2015).

[229] N Countouris, 'The legal determinants of precariousness in personal work relations: A European perspective' (2012) 34(1) *Comparative Labor Law & Policy Journal* 21–46.

[230] A Lindbeck and DJ Snower, 'Insiders versus outsiders' (2001) 15(1) *Journal of Economic Perspectives* 165–88. J Lindvall J and D Rueda, 'The Insider-Outsider Dilemma' (2014) 44(2) *British Journal of Political Science* 460–75.

[231] S Fredman, 'Women at work: The broken promise of flexicurity' (2004) 33(4) *Industrial Law Journal* 299–319.

[232] K Purcell, 'Changing Boundaries in Employment and Organizations' in K Purcell (ed), *Changing Boundaries in Employment* (Westbury-on-Trym, Bristol Academic, 2000).

[233] International Labour Office, *Non-standard employment around the world: Understanding challenges, shaping prospects* (Geneva, ILO, 2016).

[234] JR Henly, HL Shaefer and E Waxman, 'Nonstandard Work Schedules: Employer- and Employee-Driven Flexibility in Retail Jobs' (2006) 80(4) *The Social Service Review* 609–34.

[235] See https://ec.europa.eu/eurostat/web/products-eurostat-news/-/DDN-20180608-1.

[236] O Nachtwey, *Germany's Hidden Crisis: Social Decline in the Heart of Europe* (London, Verso, 2018).

[237] R Partington, 'More Regular Work Wanted by Almost Half Those on Zero-Hours' *The Guardian* (3 October 2018) www.theguardian.com/uk-news/2018/oct/03/regular-secure-work-wanted-by-almost-half-on-zero-hours-contracts-flexible-gig-economy.

[238] A Burke (ed), *The Handbook of Research on Freelancing and Self-employment* (Dublin, Senate Hall, 2015). M Del Conte and E Gramano, 'Looking to the other side of the bench: The new legal status of independent contractors under the Italian legal system' (2017) 39(3) *Comparative Labor Law & Policy Journal* 579–606.

[239] H Collins H, 'Independent contractors and the challenge of vertical disintegration to employment protection laws' (1990) 10(3) *Oxford Journal of Legal Studies* 356–60.

[240] A Thörnquist, 'False Self-Employment and Other Precarious Forms of Employment in the "Grey Area" of the Labour Market' (2015) 31(4) *International Journal of Comparative Labour Law and Industrial Relations* 411–29.

[241] F Rosioru, 'Legal Acknowledgement of the Category of Economically Dependent Workers' (2014) 5(3–4) *European Labour Law Journal* 279–305.

[242] Garben (n 221).

[243] M Wouters, 'International labour standards and platform work: an analysis based on the instruments on private employment agencies, home work and domestic work' (Doctoral dissertation, KU Leuven, 2021).

[244] L Ratti, 'Online Platforms and Crowdwork in Europe: A Two-Step Approach to Expanding Agency Work Provisions' (2016) 38(2) *Comparative Labor Law & Policy Journal* 477–511. J Prassl and M Risak, 'Uber, Taskrabbit, and Co.: platforms as employers? Rethinking the legal analysis of crowdwork' (2016) 37(3) *Comparative Labor Law & Policy Journal* 604–19.

[245] In May 2020, the Tribunal of Milan placed Uber Eats Italy under special administration over alleged criminal gangmastering offences. The company's food delivery business was alleged to have been using small firms to recruit vulnerable workers, through practices that have been associated with unlawful labour intermediation and exploitation. The company had to spend several months in this special administration to roll back the contested practices. E Allaby, 'The rise of Uber Eats gang masters is tearing the gig economy apart' (*Vice*, 15 February 2021) www.wired.co.uk/article/uber-eats-italy.

[246] AL Booth, M Francesconi and J Frank, 'Temporary jobs: stepping stones or dead ends?' (2002) 112(480) *The Economic Journal* 189–213.

[247] E Armano, A Bove and A Murgia, *Mapping Precariousness, Labour Insecurity and Uncertain Livelihoods: Subjectivities and Resistance* (London, Routledge, 2017).

[248] A Aranguiz, 'Spain's labour reform: less transience, more balance' (*Social Europe*, 6 January 2022) https://socialeurope.eu/spains-labour-reform-less-temporary-work-more-balance.

Conclusions

A Job Well Done

I. Future-Proof Labour Law

To summarise, the overarching theme of this book is that robots, algorithms and platforms may well turn out to be fundamental tools for growth and welfare, solidarity between genders, generations and geographies, the development of new skills and the renewal of production models. But they will only be beneficial to society if we are able to govern them better with awareness and accountability, and without shortcuts.

Too often, the seismic shifts brought about by digital innovation have been looked at through the distorting prism of utopian or dystopian lenses, prioritising beliefs over facts. In recent times, a trend has emerged that aims at identifying the impacts of the digital transformation starting from an analysis of the organisational models and operational templates which (re)design businesses. There is a strong link between how a company's organisation is engineered and the responses that rapidly changing technologies can offer to genuine flexibility needs. Discussions on the (not only digital) transformation of work cannot therefore neglect the content of any given job, its place within production processes and its value (be it social, corporate, relational, intrinsic or perceived). It is on these factors that technology is increasingly placing a strain. The consequences are worrying and lead to a knock-on effect – the depreciation of the abstract component of each task has an effect on the most labour-intensive jobs, devaluing personal contributions and making workers interchangeable, while the social safety net crumbles and welfare systems suffer.

Meanwhile, events have contributed to encouraging a feeling of distrust towards digital behemoths and innovation pundits – a sentiment that the press has defined as 'techlash' (a combination of 'technology' and 'backlash', indicating a period of reckoning).[1] This sentiment is accompanied by a change in the attitude of regulators on both sides of the Atlantic, who no longer seem so eager to let the 'silicon masters' off the hook, and who are threatening to resort to strict antitrust enforcement,[2] while attempting to pass new rules to limit abuses, promote a safe culture of personal data, and ensure that tax avoidance does not become an established pattern. This clearly is a breakthrough on the policymaking front.[3] As a result, we are witnessing a reversal of fortune. The utopian image of a transnational, individualistic, virtually unregulated cyberspace,[4] out of reach of national governments and international institutions, has disappeared. And disillusionment with this ideal does not seem to be confined to university and parliamentary halls.

Is the myth of tech being synonymous with well-being and progress finally collapsing? Looking at the past few years, it seems that disruption at any cost does not always turn out well. The negative externalities of the new digital world, ie, the costs that the tech sector imposes on the rest of society, have thus resurfaced at the centre of the debate. A varied coalition of critics has spoken out against big tech, by means of enquiries, infringement procedures and even public shaming. Digital platforms have been accused of being the new robber barons, similar to capitalists who ruled the world at the end of the nineteenth century.[5] According to a team of economists (unsusceptible to anti-capitalist sentiment), the practices of the digital giants 'not only [...] represent a tax on innovation', they also reduce 'the value new entrants can fetch alone and thus the price at which they would be acquired'. Moreover, 'in a world with switching costs, new entrants with a superior technology will find it difficult to attract customers, as customers expect that any superior technology will be incorporated by the incumbent platform after an acquisition'. The consequence is a reduction in 'the number of customers new entrants can obtain and thus the price at which these new entrants will be acquired, further reducing innovation incentives'.[6] In other words, digital rent-seeking middlemen are a mortal threat to global competitiveness. We are left with a big problem: self-proclaimed disruptors are stifling innovation.[7]

The increase in scandals such as the Cambridge Analytica/Facebook data breach has exposed the unscrupulous use of profiled data to convey vitriolic messages tailored to individual users, often with the aim of radicalising opinions that are in themselves already violent, or influencing election results.[8] During the COVID-19 pandemic, the role of social media in spreading conspiracy theories about the virus and against vaccination programmes has also been extremely contentious. The most destabilising mobilisations, including the 2021 United States Capitol storm, seem to have been fuelled by the inaction, if not the deliberate appeasement, of media platforms towards self-reinforcing bubbles of ever more radicalised extremists, sometimes also stirred up by foreign powers.[9] Not a week passes without similar incidents coming to light, thanks to the actions of investigative journalists, researchers, civil society organisations and whistleblowers. There is a growing fear that our private lives, societies and democracies are vulnerable to an unscrupulous group of 'parasites', who are taking advantage of their powers. Seduced by the once inspiring, now enraging parable of the genius struggling in a Californian garage, facing pressure from investors and the desire to conquer the world, we have found ourselves dealing with young adults who have never grown up and who are responsible for a large part of our future.[10] The general sense of dissatisfaction felt is the result of the betrayed hopes and unfortunate consequences we all have.

What we have been mistakenly calling the 'sharing economy' for some years has innovated almost nothing. No new objects, no new languages, no new ideas. It can be argued that, since the invention of the microprocessor – and then of the personal computer – and the launch of the internet, little progress has been made, resulting in the stagnation of productivity rates and wages in many parts of the world. If you think this is an exaggeration, consider how many benefits have remained inaccessible to many workers and businesses, and therefore they have been severely confined in their exclusively 'extractive' use. As labour economist David Autor puts it, 'we're automating a lot of trivial stuff rather than important stuff. If you compare antibiotics and indoor plumbing and electrification and air travel and telecommunications to [food-delivery apps] and smartphones or self-checkout, it may just not be as consequential'.[11] Unfortunately, use of digital devices is largely passive. We are deeply dependent on them, to the point of using laptops and smartphones in bed; we are docile users, unable to adopt a critical perspective.[12] Where does that leave us?

Now that the era of naivety seems to be over, there are no more excuses. Let us therefore ask ourselves how to mitigate the risks of a flawed system that is eager to erode any rights and protection. We must act now if we are to enjoy a future of reliable work and shared prosperity. The argument 'it's always been like this' is a terrible excuse.[13] It is both lazy and unambitious, using our own failings (and those of our ancestors) to judge the faults of those who design, sell or use digital tools.[14] Failing to explore what might happen under different conditions is a main reason for inaction. As long as technology merely perpetuates our biased ideas, it's no big deal, and things could have been much worse! It seems rather odd that the 'banality of progress' emerges as a justification alongside high praise for a bright future to be welcomed with open arms. Managerial despotism, elusive attitudes, ethical failures, the undercutting of competitors, and discriminatory abuses cannot be allowed to be perpetuated through digital technologies.[15] One of two things is true. Either these technologies (also) serve to change the course of history, or we might as well consider them as aiding and abetting human weakness and renounce worshipping 'the new' once and for all.

One of the main aims of digital innovation should be to improve society and the human condition, and not to negatively impact work, tighten up forms of control, or create inequity on the basis of race, sexual orientation, education background or postcode. And yet, according to a report by AInow institute: 'across diverse domains and contexts, AI is widening inequality, placing information and control in the hands of those who already have power and further disempowering those who don't'.[16] The fact that this has always been the case only makes it worse. The aspiration to bring about positive change should inform the choices of those who are not content with work as it is today.

A changing world of work must contribute in terms of equality, widespread access to meaningful professional opportunities and fair competition, but also inclusion and effectiveness in the allocation of social benefits, and the ability to combat hard-wired misconceptions, frauds and malpractices. Machines should be tasked with freeing us from drudgery. With their low entry point, platforms can enable the matching of labour supply and demand in a smooth and sustainable way, encouraging job security and benefiting marginalised communities.

Algorithms could facilitate the enforcement of occupational health and safety and working time regulation and the contrast to wage theft. Technologies should help us identify our interpersonal blind spots that have long plagued human decision-making processes rather than replacing them with the vagaries of their programmers and providers (or, even worse, with institutional and systemic biases).[17] The very same instruments that are currently adopted to monitor and manage workers could be used to improve transparency, verifiability and openness of workplace decisions, thus reducing socio-economic gaps.[18]

In this respect, we need technology that can produce better results than humans can. We also need new and stronger mechanisms of redistribution and social protection, as discussed in the next section.

A. Universal Basic Income, Radical Measures in Search of Sustainability

There is one thing that unites radical left-wing intellectuals like Nick Srnicek and Alex Williams, liberal philosophers like Matt Zwolinski and tech tycoons like Mark Zuckerberg and Elon Musk.[19] They all think that the only policy that can tackle the mass unemployment created by automation is universal basic income (UBI for short).[20]

Make no mistake: they do not have in mind clumsy experiments that just rebrand old-style workfare policies under fake universalistic labels. Universal basic income has nothing to do with the Universal Credit scheme introduced in the UK by the conservative-libdem coalition government in 2012, to replace various existing benefit schemes, nor with the so-called 'citizenship income', initiated in Italy in 2019. The latter measure is a jumbled combination of two different instruments: a guaranteed minimum income (ie, a sum paid to those whose income is below the poverty line) linked to a system of active labour policies (ie, programmes that should facilitate the integration of unemployed and inactive people into the labour market). The UBI, instead, must be understood as a sum distributed to all citizens or residents regardless of income and with no strings attached. Even billionaires would pocket it, and it would not be necessary to make oneself available for work.

The moral and political philosopher John Rawls was critical of the fact that his student Philippe Van Parijs would derive his influential proposal to introduce a basic income from his mentor's work. He disapprovingly asked why surfers who spend all their time on the waves in Malibu should receive a monthly check.[21] The idea of universal basic income, however, is, with due respect to Rawls, that everyone should receive it without any scrutiny over how the money is spent, and without investigating personal preconditions. No expensive and imperfect bureaucracy, no need to prove one is poor or jobless, no social control over people. The underlying vision is that giving each person an income, emancipating them from the constant need to work at all costs, will help to liberate creative energies and free the beneficiary from fears and anxieties that otherwise spread to the rest of society.

Providing a sum of money to enable the entire population to live without work-ing for a lifetime is an admittedly utopian goal. UBI's biggest supporters, such as the aforementioned Van Parijs and his colleague Yannick Vanderborght, explicitly recognise that a genuine universal income programme is out of reach in the short to medium term.[22] According to Professor Cynthia Estlund, estimated costs would be approximately 35 per cent of France's gross domestic product to give all its citi-zens a monthly income of 1,100 euros. Belgians, if they are content with 600 euros a month, could get by with 6 per cent of GDP. In the US, even if the UBI were to replace other welfare programmes, we would be talking about trillions of dollars a year to guarantee everyone $1,000 a month.[23]

This sounds like political fiction, for now. Why then is this being so widely discussed, advocated and opposed? Why has a proposal that was initially confined to academic circles become a subject on which even mainstream politics debate?

We believe that the UBI is not a realistic proposal as things stand. Among other things, the impact of UBI on a more equitable distribution of income in society cannot be taken for granted. At the same time, we think that a discussion on redis-tribution and welfare models is unavoidable and urgent. It is essential to reflect on how and how much we will work when automation and new business models will have even more profoundly changed our way of working and our understanding of work.[24] We cannot pretend that this is discussion that can be put off for another day. As we have reported, digital technologies allow companies to rotate staff by offering increasingly short and precarious contracts and shifts, while continuing to take advantage of a stable pool of available workers. Production cycles themselves are shifting towards more contingent and unpredictable models. It is not just the fault of bad business practices that jobs and, with them, incomes are becoming more unstable, although those unscrupulous practices do exist. There are many ways to react to this paradigm shift. The most foolish one would be to use universal income proposals as Trojan horses to replace or unseat social institutions.

Even though the libertarian wing of UBI proponents, in its different variants, claims that this policy is an opportunity to get rid of all other welfare programmes and state interventions, including labour protections, the hypothesis that labour and employment regulation can be replaced by the UBI is farcical. If basic income ever comes into being, and even if it is sufficient to lead a jobless existence, there will still be people who will continue to work in an increasingly algorithm-driven society, and working people must be protected. Labour and employment law does not generically serve the purpose of safeguarding 'people in need'. Nor does it have the sole aim of guaranteeing a minimum income. It is about countering the abuse of managerial powers, including when they are exerted through technologies. We have discussed this at length: these powers are crucial to making businesses work, and they are not going anywhere. There can be no possible 'accelerationist' exception,[25] the role of labour regulation in combating discrimination and arbi-trariness, limiting invasions of workers' privacy and giving them power and a voice through trade unions, would not become redundant in the presence of a version of UBI.

Other – genuine – ambitious goals should be aimed for. Anti-poverty programmes or active labour market policies aimed at integrating the unemployed or economically inactive people into the labour market must finally be freed from the deep-rooted prejudice that being poor or jobless is a person's fault. First of all, it must be acknowledged that, for too many people today, work is no longer a way out of poverty. The Bureau of Labour Statistics, the statistical unit of the US Department of Labor, reports that in 2017 almost 7 million people in the US were working poor, ie, people who, despite having worked or actively sought work for more than six months during the year, were below the poverty line. Almost 3 per cent of those who had worked full-time and more than 10 per cent of those who had worked part-time in the US were considered working poor in 2017.[26] Tellingly, a study prepared for the European Commission reveals that the percentage of EU workers who lived in households that are at risk of poverty was 9.4 per cent in the same year. Predictably, non-standard workers are at much higher risk than standard workers. The same study reports: 'In 2017 and for the EU-28, the [in-work poverty] rate is nearly three times higher for employees on temporary contracts (16.2%) than for those with a contract of unlimited duration (5.8%). The [in-work poverty] rate of part-time employees is double (15.6%) that of full-timers (7.7%)'.[27]

These numbers are overlooked in the policy debates on labour market trends. All too often commentators and regulators only look at the employment figures, they do not ask whether those who have a job are able to guarantee themselves an independent and dignified lifestyle. An important article of the Universal Declaration of Human Rights provides: 'Everyone who works has the right to just and favourable remuneration ensuring for [themselves] and [their] family an existence worthy of human dignity, and supplemented, if necessary, by other means of social protection'.[28] The drafters of this instrument linked pay to a dignified existence. The phenomenon of in-work poverty represents a betrayal of this principle and many other solemn promises included in national constitutions and international treaties. It is therefore vital to understand how to avoid it. Strengthening employment protection, protecting those who fall outside its scope, consolidating and extending equalisation instruments such as collective bargaining: these are all essential steps to increase income and to reduce unsustainable work patterns.

Welfare must also play its part, since it is paid for by the general public. Income support programmes should increase people's bargaining power, not reduce it. Benefits are often conditional on recipients making themselves available for work. Those who refuse job offers can lose their benefit or have it reduced. There is a real risk that a very strict 'conditionality', which does not care what kind of work, what wage and what stability is offered, ends up trapping people in underpaid and oppressive jobs. Too many conditions in welfare systems may be incompatible with the protection of human rights and dignity.[29] The over-invasiveness of technology can also be blamed. In early 2020, a Dutch court ruled that the algorithmic surveillance systems adopted in the country against welfare fraud should be stopped: predictably, AI disproportionately targeted the poorest and most vulnerable.[30]

A UN human rights body welcomed the decision.[31] Following accusations of racial profiling, the scandal led to the resignation of the prime minister.[32] Similarly disturbing stories have caused outrage in the UK and in the US,[33] and more traditional methods of surveillance have also fared poorly. At the end of 2019, the German Constitutional Court ruled that it is contrary to the Constitution to impose excessive sanctions on welfare recipients who do not accept job offers.[34]

Penalties for skipping a job interview, dropping out of a training course or refusing to collaborate with job placement schemes offered by the authorities are at the heart of the benefits system in Germany, called Hartz IV after its proponent. Consequences can be a cut in benefits (of 30–60 per cent) or their complete withdrawal for several months. The German constitutional justices have ruled that such an extreme cut is incompatible with the fundamental right to a minimum standard of living. The then German Minister of Labour and Welfare welcomed the ruling. This is not surprising: the effects of the Hartz IV system have long been disputed as counterproductive and unfair. The NGO *Sanktionsfrei* has launched a three-year experiment; 250 randomly selected beneficiaries of the Hartz IV system will be privately reimbursed for any sanctions imposed by public authorities for non-cooperation with the active labour market schemes imposed by the authorities.[35] The NGO will monitor the psychological effects of the removal of sanctions. It will be interesting to see if this will also affect the beneficiaries' propensity to accept or refuse job offers, as an unconditional subsidy system does not necessarily discourage people from working. In one of the most famous basic income pilot experiments, from 1974–79, the inhabitants of a small Canadian town received a guaranteed annual income of about $15,000 for a family of four. Hours worked decreased by only 1 per cent.[36] Other trials, such as the one conducted in Stockton, an industrial city on the edge of the Bay Area, are in line with these promising results. In this study, the labour force did not shrink and the share of participants with a full-time job grew 12 percentage points, versus five percentage points in the control group.[37]

Avoiding prejudices is essential to rethink welfare programmes. Far too often, welfare recipients are targeted by ad hoc media campaigns depicting them as 'benefit scroungers', free-riders and loafers or presenting them as 'welfare queens'. These campaigns usually have only one objective: fighting the poor instead of poverty. These operations are far from a relic of the past. In the US many Republican governors decided to reject increased unemployment benefits provided by the federal government to deal with the economic consequences of the pandemic, because they allegedly created a 'labour shortage' for 'businesses who can't find staff', including in essential services. It didn't matter that the correlation between generous pandemic benefits such as relief checks, rent moratoriums and student-loan forgiveness and this presumed shortage was highly controversial, and that President Biden took a very stern position: if businesses can't find workers, they should 'pay them more!'.

This trend is accompanied, and to a certain extent corroborated, by a widespread reaction to unsustainable work hours and burnout, mostly attributable to workers' changing expectations in the service sector.[38] Experts have defined the phenomenon of workers quitting a job they dislike as the 'Great Resignation'. Significantly, rejecting the alarmist attitudes predominant in the US and elsewhere, labour economist David Autor has also argued that temporary labour shortages are 'an opportunity, not a crisis', as they can encourage employers to voluntarily pay higher wages, offer better benefits, provide more training opportunities and use workers more productively.[39]

In Italy, since the very bland 'citizenship income' was approved, major newspapers and TV programmes have been full of stories, mostly fabricated for effect or invented from scratch, of fictitious young people – often from southern Italy – who refuse job offers 'because we have an income anyway'. The story of young people who can't be bothered to work because they are too 'laid back' because of welfare benefits is another version of 'businesses offering work but not finding staff', which in Mediterranean countries was fashionable before it was cool to talk about labour shortages.[40] As fact-checkers in Italy have shown,[41] these are almost always unlikely stories, or ludicrously cheap marketing campaigns designed by entrepreneurs looking for free visibility for their company.

It is about time we got rid of nonsense about 'choosy young people' and slackers in an era of labour scarcity and look at the reality: labour markets have not been the full employment markets of the post-war period for decades, now; new technologies, if they are not well managed, risk reducing jobs even further, especially good jobs. The only solid statistical evidence is of the in-work poverty, not of lazy southerners and welfare queens.

Conditions that were fine when there was work for everyone are no longer acceptable. Policymakers now have the task of finding resources to invest in improving societal welfare. Redistributing the wealth created by the digital economy, currently 'captured' by a few tech giants that escape tax systems and social security compliance, and redefining existing public spending and benefits cannot be taboo. Nor can we simply dismiss as impractical a welfare system that allows people to reject precarious, badly paid or exhausting jobs.

In short, priorities must be re-defined. One of them must be creating quality jobs, not forcing people to take any job, perhaps by giving subsidies to inefficient companies to hire welfare recipients. Another priority is to design a welfare model that makes citizens and workers free to choose. To do this, we need braver ideas and less class paternalism.

B. Collective Voice versus Digital Despotism: Negotiating the Algorithm

In October 2019, in one of her first public appearances as Vice-President-designate of the European Commission, Margrethe Vestager stated without hesitation that it would be necessary to 'make sure that there is nothing in the competition rules to stop [...] platform workers from forming a union, to negotiate proper wages as you would do in any other business'.[42] Predictably, only the insiders took notice, but the declaration was a major breakthrough. Vestager, in her capacity as competition commissioner, is the supreme guardian of EU antitrust law and, as such, has become well known for her investigation into the possible anti-competitive practices of tech giants such as Google, Amazon, Facebook, Apple and Microsoft.

So, what does Commissioner Vestager have to do with platform workers? Plenty. EU competition law, which directly influences the national laws of Member States, treats self-employed workers as small undertakings. Businesses, according to antitrust law, cannot agree among themselves to fix the price of a good or service. Imagine if all restaurants downtown agreed that a hamburger with fries could not cost less than €15 – that would be illegal. Undertakings should compete with each other on merit, not agree on uniform prices to the detriment of the consumers. The problem is that, being considered as businesses, self-employed workers cannot combine, among themselves and with their clients, and claim a minimum fee for their work. Nor can they access formal structures of labour representation and collective redress that, in many countries, are restricted only to specific categories of workers, as defined by national laws and practices. This implies that they cannot have a collective bargaining agreement.[43] And those unions organising them to negotiate and sign a collective agreement would violate antitrust laws and risk severe penalties. Take the example of the City of Seattle in the US: it was taken to court by pro-business lobbyists for passing an ordinance allowing drivers of Uber and other ride-hailing platforms to engage in collective bargaining.[44]

This is obviously a paradox. An Uber driver, a Helpling cleaner, an Instacart shopper or a Deliveroo rider cannot be considered on a par with a Michelin-star restaurateur or a successful surgeon just because their contract reads 'self-employed'. This illogical interpretation of competition law contributes to severely limiting the possibility of platform workers, and other vulnerable self-employed workers, to unionise to protect themselves. Collective agreements negotiated on behalf, and for the benefit, of employees everywhere have long been immune from antitrust laws. On this side of the Atlantic, while scholars have been advocating a purposive interpretation or a total reinvention of antitrust restrictions, which are no longer suited to the needs of modern labour markets,[45] the Court of Justice of the European Union seems still attached to a traditional model.[46] It confers immunity from antitrust laws only to subordinate employees as an exception to the general prohibition and under limited circumstances, a position that, as we will explain below, is also incompatible with international law.[47] In many countries, that interpretation means that top managers of platform companies, with their rising salaries, can join a union and enjoy the protections of a collective agreement as they are almost always hired as employees; riders, drivers, or self-employed domestic workers cannot, because they run the risk that the result of their bargaining activity will be deemed a restriction of competition.

Commissioner Vestager referred to this absurdity in the early days of her mandate and now intends to correct it. This is no small challenge: while on the one hand the Commission wants to admit vulnerable workers to collective bargaining, on the other hand the EU institutions fear that allowing the unionisation of self-employed workers will jeopardise competition in the field of small businesses and the liberal professions.

On the very same day of the publication of the draft Directive on platform work, the EU Commission published its guidelines on collective bargaining of some categories of self-employed people.[48] The guidelines cover 'only solo self-employed persons, namely, service providers who do not have any employees and who rely primarily on their own personal labour for the provision of the services.'[49] Some categories of collective agreements are in principle considered to fall outside the scope of competition law and beyond the Commission's antitrust enforcement priorities.

These Guidelines can be seen as a step forward compared to the existing situation where most vulnerable self-employed, including those working with platforms, are on shaky ground vis-à-vis competition law when trying to bargain collectively. However, they are still not sufficient to provide effective and solid collective bargaining protection to all workers who need it and have a right to collective bargaining under ILO's and Council of Europe's standards.[50] The predominantly personal work approach discussed in the previous Chapter is arguably much more suitable to provide such a protection without upending existing antitrust standards.[51]

A hostile legal framework is only one of the impediments experienced by non-standard workers. Moving on to consider some practical hurdles, casual and platform workers often lack bargaining power, which is in turn exacerbated by the short-lived nature of assignments and the fear of retaliation.[52] There are sometimes physical (there may be no fixed workplace), temporal (shifts are scattered among days and weeks) and language (migrant workers from different countries are over-represented among them) barriers to forming coalitions. Workers may also have conflicting agendas as well as opposite needs and preferences, thus making the building of effective alliances over common demands complex. In addition, businesses have adopted a range of strategies to frustrate attempts of these workers to organise: from top-down initiatives of customer mobilisation against progressive legislative reforms to opposition and intimidation from the management.[53] In particular, technology has been used by employers to uncover and deter emerging conflicts or root out protest leaders and organisers,[54] thus diluting the original core of activism.[55] Furthermore, where reputation and ratings play a significant role in securing the relationship with a platform or access to better-paid jobs, some workers may feel particularly hesitant to embark on any collective initiative as this could adversely impact them.

On the positive side, however, many 'dependent' self-employed workers, including platform workers, are starting to organise themselves anyway without being intimidated or waiting for concessions, joining existing unions or launching new repertoires of grassroots initiatives, much to the annoyance of pro-business lobbies and attracting the wrath of some national antitrust authorities.[56] This is undoubtedly a positive development because, without this unionisation activity on the thin edge of competition law, the European Commission would have been unlikely to address the problem.

Practices of (self-)organisation of non-standard workers have come to the forefront of journalists' and scholars' attention, coinciding with platform workers' mobilisations of all kinds and all over the world. Not only New York, Milan, London, Paris, Barcelona, but also Buenos Aires, Nairobi, Delhi and Bangalore, have seen collective action balloon in recent years.[57] Uber drivers went on strike to protest against a cut in fares or to demand a software update to allow them to receive tips form customers. Food delivery drivers for platforms such as Deliveroo, UberEats, Rappi, Just Eat and Glovo have been striking in Belgium, Italy, Spain, France, Latin America and the UK to demand pay rises or to oppose the move from hourly to piecework pay, which they consider damaging and unfair. In the US, not only daily workers in fast food chains, but also domestic workers and academics, took to the streets to demand recognition of the $15 minimum hourly wage, launching the 'Fight-For-15' campaign which brought together grassroots unionism initiatives and support from historic unions in sectors such as retail, restaurant, hotel, and janitorial services, and even in some professional occupations.[58]

Recently, a burst of activity has sprung up among computer scientists and programmers who have tried to alert against military initiatives commissioned by the US administration for facial recognition through drones and AI in which Google seems to be involved (the company, in response, has fired some of them).[59] Tech workers at Salesforce, Microsoft, Accenture, Google, Tableau, and GitHub are increasingly pushing back against the use of technology to perpetrate human rights abuses of migrants and Latinx residents at the southern US border.[60] There are increasingly frequent initiatives of collective action, the 'walk-outs', as the San Francisco tech bubble has dubbed strikes. Progress may take time, but it is facts that count, and the fact is that collective organisations have definitely reached the world of tech. As proof, one of the industry's iconic companies, Kickstarter, was successfully unionised in February 2020.[61]

Despite the common objectives, however, these battles often remain confined to the specific industry. Nonetheless, as the EU institutions attempt to define a regulatory framework within which to reconcile innovation with fair working conditions, these collective campaigns shatter the monopolistic dreams of the Silicon Valley 'unicorns', as successful start-ups valued at over a billion dollars are sometimes called in the financial sector.[62] The protests of the platform workers have certainly helped to dissolve the aura of mystical deference of commentators and policymakers to the unicorns themselves. Someone had to point out that there was something wrong with the 'tech's new clothes'.

Even the trade unions sometimes are caught off guard in the face of these actions, uncertain whether to invest in defending traditional crafts 'under siege' or to lead a new generation of activists. The international landscape varies widely, ranging from universalistic projects to 'sector-based' ones. In the UK, unions such as General Municipal and Boilermakers Union (GMB) and 'grassroots' movements such as Independent Workers' Union of Great Britain (IWGB), the United Voices of the World (UVW), the Industrial Workers of the World Union (IWW) and ADCU (App Drivers and Couriers Union) offer legal assistance to drivers and delivery couriers who want to take platforms to court in a broad variety of cases such as discrimination, anti-union practices, automated decision-making and data protection violations. In the US, riders are allied with drivers represented by the AFL-CIO, the largest trade union federation. Some video game developers, a much more labour intense activity than people imagine, have started to organise and even the creators of original YouTube videos and Twitch or OnlyFans contents have made collective demands to the platforms, in some instances supported by the main German union, the legendary IGMetal.[63]

Not content with that, the IGMetal brought together fellow trade unionists from Austria, Denmark, Sweden, the US and Canada and – with the help of lawyers and economists – drew up the first programme calling for multi-stakeholder transnational cooperation 'to avoid digital feudalism' and 'bring democracy to these new digital workplaces'. The document points out that there is a close tie between the organisation of workers and the economic well-being of the middle class in developed countries, and proposes to make internal systems for performance ratings, workload allocation, content of tasks and disciplinary measures more transparent.[64]

Forms of resistance in the platform economy draw on the traditional repertoires of trade union action, from picket lines to sit-ins, but are also inspired by more recent practices, such as twitterstorms or flash mobs, and collect resources to support striking colleagues through online petitions; this has already happened in the UK, where workers and organisers have used crowdfunding to economically support workers on strike. Concomitantly, advocates of digital cooperativism, a movement heralded by the sociologist Trebor Scholz have chosen to challenge tech giants on the same playing field, aiming to build 'ethical' and 'democratic' platforms owned by workers and users.[65]

All these initiatives aim not only to hit the platforms financially, but also to make customers aware and stimulate responsible consumption. They focus on corporate reputation, and therefore use caricatures of promotional slogans, viral hashtags, thumbs down and negative feedback in review systems. In Greece and the US, workers and customers have mobilised to get some apps deleted or their rating downgraded on app marketplaces.[66] Coordinators are very familiar with social media and use it as much as, and often better than, their counterparts. If managers use WhatsApp to summon them, workers populate groups on Telegram, Slack, Discord or Signal to coordinate actions and exchange information.[67] Digital tools are surging that provide information about the workload and increase awareness about workers' options and goals. When it comes to online work, the Turkopticon is an ingenious web browser plugin that scans the Amazon Mechanical Turk platform, helping crowdworkers to avoid poor quality jobs, delayed payment, bad payers and outright wage theft.[68] Workers also resort to more traditional industrial action (mass disconnection from the software during promotional initiatives or in peak periods or the distribution of flyers inviting customers and restaurants to boycott unscrupulous platforms).

All in all, these positive developments corroborate the idea that strong awareness, resistance and experimental solutions are emerging amongst workers who are often wrongly assumed to be structurally 'unrepresented' and 'unorganised'. In Italy, in May 2018, traditional unions and grassroots collectives of food-delivery riders signed a territorial collective agreement with delivery companies, assisted by the municipal council of Bologna. This 'Charter of fundamental rights of digital work in the urban context' sets an hourly wage no lower than that mandated by collective agreements signed by the most representative unions in the industry, grants paid holidays and overtime, as well as obligations to provide information on working conditions and rating mechanisms, and insurance against accidents and illnesses.[69] The agreement also recognises trade union rights for all digital platforms workers operating in the area.

In July 2018, another collective agreement was signed between the Danish trade union 3F and the cleaning services platform Hilfr.dk. Accordingly, domestic workers, previously classified as self-employed, are considered employees if they complete 100 hours of work, unless they opt to remain self-employed. This agreement recognises trade union rights. There is also a minimum hourly wage, a system of protection in case of dismissal and personal data and reputation safeguards. Hilfr.dk had adopted a policy to provide a minimum fee for those workers that remained classified as self-employed. This policy, however, came under the scrutiny of the Danish Competition Policy under the assumption that self-employed people working in households can seriously be equated to undertakings.[70]

In February 2019, Hermes, a British delivery company, negotiated an agreement with the GMB union that guarantees minimum wage and paid holidays. A new specific framework agreement concerning delivery riders was signed in November 2020 by major Italian labour unions and employers' organisations in the logistics and transport sector. Between 2021 and 2022, the food-delivery company Just Eat also reached a company agreement with the major Italian and Spanish sectoral trade unions.[71] In both cases, riders are classified as employees and have access to protection traditionally granted to standard workers in the relevant sector. In Austria, Germany and Norway, riders have succeeded in setting up worker representation bodies and works councils at the company level, a vehicle for significant collective information and consultation rights for workers.

Not only do all these cases shatter the myth of the alleged economic unsustainability of organisational models other than those typical of the digital 'pirates', they also show that employment status is not at odds with flexible schedules in labour intensive businesses. More importantly, these examples are proof of coalition-building between institutional unions and self-organised movements, notwithstanding the initial (sometimes persistent) mutual distrust.

Finally, these agreements challenge an up till now too conservative view of competition law, according to which establishing minimum compensation rates for the benefit of non-waged workers should be seen as a prohibited cartel activity. At a European and international level, trade union rights are recognised for workers without distinction between the self-employed and employees. These rights are widely recognised as fundamental and human rights that should cover everyone, including the self-employed. The case law of the European Court of Human Rights has established that the right to collective bargaining is an essential element of 'freedom of association with others, including the right to form and to join trade unions for the protection of [one's] interests'[72] and has progressively broadened its personal scope to even include priests.[73] A similar 'universalistic' approach can be found in the European Social Charter, another treaty that is binding on many EU countries, as recently noted by the European Committee of Social Rights, which monitors compliance with the Charter. According to the Committee, the right of the self-employed to bargain collectively is protected under the Charter.[74]

Wherever they come from, restrictions on collective rights appear increasingly unjustified, particularly in the light of changes we have attempted to describe in this book. Looking beyond Europe, the Universal Declaration of Human Rights guarantees the right of 'everyone' to form and to join trade unions for the protection of their interests. The International Labour Organisation counts freedom of association and the effective recognition of the right to collective bargaining among its Fundamental Principles and Rights at Work, applicable to all workers in all countries around the world, 'without distinction whatsoever', according to the text of its fundamental Freedom of Association and Protection of the Right to Organise Convention, 1948 (No. 87) and Right to Organise and Collective Bargaining Convention, 1949 (No. 98). When blindly applied to vulnerable self-employed workers, competition law therefore risks violating internationally recognised human rights.[75]

It is not just a matter of antitrust law. Too often, non-standard workers, including platform workers, are too easily deprived of these fundamental rights, following a rigid interpretation of existing labour regulations. In the UK, for instance, it was sufficient for Deliveroo to include a boilerplate substitution clause allowing delivery riders to pass work to another person, for these riders to be denied essential collective rights, based on the idea that the work they performed was not 'personal'[76] – it didn't matter if that clause was only included shortly before the hearing to reinforce the platform's claim. This interpretation seems hardly consistent with various international standards, including the ILO's instruments.[77]

Despite all these obstacles, the collective claims and actions of riders, drivers and other non-standard workers are on the rise, and represent a newfound vitality in industrial relations. It is also for this reason that, after some initial hesitation, the 'institutional' trade unions have mobilised alongside informal initiatives, energised by this surprising resurgence of labour militancy. In an era of supposed 'disintermediation', there is still a need for organised bodies and representative communities capable of negotiating the digital transformation and governing the current shift. From a legal standpoint, it will be important to overcome the old reflex that causes the dichotomy between employment and self-employment to reappear, with undesirable effects. Practically speaking, the resurrection of old-fashioned schemes of personnel management and augmented supervision, the prevalence of bogus self-employment and the near-monopsonist nature of digital markets mean that the instruments of collective voice and power such as collective bargaining agreements, which by their very nature are more flexible than litigation and legislative reforms, must be encouraged.[78]

Bearing this in mind, overcoming the distinction between the self-employed and waged workers has been proposed in order to extend employment and labour protection, including all collective rights, to anyone who 'works predominantly personally' (where the 'predominantly' should serve also to defuse 'carefully choreographed' substitution clauses such as the ones successfully used by platform companies in the UK).[79] In spite of all the ongoing initiatives, it is hard to bust the myth that self-employed workers should not be legally entitled to any trade union rights. This belief, over time, has triggered a vicious circle that ends up discouraging solidarity initiatives to the benefit of non-standard workers, on the one hand, and inhibiting the expansive efforts of traditional unions in new industries, on the other.

The future of collective rights is not limited to organising platform workers. Automation, AI, algorithms and big data impose a need for crucial reflection and consequent urgent action. We cannot react as individuals to the momentous changes currently occurring in work and everyday life. If everyone is to benefit from innovation, collective responses are needed to combat excesses and avoid techlashes. Rules are essential to limit the amount of personal data collected on workers' performance and characteristics, as well as how they are collected and processed. The 'relational' nature of data necessitates responses at the collective level.[80] This is not just a privacy issue. The way work is coordinated through new tech, including wearables and other invasive devices, must be regulated to ensure that the pursuit of higher productivity does not translate into discrimination or health risks and increased stress for the workers involved.

Work discipline mechanisms enabled by technology and algorithmic management systems are another key element in need of regulation. Wherever AI is employed to decide on issues such as increasing work pace or intensifying production, it is crucial that humans have the final say (especially where evaluation criteria can be updated through machine-learning processes). The same applies to any disciplinary sanction taken in the light of data collected through automated monitoring systems or algorithmic processes. In addition to this, any job performance evaluation based on metrics should also be collectively negotiated and agreed upon. Assessment criteria must be easy to understand and explain and made available to workers in order to avoid arbitrary or discriminatory outcomes.[81] The task of taming the domination exerted by 'augmented' employers over employees requires mobilising existing regulation to exercise power preemptively and collectively since managerial functions impact on vulnerable categories and groups.[82] This is the bare minimum needed to ensure a 'human-in-command' approach in the modern world of work.

To ensure that automated managerial decisions are subject to human over-sight, responsive regulation adaptable to new tech is needed. In addition to a general legislative framework, tailor-made rules are essential, the definition of which is the crucial task of collective bargaining, at the transnational, national, sectoral and company level.[83] Individual rights to access data and to contest the results of automated decision-making, as sometimes provided for in data protec-tion law, are indispensable but not sufficient. Individuals wishing to understand, control and challenge the far-reaching implications of these systems cannot be left to their own devices when it comes to dealing with the intricacies of these innovations. For this reason, collective agreements should cover the use of digital technology, data collection and algorithms that manage the workforce, ensuring transparency, sustainability and respect for human rights at work, going beyond the ex-post damage-control approach. They could also regulate matters such as the ownership of information collected from workers' activities and set up bilateral or independent funds to manage this data and redistribute the value created. Where the coverage of collective bargaining is not broad enough, as is the case in many countries and in small and medium enterprises, dedicated administrative bodies should intervene.

Some first legislative steps are timidly moving in the right direction. According to the new Spanish *Ley Rider*, the workers' legal representatives shall have the right to be meaningfully informed about AI or algorithm-fuelled metrics, rules and instructions that result in decisions on working conditions and access and retention of work, including through profiling. The text resembles an expansive transposi-tion of the GDPR's Articles 13 and 14 on information to be provided, Article 15 on the right of access and Article 22 on automated individual decision-making, including profiling.[84] Its personal scope of application includes all workers who are in a relationship with an undertaking operating by means of AI-driven tools. This collective right may contribute to making algorithms more contestable, but there are inadequate systems of objection and redress. Information rights fall short of the right to negotiate in good faith that is sorely needed in this field. Nonetheless, by operating in conjunction with the GDPR, this new provision could pave the way to a modern understanding of algorithmic legibility, combining national efforts and practices on limiting workplace monitoring with the general EU frame-work on data protection. Regrettably, while the European Data Protection Board (EDPB) and national data protection authorities have proven vigilant and proac-tive, instruments such as the brand-new AI Act, which, as mentioned, is based on an EU market liberalisation legal basis, risk jeopardising many domestic protec-tions safeguarding labour rights, including those mandating for information and consultation, codetermination and veto power for worker representatives.[85]

We have long maintained that 'negotiating the algorithm' must become a primary objective for workers and companies.[86] This is a slogan that has also recently been embraced by some national trade union movements. In 2017, the UNI Global Union had published a series of cutting-edge proposals on Ethical Artificial Intelligence and the treatment of workers' data.[87] As regards human resource practices 'such as recruitment, evaluation, promotion and dismissal, performance analysis', the new European Social Partners Framework Agreement on Digitalisation imposes data transparency and states that workers have the right to human intervention, objection and 'testing of the AI outcomes'.[88] Moreover, albeit limited in its scope and improvable, the draft Directive on platform work requires labour platforms to inform and consult workers' representatives on algorithmic management when they consider adopting or amending automated monitoring or decision-making systems.[89]

More and more collective agreements in force in various countries regulate the use of technology not only in the surveillance of workers but also in the management of the personnel, to protect human dignity and health and safety at work. Trade unions and employers are already tackling these issues pragmatically.[90] This will not be an easy process and will require efforts from all parties involved. Among other things, massive resources will need to be invested to ensure that workers, executives, trade unionists and HR managers are properly trained to deal with the challenges and opportunities that technology can offer. The regulation and collective governance of these processes take time. However, they are essential to ensure that the benefits of technological advances improve our societies in an inclusive and cohesive way.

C. And They Lived Happily and Connected Ever after: Saving the Digital Transformation from Itself

Everyone is talking about the future(s) of work, and rightly so. The wealth of predictions runs the risk of muddying the waters, as well as discouraging general interest. All analysis of production models, industrial policies, the state of rights and the quality of work therefore risks being perceived as an exercise in futurology, the prerogative of a handful of privileged people who – as Jerome K Jerome said – like work so much that they 'can sit and look at it for hours'. Tackling digital transformation head on serves to reiterate a vital message: change is afoot, but technology can be governed, and progress can go hand in hand with respect for and enhancement of the rights of working people.

Humankind is not defenceless. In a debate where policy is often presented as a binary choice between 'less' and 'more' regulation, we intend to introduce practical realism, and concrete ideas with the aim of raising a greater sense of public urgency. A few years ago, together with Six Silberman, a software engineer hired by the German trade union IGMetall to coordinate unionisation campaigns for digital workers and then by the Organise Platform, we had drafted a 'manifesto' to save the gig economy (first and foremost from itself). In the wake of other international initiatives, we had put together a list of suggestions for improvement. We think it is useful to re-advance and update some of its contents with the aim of striking a balance between advancing social rights, ensuring a level playing field for all economic operators, and unlocking authentic innovation. Our proposals apply not only to those who work for platforms or are governed by algorithms, but also to the many workers with fragmented contracts, unpredictable hours and unstable pay. Our recommendations are obviously not a definitive version. They are addressed not only to the 'silicon masters', but also to legislators, employers, trade unions and, above all, to workers. Assuming that the digital revolution requires us to abdicate policies of solidarity, welfare and redistribution is wrong and intellectually inept. Much can be achieved. Our short list of proposals includes:

- *Standard employment contracts.* Those platforms that have conquered large parts of the market should offer employment contracts for the portion of the workforce that guarantees the bulk of the orders. After an initial phase, the statistics and data collected can help to define a number of stable hirings, including through regular part-time work and other flexible formats, taking into account time slots and periods when certain services are most in demand. Businesses can legitimately continue to use other staff to cope with genuine peaks and troughs. Several experiences demonstrate that this is feasible. Having a stable workforce would thus send a clear message about the sustainability and viability of many business models in the platform economy, and would also help them to divest themselves of strategies that have alienated many consumers and investors.

- *A code of conduct for digital players.* In order to regulate minimum levels of payment by platforms, to enhance the understanding of the criteria applied by the algorithms and to guarantee the lawfulness of the content exchanged online, there is a need for a code of conduct within everyone's reach, along the lines of the one adopted by some German crowdwork platforms in 2017.[91] This is an agile tool that aims to promote best practices for non-standard work and offer a catalogue of conducts to be sanctioned (eg, by excluding undisciplined companies from public procurement). Initiatives such as the Oxford Internet Institute's *Fairwork* project, committed to highlighting best and worst labour practices in the platform economy, are also extremely useful tools in this direction.[92] Technical design plays a decisive role when it comes to shaping expectations, interactions and outcomes in the relationship between platforms, clients and workers. It is time to define a model of social responsibility that promotes the transparency and contestability of internal processes.

- *Clear rules on payments for online work.* Transparent rules on payments and the consequences of the rejection of finished work by clients on platforms must be established. Unacceptably, the terms and conditions of many online platforms allow dissatisfied customers to withhold a final product without compensating the worker, to whom no explanation is due. The possibility of challenging a rejection should be given, offering workers a channel to seek information and present their own views (without risking retaliation or account deactivation, as often happens today). An impartial system for dispute resolution on the quality of work provided can be envisaged, with a committee of arbitrators to ensure fairness of adjudication. Otherwise, it must be possible to seek redress in court in the country where the worker habitually works (this already happens for on-location work when someone works in a country other than that of the employer).

- *Obligations for those who want to outsource.* The idea, supported by some unfortunate recent reforms and business developments, that outsourcing can simply be justified by the desire to cut labour costs must be dismissed. In cases where it can be shown that recourse to casual work disguises a deliberate process of *'intra moenia'* outsourcing (ie, when an internal position is first suppressed and then entrusted to workers who find themselves performing the same tasks side by side with standard workers, but with poorer treatment), reference should be made to an existing collective agreement for related job positions as a parameter for measuring the fairness of the conditions applied, in terms of working hours, remuneration, employment protection, health and safety insurance and working tools. This does not only apply to platforms. The legal and industrial tradition of many countries has plenty of measures to counter these phenomena: most of them have been set aside too hastily. A feasible, EU-wide solution could be the adoption of a Directive that ensures real equal treatment between all forms of non-standard and standard work, also solving some of the problems and loopholes that have emerged over time concerning the equal-treatment provisions in the Directives on atypical work.

- *Protections and rights beyond employment.* Well beyond platforms, legislators should address the issue of broadening the scope of labour and employment protection. If new forms of work are poorly covered, the classical notions of employment and self-employment can be reformed and, if necessary, overcome. Moving towards universal protection, irrespective of the distinction between self-employed and waged workers, is a way forward. The new paradigm would also provide greater certainty and reduce the number of court lawsuits over the correct classification of workers, which are costly, unpredictable and detrimental for all parties involved and society in general. For some rights, first of all trade union protection, data protection, health and safety and anti-discrimination, the trail has already been blazed thanks to international law and litigation at the European level.

- *Guaranteed minimum hours.* In the era of 'mass freelancing' and online piecework, understanding how to reverse precarisation trends is essential. We can make casual work less unpredictable and irregular, on and off platforms. It is possible to take a cue from rules such as those limiting zero-hour contracts in the Netherlands. Under this regulation, after a few months, workers are guaranteed a minimum hourly rate based on the average hours worked in the previous quarter, in order to prevent abuse of 'on tap' jobs in the services sector. Under the new European Directive on transparent and predictable working conditions, Member States are required to adopt similar solutions as of 2022. In the absence of such rules, the European instruments envisage that 'on-call' work will be restricted and confined to a physiological use, avoiding it becoming a generalised low-cost management option.

- *Flexible jobs, stable rights.* Customised shifts, long-term deliverables or complex projects with reasonable deadlines must be guaranteed for those who turn to digital platforms and, generally, to workers in search of authentic organisational flexibility. As long as the distinction between employment and self-employment is maintained, if the worker is considered genuinely self-employed, any intrusion from platforms, clients and other principals should be limited as much as possible, especially if it borders on direct supervision or detailed orders. In the EU, this can be done also by resorting to the application of the provisions of the recent P2B Regulation.[93] If, on the other hand, the relationship is of a subordinate nature, solutions such as remote work schemes that became widespread during the peaks of the COVID-19 pandemic can remain useful, but they need to be improved, ensuring a proper right to disconnection, to guarantee organisational self-government for workers and a healthy work-life balance. Technology can help, when it is not counterproductively used to proctor people and micromanage workers.

- *Trade unions for non-standard workers.* Despite their fragmentation and isolation, platform workers and other – genuine and bogus – self-employed workers are organising into collective movements or trade unions and have every right to do so under international law. On the domestic and EU legal side, outdated interpretations of competition law need to be overcome, as admitted by the Commission itself. At the same time, on the practical front, traditional trade unions must support the initiatives of organisation and demands. Intercepting spontaneity and gaining traction from it to enhance bargaining power is, after all, one of the founding missions of labour movements especially in hard-to-organise industries. This would encourage grassroots groups to communicate with more established trade unions, not least to take advantage of the experience and resources that the latter can provide. Campaigns such as Fight-for-15 have shown how much cooperation between traditional trade unions and independent collectives pays off.

- *Data portability and interoperability.* The logged digital traces of our lives are increasingly important. Even more so for workers who rely on their online reputation. The rating earned on a platform, as well as the work history that led to that score (customers served, services rendered), represent a personal portfolio of credibility and professionalism. It must be 'portable', as several data protection authorities have called for. In addition, the adaptability and interoperability of digital careers on other platforms must be guaranteed. In this regard, exclusivity clauses that bind workers must be removed, unless we decide to consider them non-compete agreements that should therefore be monetised. The challenge for the future is also to reinvent social protection models by adopting more flexible solutions based on the transferability and interoperability of acquired social rights instead of implementing exemptions and exclusions. This opportunity should be capitalised on to extend protection to non-standard workers in an incremental, systemic and permanent manner.

- *Universal benefits and less conditionality in welfare.* The forced conditionality of benefits pushes recipients to take low quality jobs for the benefit of inefficient firms and to the detriment of productivity and prosperity for all. For this reason, too, redesigning benefits for those temporarily out of a job is significantly overdue. We have the opportunity to rethink existing models and question old ideas such as the excessive conditionality of benefits, often resulting in punitive downward spirals. Less virtue signalling, more opposition to in-work poverty and freedom from need are essential objectives. At both the supranational and local level, this should be combined with an in-depth collective reflection on bolstering minimum wage protection for workers who are not adequately covered by collective agreements.

- *Bringing algorithmic bosses to account.* Since AI and algorithms are complementing or substituting managers in various functions, solutions must be wide-ranging, including complementary tools from different legal domains, such as data protection, anti-discrimination law and occupational health and safety, based on the final use of data-driven tools. Individual information is seldom used in isolation. Therefore, despite the gradual decline in trade union density, information and consultation are among the most successful tools to accomplish the goal of comprehensible, verifiable and fair organisational practices in a swift and bespoke fashion. Workers' involvement and codetermination in all phases (design, introduction, implementation, maintenance and improvement) is a way to enhance their agency and build trust in professional communities in a 'privacy-by-default' model, whereby an organisation ensures that only data strictly necessary for each specific purpose are processed. The proposed EU Directive on platform work is a step in the right direction, albeit its provisions on algorithmic management still need to be strengthened.

- *Negotiating the digital transformation.* Workers, trade unions and businesses must negotiate job substitution, the introduction of new technology in the workplace, the use of big data and AI, and the deployment of algorithmic management. Public and private decisions that have a significant impact on people's lives and work should not be made by machines, under the pretext of their supposed objectivity. Collective agreements, good practices and labour regulation can guarantee a human-in-command approach at work, ensuring the good use of data. As documented,[94] this participatory method, in turn, will have positive effects on productivity. Governments must promote social dialogue in this area, including by making any public incentives for restructuring and modernising company technology conditional on the conclusion of and compliance with agreements with the social partners. Similarly, critical digital literacy and firm-provided training must be used to counter skill depreciation and enforce data rights. More encompassing, anticipatory agreements should also aim at incorporating provisions covering workers regardless of their employment status to avoid furthering labour market segmentation. This would ensure that mutual trust flourishes while averting a loss of competitiveness and engagement.

In short, the future of technology and the future of work are not set in stone. They will not develop on the basis of inscrutable and unchangeable laws of nature. Digitalisation, work, automation and social rights are all too human: they depend on the rules that a society decides to set for itself. Since this fate concerns everyone, it cannot be left solely to the decisions of computer programmers, the CEOs of tech unicorns, or those who create and market instruments of mass digital surveillance and algorithmic management. The debate on innovation is inextricably linked to the urgency of creating good jobs. The discussion is becoming clearer, allowing us to see the common threads linking seemingly disconnected issues and reminding us of our responsibilities. 'Labour is not a commodity', as the International Labour Organisation has asserted since its foundation. However, labour is not a technology either.

---

[1] See generally M Moore and D Tambini (eds), *Regulating Big Tech: Policy Responses to Digital Dominance* (Oxford, Oxford University Press, 2021).

[2] LM Khan, 'Amazon's antitrust paradox' (2016) 126(3) *Yale Law Journal* 710–805; S Rahman, *Democracy Against Domination* (Oxford, Oxford University Press, 2016).

[3] *The Economist*, 'Calls to rein in the tech titans are getting louder' (*The Economist*, 16 July 2019) www.economist.com/graphic-detail/2019/07/16/calls-to-rein-in-the-tech-titans-are-getting-louder. See also A Prat and TM Valletti, 'Attention oligopoly' (2021) *American Economic Journal: Microeconomics*.

[4] M Castells, *Networks of Outrage and Hope: Social Movements in the Internet Age* (Cambridge, Polity Press, 2015).

[5] JA Knee, *The Platform Delusion: Who Wins and Who Loses in the Age of Tech Titans* (London, Penguin, 2021). See also AC Madrigal, 'The coalition out to kill tech as we know it' (*The Atlantic*, 4 June 2019) www.theatlantic.com/technology/archive/2019/06/how-politicians-and-scholars-turned-against-big-tech/591052/.

[6] L Zingales, '"The digital robber barons kill innovation": the Stigler Center's report enters the senate' (*ProMarket*, 15 September 2019) https://promarket.org/2019/09/25/digital-robber-barons-kill-innovation-stigler-center-senate/. See also D Mattioli, 'Amazon Scooped Up Data From Its Own Sellers to Launch Competing Products' (*The Wall Street Journal*, 23 April 2020) www.wsj.com/articles/amazon-scooped-up-data-from-its-own-sellers-to-launch-competing-products-11587650015.

[7] See UNCTAD, 'Trade and Development Report 2018: Power, Platforms and the Free Trade Delusion' (2018). See also G Standing, *The Corruption of Capitalism: Why Rentiers Thrive and Work Does Not Pay* (London, Biteback Publishing, 2016).

[8] B Kaiser, *Targeted: My Inside Story of Cambridge Analytica and How Trump, Brexit and Facebook Broke Democracy* (London, HarperCollins, 2019).

[9] C Silverman, R Mac and D Pranav Dixit, '"I Have Blood on My Hands": A Whistleblower Says Facebook Ignored Global Political Manipulation' (*Buzzfeed News*, 14 September 2020) www.buzzfeed-news.com/article/craigsilverman/facebook-ignore-political-manipulation-whistleblower-memo.

[10] D Ghosh, *Terms of Disservice: How Silicon Valley is Destructive by Design* (Washington, Brookings Institution Press, 2020); A Wiener, *Uncanny Valley: A Memoir* (NY, MCD Books, 2020).

[11] E Stewart, 'Robots were supposed to take our jobs. Instead, they're making them worse' (*Vox*, 2 July 2021) www.vox.com/the-goods/22557895/automation-robots-work-amazon-uber-lyft.

[12] J Lanier, *You Are Not a Gadget* (London, Penguin, 2011).

[13] S Wachter, 'The Other Half of the Truth: Staying human in an algorithmic world' (*The Forum Network*, 7 June 2019) www.oecd-forum.org/posts/49761-the-other-half-of-the-truth-staying-human-in-an-algorithmic-world.

[14] S Costanza-Chock, *Design Justice* (Cambridge, MIT Press, 2020).

[15] D Acemoglu and P Restrepo, 'The Wrong Kind of AI? Artificial Intelligence and the Future of Labour Demand" (2020) 13(1) *Cambridge Journal of Regions, Economic, and Society* 25–35. See also P Kalluri, 'Don't ask if artificial intelligence is good or fair, ask how it shifts power' (2020) 583(7815) *Nature* 169.

[16] K Crawford, R Dobbe, T Dryer, G Fried, B Green, E Kaziunas, A Kak, V Mathur, E McElroy, AN Sánchez, D Raji, J Lisi Rankin, R Richardson, J Schultz, S Myers West and M Whittaker, *AI Now 2019 Report* (New York, AI Now Institute, 2019).

[17] C Criado Perez, *Invisible Women: Data Bias in a World Designed for Men* (Abrams Press, New York 2019).

[18] I Ajunwa and D Greene, 'Platforms at Work: Automated Hiring Platforms and Other New Intermediaries in the Organization of Work' in SP Vallas and A Kovalainen (eds), *Research in the Sociology of Work* (London, Emerald Publishing Limited, 2019) 61–91; P Hacker, 'Teaching fairness to artificial intelligence: Existing and novel strategies against algorithmic discrimination under EU law' (2018) 55(4) *Common Market Law Review* 1143–86.

[19] N Srnicek and A Williams, *Inventing the Future: Postcapitalism and a World Without Work* (New York, Verso, 2015); M Zwolinski, 'A Hayekian case for free markets and a basic income' in M Cholbi and M Weber (eds), *The Future of Work, Technology, and Basic Income* (Abingdon, Routledge, 2019); K Lui, 'Mark Zuckerberg Calls for Universal Basic Income in His Harvard Commencement Speech' (*Fortune*, 26 May 2017) https://fortune.com/2017/05/26/mark-zuckerberg-universal-basic-income/; A Sheffey, 'Elon Musk says we need universal basic income because 'in the future, physical work will be a choice' (*Business Insider*, 20 August 2021) www.businessinsider.com/elon-musk-universal-basic-income-physical-work-choice-2021-8?r=US&IR=T.

[20] R Bregman, 'Has the time finally come for universal basic income? (*The Correspondent*, 2 April 2020) https://thecorrespondent.com/386/has-the-time-finally-come-for-universal-basic-income/51070573796-cb9a9b6f.

[21] RJ Van der Veen and P Van Parijs, 'A capitalist road to communism' (1986) 15(5) *Theory and Society* 635–55.

[22] P Van Parijs and Y Vanderborght, *Basic Income: A Radical Proposal for a Free Society and a Sane Economy* (Harvard, Harvard University Press, 2017); P Van Parijs, *Real Freedom for All: What (if anything) Can Justify Capitalism?* (Oxford, Oxford University Press, 1998).

[23] C Estlund, 'Three big ideas for a future of less work and a three-dimensional alternative' (2019) 82 *Law and Contemporary Problems* 1–43.

[24] G Standing, *The Precariat: The New Dangerous Class* (London, Bloomsbury, 2016).

[25] F Gildea, 'Accelerating down a Road to Nowhere: On Inventing the Future by Nick Srnicek and Alex Williams' (2020) 91(2) *The Political Quarterly* 359–63.

[26] U.S. Bureau of Labor Statistics, A profile of the working poor, 2017. Available at www.bls.gov/opub/reports/working-poor/2017/home.htm.

[27] R Peña-Casas, D Ghailani, S Spasova and B Vanhercke, *In-work poverty in Europe: A study of national policies* (European Commission, 2019).

[28] Article 23, Universal Declaration of Human Rights, *UN General Assembly*, 1948.

[29] V Mantouvalou, 'Welfare-to-work, structural injustice and human rights' 83(5) *The Modern Law Review* 929–54. See also V Gantchev, 'Data protection in the age of welfare conditionality: Respect for basic rights or a race to the bottom?' (2019) 21(1) *European Journal of Social Security* 3–22.

[30] J Henley and R Booth, 'Welfare surveillance system violates human rights, Dutch court rules' *The Guardian* (5 February 2020) www.theguardian.com/technology/2020/feb/05/welfare-surveillance-system-violates-human-rights-dutch-court-rules.

[31] Office of the High Commissioner for Human Rights, 'Landmark ruling by Dutch court stops government attempts to spy on the poor – UN expert' (*UN Human Rights*, 5 February 2020) www.ohchr.org/EN/NewsEvents/Pages/DisplayNews.aspx?LangID=E&NewsID=25522.

[32] J Henley, 'Dutch government faces collapse over child benefits scandal.' *The Guardian* (14 January 2021) www.theguardian.com/world/2021/jan/14/dutch-government-faces-collapse-over-child-bene-fits-scandal. See also M Loi, 'Automated Decision-Making Systems in the Public Sector An Impact Assessment Tool for Public Authorities'. Available at https://algorithmwatch.org/en/wp-content/uploads/2021/09/2021_AW_Decision_Public_Sector_EN_v5.pdf.

[33] ME Gilman, 'Poverty Lawgorithms: A Poverty Lawyer's Guide to Fighting Automated Decision-Making Harms on Low-Income Communities' *Data & Society* (2020); Human Rights Watch, 'UK: Automated Benefits System Failing People in Need' (*Human Rights Watch*, 29 September 2020) www.hrw.org/news/2020/09/29/uk-automated-benefits-system-failing-people-need.

[34] V Gantchev, 'Welfare Sanctions and the Right to a Subsistence Minimum: a troubled marriage' (2020) 22(3) *European Journal of Social Security* 257–72.

[35] B Knight, 'Germany's welfare experiment: Sanction-free basic security' (*Deutsche Welle*, 8 December 2018) www.dw.com/en/germanys-welfare-experiment-sanction-free-basic-security/a-46629933.

[36] A Romano and A Zitelli, 'Il reddito di base è una cosa seria. Disuguaglianze, qualità della vita, robot: immaginare una società diversa' (*Valigia Blu*, 7 March 2017) https://storie.valigiablu.it/reddito-di-%20 base/.

[37] D Thompson, 'Busting the Myth of 'Welfare Makes People Lazy'' (The Atlantic, 8 March 2018) www. theatlantic.com/business/archive/2018/03/welfare-childhood/555119/. See also J Henley, 'Finnish basic income pilot improved wellbeing, study finds' The Guardian (7 May 2020) www.theguardian. com/society/2020/may/07/finnish-basic-income-pilot-improved-wellbeing-study-finds-coronavirus.

[38] D Thompson, 'The Great Resignation Is Accelerating' (*The Atlantic*, 15 October 2021) www. theatlantic.com/ideas/archive/2021/10/great-resignation-accelerating/620382/; KL Miller, 'During the "Great Resignation," workers refuse to accept the unacceptable' *The Washington Post* (30 September 2021) www.washingtonpost.com/business/2021/09/30/during-great-resignation-workers-refuse-accept-unacceptable/.

[39] D Autor, 'Good News: There's a Labor Shortage' *The New York Times* (3 September 2021) www. nytimes.com/2021/09/04/opinion/labor-shortage-biden-covid.html?smid=url-share. See generally EO Wright, *Envisioning Real Utopias* (London, Verso, 2010).

[40] K Roose, 'Welcome to the YOLO Economy' *The New York Times* (21 April 2021) www.nytimes. com/2021/04/21/technology/welcome-to-the-yolo-economy.html.

[41] A Ciccone, 'Il kit definitivo per contrastare il format pseudo-giornalistico "Il lavoro c'è, ma i giovani non vogliono lavorare"' (Valigia Blu, 14 June 2019) www.valigiablu.it/articoli-lavoro-giovani-fannulloni/.

[42] J Espinoza, 'Vestager Says Gig Economy Workers Should "Team Up" on Wages' *Financial Times* (24 October 2019) www.ft.com/content/0cafd442-f673-11e9-9ef3-eca8fc8f2d65.

[43] See generally V Daskalova, S McCrystal and M Wakui, 'Labour protection for non-employees: how the gig economy revives old problems and challenges existing solutions' in J Meijerink, G Jansen and V Daskalova (eds), *Platform Economy Puzzles* (Cheltenham, Edward Elgar Publishing, 2021) 68–99.

[44] C Garden, 'The Seattle Solution: Collective Bargaining by For-Hire Drivers & Prospects for Pro-Labor Federalism' (2017) 12 *Harvard Law & Policy Review Online*. See also A Aloisi and E Gramano, 'Workers without workplaces and unions without unity: Non-standard forms of employment, platform work and collective bargaining' *Employment Relations for the 21st Century*, Bulletin of Comparative Industrial Relations (Alphen aan den Rijn, Kluwer Law International, 2019) 107, 37–57.

[45] S Paul, S McCrystal and E McGaughey (eds), *The Cambridge Handbook of Labour in Competition Law* (Cambridge, Cambridge University Press, 2022).

[46] Court of Justice of the European Union, Case C-67/96 *Albany International BV v Stichting Bedrijfspensioenfonds Textielindustrie* [1999] ECR I-5751. However, the Court exempted the collective agreements also covering workers in a situation 'comparable' to that of employees by relying on the (somehow artificial) category of 'false self-employed' workers. Court of Justice of the European Union, Case C-413/13 *FNV Kunsten Informatie en Media v Staat der Nederlanden* [2014].

[47] In particular, it is not compatible with the notion that collective bargaining is a fundamental right, protected under the European Convention of Human Rights, the European Social Charter, ILO Fundamental Conventions and the Charter of Fundamental Rights of the European Union. See N Countouris and V De Stefano, 'The Labour Law Framework: Self-Employed and Their Right to Bargain Collectively' in B Waas and C Hießl (eds), *Collective Bargaining for Self-Employed Workers in Europe*, Bulletin of Comparative Industrial Relations (Alphen aan den Rijn, Kluwer Law International, 2021) 3–17.

[48] Annex to the Communication from the Commission, Approval of the content of a Draft for a Communication from the Commission, Guidelines on the application of EU competition law to collective agreements regarding the working conditions of solo self-employed persons, C(2021) 8838 final. Moreover, the Commission also requires that strikes in support of the collective agreements allowable or 'tolerated' under the Guidelines be 'necessary' and 'proportionate' to the conclusions of these agreements. Such scrutiny of the endgame and aims of a strike seems hardly compatible with several national constitutional traditions concerning the right to strike, also protecting self-employed workers, and with ILO standards.

[49] See n 1, ibid.

[50] N Countouris, V De Stefano and I Lianos, 'The EU, Competition Law and Workers' Rights' in Paul, McCrystal and McGaughey (n 45).

[51] Countouris and De Stefano (n 47).

[52] H Johnston and C Land-Kazlauskas, 'Organizing on-demand: Representation, voice, and collective bargaining in the gig economy' (Geneva, Conditions of work and employment series 94, 2018).

[53] A Griswold, 'This is the script Uber is using to make anti-union phone calls to drivers in Seattle' (*Quartz*, 22 February 2016) https://qz.com/621977/this-is-the-script-uber-is-using-to-make-anti-union-phone-calls-to-drivers-in-seattle/. See also A MacGillis, 'The Union Battle at Amazon Is Far from Over' *The New Yorker* (13 April 2021) www.newyorker.com/news/news-desk/the-union-battle-at-amazon-is-far-from-over.

[54] W Negrón, 'Little Tech is Coming for Workers. A Framework for Reclaiming and Building Worker Power' (CoWorker.org, 2021); S Kessler, 'Companies Are Using Employee Survey Data to Predict – and Squash – Union Organizing' (*OneZero*, 30 July 2020) https://onezero.medium.com/companies-are-using-employee-survey-data-to-predict-and-squash-union-organizing-a7e28a8c2158.

[55] A Tassinari and V Maccarrone, 'Riders on the storm: Workplace solidarity among gig economy couriers in Italy and the UK' (2020) 34(1) *Work, Employment and Society* 35–54. See also S Greenhouse, 'Unionized but impotent? Row erupts over gig workers' labor proposal' *The Guardian* (27 May 2021) www.theguardian.com/us-news/2021/may/27/gig-workers-unionized-but-impotent-new-york-bill.

[56] A Forsyth, *The Future of Unions and Worker Representation. The Digital Picket Line* (Oxford, Hart, 2022). See also A Bertolini and R Dukes, 'Trade Unions and Platform Workers in the UK: Worker Representation in the Shadow of the Law' (2021) 50(4) *Industrial Law Journal* 662–88; T Katsabian, 'Collective Action in the Digital Reality: the Case of Platform-Based Workers' (2021) 85(5) *The Modern Law Review* 1005–40.

[57] A Donini, M Forlivesi, A Rota and P Tullini, 'Towards collective protections for crowdworkers: Italy, Spain and France in the EU context' (2017) 23(2) *Transfer: European Review of Labour and Research* 207–23. See also J Schor, *After the Gig: How the Sharing Economy Got Hijacked and How to Win It Back* (Oakland, University of California Press, 2021).

[58] See https://fightfor15.org/. KVW Stone, 'Unions in the Precarious Economy' (*Prospect*, 21 February 2017) https://prospect.org/labor/unions-precarious-economy/; AJ Wood, 'Three lessons the labour movement must learn from the Fight for 15 at Walmart' (*SPERI.Comment: The Political Economy Blog*, 8 June 2018) http://speri.dept.shef.ac.uk/2018/06/08/three-lessons-the-labour-movement-must-learn-from-the-fight-for-15-at-walmart/.

[59] N Scheiber and K Conger, 'The Great Google Revolt' (*The New York Time Magazine*, 18 February 2020) www.nytimes.com/interactive/2020/02/18/magazine/google-revolt.html.

[60] S von Struensee, 'The Role of Social Movements, Coalitions, and Workers in Resisting Harmful Artificial Intelligence and Contributing to the Development of Responsible AI' (16 June 2021). Available on SSRN: https://ssrn.com/abstract=3880779.

[61] K Conger and N Scheiber, 'Kickstarter employees vote to unionize in a big step for tech' *The New York Times* (18 February 2020) www.nytimes.com/2020/02/18/technology/kickstarter-union.html.

[62] E McGaughey, 'Will robots automate your job away? Full employment, basic income, and economic democracy' *Centre for Business Research, University of Cambridge, Working Paper* (2018) 496.

[63] K Vandaele, 'Collective resistance and organisational creativity amongst Europe's platform workers: A new power in the labour movement?' in J Haidar and M Keune (eds), *Work and labour relations in global platform capitalism* (ILERA Publication series, 2021). See also S O'Connor, 'Trade unions are back after a long absence' *Financial Times* (9 March 2021) www.ft.com/content/ea709746-f4c9-4fc3-80c9-8977b2dbd82d.

[64] M Silberman, V Barth, R Fuss and C Benner, *Frankfurt Declaration on Platform-Based Work: Proposals for Platform Operators, Clients, Policy Makers, Workers, and Worker Organizations* (2016). Available at https://wtf.tw/pubs/frankfurt_decl_en.pdf.

[65] T Scholz, 'Platform cooperativism vs. the sharing economy' (2014) 47 *Big Data & Civic Engagement* 47–52. See also T Scholz and N Schneider (eds), *Ours To Hack and Own: The Rise of Platform Cooperativism, a New Vision for the Future of Work and a Fairer Internet* (New York, OR Books, 2016); A King, 'This rider-owned food delivery service is taking back power from Deliveroo' (*EuroNews*, 1 October 2021) www.euronews.com/green/2021/10/01/this-rider-owned-food-delivery-service-is-taking-back-power-from-deliveroo.

[66] L Kaori Gurley, 'Instacart Workers Are Asking Users to #DeleteInstacart' (*Vice*, 20 September 2021) www.vice.com/en/article/xgxjbj/instacart-workers-are-asking-users-to-deleteinstacart.

[67] L Lawrence and A Kramer, 'How Slack and Discord became tools for worker revolt' (*Protocol*, 13 October 2021) www.protocol.com/workplace/slack-discord-worker-protest-tools#toggle-gdpr.

[68] S Silberman and L Irani, 'Operating an employer reputation system: Lessons from Turkopticon. 2008–2015' (2016) 37(3) *Comparative Labor Law & Policy Journal* 505–42; N Salehi, LC Irani, MS Bernstein, A Alkhatib, E Ogbe and K Milland, 'We are dynamo: Overcoming stalling and friction in collective action for crowd workers' (2015) *Proceedings of the 33rd annual ACM conference on human factors in computing systems* 1621–30.

[69] See www.comune.bologna.it/sites/default/files/documenti/CartaDiritti3105_web.pdf.

[70] N Countouris and V De Stefano, 'Collective-bargaining rights for platform workers' (*Social Europe*, 6 October 2020) https://socialeurope.eu/collective-bargaining-rights-for-platform-workers.

[71] L Rodríguez, 'First collective agreement for platform workers in Spain' (*Social Europe*, 13 January 2022) https://socialeurope.eu/first-agreement-for-platform-workers-in-spain.

[72] ECtHR, 12/11/2008 (GC), *Demir a. Bayjara v Turkey*, No. 34503/97.

[73] ECtHR, 9/7/2013 (GC), *Sindicatul 'Păstorul cel Bun' v Romania*, No. 2330/09.

[74] European Committee of Social Rights, *Irish Congress of Trade Unions (ICTU) v Ireland*, Complaint No.123/2016, 12 September 2018.

[75] C Stylogiannis, 'Freedom of association and collective bargaining in the platform economy: A human rights-based approach and an over increasing mobilization of workers' (2022) *International Labour Review*.

[76] *The Independent Workers Union of Great Britain v The Central Arbitration Committee* [2021] EWCA Civ 952 (24 June 2021). See J Atkinson and H Dhorajiwala, 'IWGB v RooFoods: Status, Rights and Substitution' (2019) 48(2) *Industrial Law Journal* 278–95.

[77] A Bogg, 'Taken for a ride: Worker in the gig economy' (2019) 135 *Law Quarterly Review* 219–26.

[78] See generally G Mundlak, *Organizing matters: Two logics of trade union representation* (Cheltenham, Edward Elgar Publishing, 2020); BI Sachs, 'Law, Organizing, and Status Quo Vulnerability' (2017) 96 *Texas Law Review* 351–77. See also J Stanford, 'The Resurgence of gig work: Historical and theoretical perspectives' (2017) 28(3) *The Economic and Labour Relations Review* 382–401.

[79] *Supreme Court of the United Kingdom, Pimlico Plumbers Ltd and another v Smith* [2018] UKSC 29.

[80] S Viljoen, 'Democratic Data: A Relational Theory For Data Governance' (2021) 13(2) *Yale Law Journal* 573–654.

[81] R Hamon, H Junklewitz and I Sanchez, *Robustness and Explainability of Artificial Intelligence – From technical to policy solutions* (Luxembourg, Publications Office of the European Union, 2020).

[82] B Mittelstadt, 'From individual to group privacy in big data analytics' (2017) 30(4) *Philosophy & Technology* 475–94.

[83] K Ewing and J Hendy, 'New Perspectives on Collective Labour Law: Trade Union Recognition and Collective Bargaining' (2017) 46(1) *Industrial Law Journal* 23–51.

[84] A Aranguiz, 'Spain's Platform Workers Win Algorithm Transparency' (*Social Europe*, 18 March 2021) https://socialeurope.eu/spains-platform-workers-win-algorithm-transparency (welcoming the law as 'ambitious at first sight' for its novelty). C Villarroel Luque, 'Workers vs Algorithms: What Can the New Spanish Provision on Artificial Intelligence and Employment Achieve?' (*VerfBlog*, 7 May 2021) https://verfassungsblog.de/workers-vs-ai/. See also M Flyverbom, *The Digital Prism. Transparency and Managed Visibilities in a Datafied World* (Cambridge, Cambridge University Press, 2019).

[85] J Niklas and L Dencik, 'What rights matter? Examining the place of social rights in the EU's artificial intelligence policy debate' (2021) 3 *Internet Policy Review* 10. Several attempts to limit to efficacy of the Act are ongoing, see M Heikkilä, 'POLITICO AI: Decoded: Big Tech on the AI Act – AI inventors – Deepfakes' ('Corporations say they want laser-sharp laws to create "legal certainty." Ironically that also gives them more wiggle room, as researchers can develop new technologies far faster than regulation keeps up. If a regulation is too broad, it might end up capturing large parts of tech companies' money-making products, and embroil them in long, costly court battles').

[86] V De Stefano, 'Negotiating the algorithm': automation, artificial intelligence and labour protection (ILO Employment Working Paper, No. 246, 2018). One of the most critical downsides of current approaches lies in an individualistic conception of data protection, which is also evident in the preliminary achievements in strategic litigation. M Tisné, 'The Data Delusion: Protecting Individual Data Isn't Enough When the Harm Is Collective' (2020) https://cyber.fsi.stanford.edu/publication/data-delusion; P Townsend, 'Data Privacy Is Not Just a Consumer Issue: It's Also a Labor Rights Issue' (*The Century Foundation Next 100*, 14 May 2021) https://thenext100.org/data-privacy-is-not-just-a-consumer-issue-its-also-a-labor-rights-issue/.

[87] See www.thefutureworldofwork.org/opinions/10-%20principles-for-ethical-ai/.

[88] Available at www.etuc.org/en/document/eu-social-partners-agreement-digitalisation. See D Mangan, 'Agreement to Discuss: The Social Partners Address the Digitalisation of Work' (2021) 50(4) *Industrial Law Journal* 689–705.

[89] Article 9, Proposal for a Directive of the European Parliament and of the Council on improving working conditions in platform work COM(2021) 762 final 2021/0414 (COD).

[90] I Armaroli and E Dagnino, 'A seat at the table: negotiating data processing in the workplace. A national case study and comparative insights' (2019) 41(1) *Comparative Labor Law & Policy Journal* 173–95. See also F Flanagan and M Walker, 'How can unions use Artificial Intelligence to build power? The use of AI chatbots for labour organising in the US and Australia' (2021) 36(2) *New Technology, Work and Employment* 159–76 (re-imagining AI technologies developed in the context of customer service as instruments of solidarity and activism).

[91] See http://faircrowd.work/2017/11/08/ombudsstelle-fuer-crowdworking-plattformen-vereinbart/.

[92] See www.oii.ox.ac.uk/research/projects/a-fairwork-foundation-towards-fair-work-in-the-platform-economy/.

[93] Regulation (EU) 2019/1150 of the European Parliament and of the Council of 20 June 2019 on promoting fairness and transparency for business users of online intermediation services (OJ L186/57 11.07.2019).

[94] T Kato and M Morishima, 'The productivity effects of participatory employment practices: Evidence from new Japanese panel data' (2002) 41(4) *Industrial Relations: A Journal of Economy and Society* 487–520.

INDEX